THE CHURCH

ALWAYS IN NEED
OF REFORM

D1158773

Experience and history have taught me that one must ALWAYS protest when one feels in conscience or by conviction that there are grounds for doing so. Of course, one thereby makes trouble for oneself, but something positive is nevertheless achieved.

Yves Congar, O.P.

Gabriel Daly OSA

The Church

ALWAYS IN NEED
OF REFORM

DOMINICAN PUBLICATIONS

Published (2015) by
Dominican Publications
42 Parnell Square
Dublin 1
Ireland

www.dominicanpublications.com

ISBN 978-1-905604-26-5

British Library Cataloguing in Publications Data.
A catalogue record for this book is available
from the British Library.

Origination by Dominican Publications
Cover design by David Cooke
Printed by Gemini International, Dublin 15

Contents

Preface

The opening chapter of this book is deliberately autobiographical in character. This has not been my usual practice; but I have written the book towards the end of a life devoted mainly to theology, and I thought that I should give the reader some indication of how my mind has changed over the years. I have gone from being an uncritical Roman-trained candidate for the priesthood, more than 60 years ago, to being a theologian who has the same Catholic faith today as he had in his youth, but whose theology, especially of church, has changed comprehensively.

Like many others with views similar to mine, I continue to value my membership of the Catholic Church while experiencing considerable alienation from its structures of governance and acute disapproval of the actions of some of those who have power in the institution. As a theologian I feel bound to criticise, from a theological point of view, what has been happening, and to call for reform, not as an institutional convenience, but as an evangelical necessity.

There have been two critical approaches to the Catholic Church's life, attitudes and methods of government: one, broadly speaking, may be described as journalistic; the other is theological in origin. Both approaches are necessary and ideally each should complement the other. Criticism of the institution can often be found in the writing of journalists who pay little attention to the theology of church; while academic ecclesial theology usually steers clear of institutional controversy and pursues an untroubled course of theoretical and detached reflection.

I have come to regret this unnecessary division of labour, and in this book I try to bring the two together. The result, however, may displease some readers. Some of those who have an interest in the theology of church may disapprove of my critique of the institution, while those whose interests are journalistic may dislike my excursions into theology, philosophy and history. I can see no way of avoiding this problem, and I therefore ask for the reader's forbearance. Discussion of church reform is not solely an academic exercise; it is a moral task, because it may involve issues of natural justice and human happiness. Worthy and faithful people have suffered from the absence of institutional reform and its spirit.

I have also come to believe that it is a theological and moral duty to take issue with some current church structures and practices, in spite of the fact that some Catholics will disagree with what I have to say. I ask only that they concede my right to say it without being regarded as a disloyal Catholic. I believe that some controversial matters in the church call for a conscientious choice of which side one is on, instead of acquiescing in a careless indifference to the realities of the situation. I began my adult life accepting unquestioning theological uniformity; I now appreciate the vital importance of theological diversity as an enrichment of, not a threat to, the unity of the church. If this change of attitude is described as liberalism, then I am happy to be seen as a liberal, while I respect fellow Catholics who take issue with it.

These have not been easy times for Catholics who have remained in their church in spite of scandals, low morale and a dictatorial system of government. Pastors have a duty of care for the intellectually and culturally disillusioned as well as for those who apparently have no problems with their church or their faith. Pope Francis speaks of the need for genuine consultation with the people of God; and this means having the courage to listen to questions and observations that may prove uncomfortable to hear. To regard people like the Association of Catholic Priests in Ireland as irresponsible 'troublemakers', for example, simply evades a pastoral duty by falling back on passive aggression – which is a regrettable tactic for those who have a serious ministerial vocation to care not only for the untroubled but also for those who ask difficult questions about the church and its beliefs. There are people for whom the choice is either no faith or else a faith that is critically aware and is courageous enough to put honest questions to itself.

Choice of words to describe each side of the clear division in the church presents difficulties because it is hard to find terms acceptable to everyone. In the course of this book I frequently advocate the need for diversity in church life and thought. Diversity implies the possibility of several distinct and even conflicting attitudes and convictions. However, one conflict of opinion stands out as being particularly significant, indeed basic, to all the others: it concerns the attitude and approach to political and cultural change within the church. No reform is possible without substantial change; consequently those members of the church who oppose change on principle and speak menacingly about the binding power of 'the teaching of the Church', which they identify with their own opinions, must necessarily oppose reform. Radical conservatism, by definition, rules out the sort of reform I envisage here.

Journalists covering the Second Vatican Council (1962-1965) normally described as 'conservative' the council members who saw no reason for, and much danger in, any change of the status quo, and as 'progressive', those who recognised that things had to change if the contemporary church was to speak effectively to the men and women of today. Pope John XXIII, using the word '*aggiornamento*', made it quite clear where he stood in the matter and gave the council an exciting programme in his opening address. His successors did not fully share his vision or continue his programme. The arrival of Pope Francis marks a recognition of the need for reform. Francis speaks of the necessity of *change of attitude*, and conversion of heart, before effective action can be undertaken to reform the church. The real problem consists in the blunt fact that some members of the church see no reason to change their attitude, and they treasure the very features that others see as being in serious need of change.

When we try to name each wing of the division and seek to find words that describe the attitude of each as fairly as possible, the words that we choose almost inevitably suggest values rather than descriptions that are value-free. The terms 'conservative' and 'progressive' can be, but rarely are, used in a value-free sense. If taken in a value-free sense, 'conservative' simply means opting for no change in the way things are. 'Progressive' means wanting to move in a new, or rediscovered old, direction in order to meet the challenge of new situations, and perhaps to abandon habits and attitudes now seen to be outmoded, defective or unsuited to present needs of the church. (It is almost impossible to employ the word 'progressive' in a totally value-free sense!) The Christian vocation calls for a blend of the two. It all depends on what one wants to save and what one wants to change; and on this there can be serious disagreement, and value-judgements have to be made. How they are made constitutes the kernel of the Christian way of life. Christian faith is more a matter of attitude and action than of carefully assessed, and rigidly enforced, doctrines.

The Congregation for the Doctrine of the Faith (CDF) will figure prominently in this book, largely because it uses force in the prosecution of its aims. If it engages in discussion, it is *de haut en bas,* and normally from a judgemental viewpoint. It has a preset idea of what is orthodox and simply tries to enforce an ultra-conservative theology on the entire church. At present it has punitive powers that can destroy the lives, reputations and spiritual influence of pastoral priests and religious. Theologians, when they think this wrong, have a duty to examine what is happening from the standpoint of the Gospel and to speak up honestly and fearlessly.

I appreciate that my preoccupation with the CDF can seem rather clericalist, but it should be remembered that the work of priests, bishops and members of religious orders impinges, with greater or lesser effect, on the lives of the laity and of the church in general. Clerics and religious are the people most vulnerable to institutional attack. If an atmosphere of threat and fear is created at the senior levels of an institution like the church, it may damage the morale and vision of those further down the institutional ladder, to the detriment of all. We have a duty to protest against any kind of official behaviour that gratuitously destroys the attractiveness of the Good News. This is a thought that never seems to occur to those who exercise unchecked power in the church, and like to project an authoritative image. They may fail to see how their attitude seems to have little of the Gospel in it, and consequently discourages many people by its forbidding manner.

No matter what terms we use, there can be no credible denial that there *is* a radical division of attitudes in the Catholic Church, and that these attitudes resist any attempt to bring about consensus between them. We are faced with the unavoidable fact of logic that they are mutually contradictory. The only consensus that is possible from a Christian standpoint is an agreement to live together in tolerant and perhaps sometimes humorous disagreement about ideas and ideals. This is a difficult enough challenge, but it is the truly Christian one; and the search for consensus between two mutually contradictory positions is a diversion from the challenge that will have to be faced eventually in a church that takes the Gospel with any degree of seriousness.

In some respects this challenge is more difficult than that of interchurch relations; and it receives much less attention. The Archbishop of Canterbury, Justin Welby, recently expressed his fear that the Anglican Church might disintegrate as a result of differences between liberals and traditionalists. However, the Anglican Church has a long tradition of 'comprehensiveness', which is lacking in the Roman Catholic Church. Nevertheless, both churches are faced with the same difficult situation, caused by the two conflicted wings. Perhaps both churches could make a sterling contribution to church unity by seeking *together* an answer to a situation that threatens many Christian churches. It might come to be seen as deeper, more realistic and more practical than theoretical questions about Baptism, Eucharist and Ministry, on which many hours of labour have been spent in a bilateral search for theoretical agreement.

I hope that this book will be seen as a contribution not merely to Roman Catholic life and theology, but also to interchurch relations. There is no practice more bonding than a challenge met together by bodies that find themselves in a similar situation. We can no longer afford to act separately in pursuit of a goal that can be more effectively faced together. Reform as a shared task is such a goal, especially when it bears on unity, and is a response to Jesus' exhortation to love one another.

I am indebted to my colleagues and friends, Dr Andrew Pierce and Dr Geraldine Smyth, for helpful suggestions on clarifying passages in earlier drafts of this book. Neither is of course responsible for anything I have written on what I know is a controversial subject.

1

An Autobiographical Note

I have written this book as a theologian who happens to be a Roman Catholic and has long retired from regular work. My reason for writing it is that after an illness a few years ago, I recovered my health only to notice that I and others were living in a church the authorities of which were continuing the practice of condemning and punishing fellow Catholics who cannot always share their views. The Pope at that time was Benedict XVI. He had once been seen as a moderately progressive theologian and an associate of reformers like Karl Rahner and Hans Küng. Then in the late 1960s he underwent a startling metamorphosis from progressive theologian to an anxious and defensive one who believes that the church is in urgent need, not of reform but of a reaffirmation of its authority. Under John Paul II in 1981 Joseph Ratzinger became Prefect of the Congregation for the Doctrine of the Faith (CDF), the most conservative and powerful dicastery[1] in the Vatican Curia. In 2005 he succeeded John Paul as pope. Between them they made the Catholic Church a cold place for many members who were unable to see the church and the world as they did.

The greater part of this book was written during Benedict's papacy. The arrival of Pope Francis has necessitated considerable revision of my original text, the mood of which was sombre and rather negative. The mood in the church today is brighter because of what Pope Francis is doing. It is not my intention to use Pope Francis in order to disparage Pope Benedict. I recognise that Joseph Ratzinger is a reputable theologian; but I disliked some of the trends in his theology before he became pope; and I do not believe that becoming pope made any significant difference to

---

1. The Roman Curia is made up of different dicasteries (departments). Although all dicasteries belong to the structure of papal governance, most are not as intolerant and oppressive as the Congregation for the Doctrine of the Faith (CDF), and some promote a more irenic, and less intolerant, approach to the church and world. When I mention 'the curia', I am referring to its general structure, and often implicitly to the CDF. Most of my complaints are levelled at the CDF, mainly because it has the power to interfere punitively in the lives of theologians and pastors throughout the church, and is most in need of reform.

his theology. Popes have every right to continue to hold theological views that they have formerly held, but they have no authority to impose their theology on the whole church. If a pope condemns 'dissenters', meaning those who do not share all of his ideas, he overreaches his authority and perpetrates an injustice, especially if he sanctions the punitive actions of a body such as the Congregation for the Doctrine of the Faith (CDF).

In this book I am especially critical of the CDF; and for this I make no apology. I believe that, as well as perpetrating injustices, it is severely damaging the image and reputation of the Catholic Church. I cannot understand why it is still allowed to behave as it does. I would have little difficulty with its *having* a notably conservative theology, provided that it did not *impose* it on the entire church with serious institutional penalties for those who cannot in conscience agree with it; and provided that there was clear institutional freedom to take issue with its opinions. It would also need to have liberal as well as conservative members, so that it could relate justly and peacefully to the entire church. It should not have the power to penalise Catholics who dissent from its views and mindset. I realise how long a history it has had; but I am convinced that it needs to come into the modern world and abandon what George Tyrrell called its medieval mindset.

I return to the activities of the CDF at several points in the book. This may strike the reader as excessive, but I do so only because attempts to reform it have fallen far short of what is needed. It continues to wield a power greater than that of bishops and even popes. It seems to me that a book on reform in the Catholic Church has to regard the CDF as its principal concern. Because of its anonymity and its obsession with secrecy, it manages to avoid the attentions of the media and thus it is able to escape the obligation of transparency, so necessary in a body that possesses such power and is prepared to use it unjustly against those who are trying to make the church more Christlike and responsive to Gospel values.

I realise that the main targets of the CDF are priests and members of religious orders, and this may suggest that the whole business is exclusively clerical. The fact is that this disorder affects the entire church because intimidation of the clergy influences how the clergy interacts with the laity. It is in the best interests of the laity to support, as far as they can, those clergy who are attempting to bring about necessary changes in church life. It will be the constant concern of this book to argue that diversity of opinion in matters that do not belong to the essence of the faith enriches the church. If a pope were publicly to recognize the importance of diversity to the health of the church; if he discouraged his curia from elevating their opinions to the status of immutable doctrines; and, above all, if he were to prohibit the CDF from penalising those who cannot in conscience share their views, it would be a crucial and heartening step towards reform.

It is obvious that there are two conflicting mentalities in the church, and logic will show that they cannot be conflated. Why should we try to seek a consensus between conservatives and liberals? It is often assumed that this is a laudably Christian aim; but it is in fact aiming at an impossible goal. Consensus of mindset and conviction between these two wings of the church is logically impossible since they have views that are mutually incompatible. What *is* possible and desirable is a willingness to live tolerantly and peacefully together in spite of their different attitudes. Why not let each abound in their own sense, and be free to discuss and dispute the issues that divide them? Pretending that a consensus is possible amounts to dissembling the truth for a well-intentioned but logically impossible reason. Discrepant attitudes are inevitable in a body as large and diverse as the Catholic Church. The demand for the suppression of views with which we do not agree can be rightly described as an unacceptable extreme, but there is nothing to be gained from ignoring the presence of conflicting views in the church. What we need is the freedom to discuss and argue the case for what we believe to be true, but to do so in a way that befits disciples of Christ.

One fact is evident: in the Catholic Church today there is a very clear division between those who are content with the church as it has been up to now, and those who want to see a change in its attitudes, structures and behaviour. I am one of an increasing number of Catholics who believe that our church is in urgent need of reform, not merely for administrative and socially responsible reasons, but principally for evangelical ones. I regret that some fellow Catholics will take offence at what I have to say. I do not ask that they share my views; and they should not insist that I share theirs. They, and especially those in authority, should, for the benefit of the whole church, appreciate, and even encourage, a range of views rather than sternly try to impose a narrow conception of orthodoxy on everybody. Pope Francis is leading the way.

If we submerge legitimate differences in an attempt to achieve unity, we impoverish the body that is enriched by these differences. This was a conviction of John Macquarrie, a distinguished Anglican theologian, and a prominent ecumenist who appreciated what he described as 'the many dangers in ecumenism'. He has written a sentence that says a great deal not merely about relations between divided Christians, but also about conditions that exist within each church: 'The genuine diversity-in-unity of the body of Christ needs to be defended against uniformity just as much as against divisiveness'. [2] When I first read these words, I realised that they expressed a sentiment that was true not only of ecumenical relations but also of domestic church divisions. Trying to find an impossible consensus can be a diversion from the more difficult faith-inspired task of living peacefully with fellow Christians who do not share one's theological convictions.

The basic thesis of this book is that people of one mindset have gained control of the entire institutional church, and are putting forward their own theology as 'the teaching of the church'. They are acting gratuitously as if the legitimate views of others who disagree with them are a 'danger' to the faithful. Some of them brandish the word 'heretic' to describe their opponents; others like to speak of 'confusion', alleged to characterise those Catholics who take issue with them. Those who do not share their views they describe as 'confused'. (Some traditionalist cardinals have suggested that Pope Francis and Cardinal Kasper were 'confusing' the synod of 2014.) In the course of the book I will try to show that while these ultra-conservatives have a right to hold their own particular ideas and convictions, and even to express them as officially binding, if they feel obliged to do so; they have no right, however, to use their executive powers to punish those who are clearly within the parameters of credal doctrine. Although I am well aware of occasional protests against 'labels' such as 'conservative' and 'progressive', we must employ something like them to describe where we stand on the controversial issues under discussion in the contemporary church and world. Condemnation of labels

2. J. Macquarrie, *Principles of Christian Theology* (London, 1977), pp. 403-4.

can be an indolent and convenient way of avoiding an issue by refusing to give it a name. It is often an attempt to rise above unavoidable debate by taking refuge in flight from difficult questions; and it patronizes those Catholics who see the urgent need for discussion and debate. Those of us who are looking for reform are not troublemakers in the vineyard of the Lord. We are trying to clear away weeds that we believe are interfering with the health and growth of the vines, and we are doing so from inside the church. Sometimes confrontation is necessary, especially when one mentality sets itself up as the arbiter of orthodoxy and uses power rather than respectable argument to promote its cause.

Pretending to be virtuously above the conflict between 'conservative' and 'progressive' views of church structures and practices, however, amounts to an appeasement of people who are striving to prevent reform. I would have greater respect for dedicated traditionalists who actually believe in the truth of their position, than for people who think that they can occupy a storm-free eminence whence they can look down with patronising pity on the combatants.

With many others, I protest against the reliance of Rome on crude tactics such as excommunication, dismissal of members of religious orders or censoring of people who hold teaching posts in institutions under church control. Although the need to call for reform has been the main spur to my writing this book, I found that the notion of reform opened up several theological, historical and philosophical issues which are not controversial in any institutional sense, but which I believe to be relevant to what I have to say. I hope to show that reform has its roots deep in Christian faith and theology, and is not just a passing trend.

I would not normally introduce an autobiographical note into what I write. For the purposes of this book, however, I think the reader should be given some notion of where I am coming from, and where I find myself today.

I learnt my first lessons in theology at the Gregorian University in Rome just after World War II. Consequently I have some personal knowledge, from the inside, of how traditionalists think today, for in many respects I was once unknowingly of their number. The Gregorian was a clerical university run by Jesuits and at that time to some extent shaped by the needs of future priests. Its dedication to neo-scholasticism was clear.

Neo-scholasticism was a nineteenth century adaptation of a medieval philosophy which in turn was an adaptation of ancient Greek philosophy, mainly expressed in the thought of Thomas Aquinas, who was heavily influenced by Aristotle. I cannot give here a full account of neo-scholasticism, and I am not taking issue with it as an estimable philosophical system. What I am concerned with here is the way it was made indispensable to orthodox Catholic theology and was imposed by Rome on centres of learning and teaching throughout the whole church. Pope Leo XIII gave Thomism a privileged place in his encyclical *Aeterni Patris* (1879), but he specifically stated that it was not his intention to displace the scientific study of nature. What he wanted was a firm philosophical base for the orthodox expression of Catholic doctrine. From that moment it became inseparable from the orthodox Catholic theology that I was taught in the late 1940s. I think of it today as an important philosophical and theological movement which can be studied in its own right, now that it has ceased to be a mandatory feature of orthodox Catholicism.

The main features of neo-scholastic theology may be briefly summarized as follows: God's existence can be proved by reason; God's self-revelation can be established by 'fundamental' theology (a bridge between philosophy and theology proper), principally by the existence of miracles and fulfilled prophecies; divine revelation consists in statements communicated by God to the church; these statements must be assented to by an act of faith made by the intellect; in the rest of dogmatic theology, deductions may be made as logical consequences drawn from an analysis of the meaning of revealed truths; Scripture is one source of revelation; Tradition is the other. Deductions may be made from scripturally based assertions (Matthew 16:18, 'Thou art Peter...') proved capable of generating a surprising number of subsequent doctrines which have been taught by the magisterium of the church and graded by its theologians as having a weight relative to the scholastically determined scheme of things. The respected French Catholic philosopher, Maurice Blondel, would stigmatise the whole scheme as 'extrinsicism' – a system that lacked an interior dimension. His disciple – or perhaps better, colleague – the Modernist Lucien Laberthonnière, later to be harried by the Roman Holy Office, remarked humorously that the liberal Protestants had faith without beliefs, while Catholics had beliefs without faith.

18

Neo-scholasticism lent itself as an intellectual basis for Catholic Church internal political action at and after the First Vatican Council. In spite of Leo XIII's openness to modern science, neo-scholasticism underwrote the tendency in the church to withdraw from engagement with the modern world and to take refuge in a medieval pre-scientific world. It was a philosophy that rooted itself in pre-ordained essences which gave the church a stability that protected it from what it saw as the ravages of post-Enlightenment thought, and enabled it to take refuge from the challenges presented by scientifically inspired materialism together with various existential and positivist theories and other kinds of inductive thinking that, in the view of Rome, threatened to destroy the settled world of fixed essences.[3] The Modernists at the end of the nineteenth century and the beginning of the twentieth challenged that world; and they were wiped out with a ferocity induced by the conviction that they were attacking the very foundations of Catholic orthodoxy. Neo-scholastic culture was still being proclaimed as indispensable to Catholic orthodoxy as late as 1950 by Pope Pius XII in his encyclical, *Humani Generis*. It was tacitly abandoned at and after the Second Vatican Council – a highly significant development.

As a result of severely restrictive rules about reading when I was a student, I quite literally knew no better, and my thought then was much like that of today's traditionalists, though, I hope, without the defensive and combative attitude that one so often encounters today. In those days we were so sure of the rightness of where we stood that there was no need for pugnacity in its defence. We were tranquilly in possession of an indisputably and triumphantly assured eminence from which we could contemplate other erroneous Christians. Most of us theology students in Rome were trained to be unthinking conservatives by men who were highly intelligent and scholarly in their own neo-scholastic fields, but who were themselves constricted in what they could teach and write. Neo-scholasticism was at that time considered to be a necessary feature of orthodox Catholicism. Rome taught one all the 'correct' answers that were in conformity with verbal orthodoxy, and it issued severe warnings about 'errors' that could be a danger to one's faith and the faith of others. It was theologians from the Roman clerical universities who wrote

---

3. I develop this topic in greater detail *infra*, Chapter 14, on essence and existence.

the first drafts submitted to, and rejected by, the fathers of the Second Vatican Council.

At the Gregorian, as in every Roman clerical university, one was examined as much in scholastic orthodoxy as in theology. The Gregorian was only a stone's throw away from the distinguished Biblical Institute, where fellow Jesuits, who lived in a totally different academic atmosphere from that in the Gregorian, worked with and taught modern critical biblical studies. The Biblical Institute, however, pursued its studies and teaching under the frequent lash of the Holy Office (as it was called in those days). The Institute had little influence on the Gregorian, which taught a theology that was virtually unaffected by critical treatment of the Bible or by modern post-Enlightenment thought in general, both of which it seriously mistrusted and condemned at every turn. We were left in no doubt about who our enemies were; and it later became clear to some of us that our 'adversaries' (the term preferred in the text-books) were some of the foremost minds of their age.

In the early 1950s I was sent to Oxford University to read history, not in any effort to broaden my mind, it must be admitted, but for the practical reason that it would prepare me for teaching history in a school run by my Order in England. It did much more than prepare me for teaching history. Where Rome had taught me all the answers, Oxford taught me to ask questions and to think for myself, both then considered theologically dangerous activities in the Roman Catholic Church.

While I am in autobiographical mode I would like to indulge in a vivid memory of three of the happiest years of my life, spent in an Oxford that was, less than ten years after the Second World War, still sparsely populated.

I lived with members of the Ampleforth community at St Benet's Hall where I was an Irish friar living among British monks – a stimulating and valuable experience. The Master, Fr. Gerard Sitwell, O.S.B., arranged for tutorials in various colleges throughout the university. His choice of tutors was wise and well informed. My first tutor was Lionel Butler, Fellow of All Souls College and a distinguished medieval historian. The tutorial system was one of Oxford's most striking educational features. It gave students the benefits of spending an hour a week with some of the finest minds in Europe. Lionel was not merely a teacher but also a friend. He was impressed by the fact that my studies in Rome had been conducted in

Latin – something I had never given much thought to while I was a theology student. My Latin was anything but Ciceronian. I was later to reflect that a dead language suits an immobile theology – an opinion held in all seriousness by Giovanni Perrone, a nineteenth century theologian who was regarded as the foremost Roman theologian of his age.

I still remember studying political theory with Beryl Smalley, vice-Principal of St Hilda's College, whose book, *The Study of the Bible in the Middle Ages*, was celebrated as a fine work of medieval scholarship. She had a razor-sharp mind, and I enjoyed writing essays for her and hearing her chuckle if I managed to write something that amused her. Writing essays for Beryl became for me an important occasion for learning how style matters. When I studied Aristotle's *Politics* with her, she expressed surprise that I did not feel obliged to acknowledge the intellectual suzerainty of Aristotle. She told me that her experience with most Catholic priests who studied with her was that they seemed to feel an obligation to behave as paid-up Aristotelians. It was a lesson for me of how Aristotelian philosophy, because of its influence on Thomas Aquinas, had become inseparable from Catholic orthodoxy – a point that was to become significant in the next decade with the reforms of the Second Vatican Council.

Lectures at Oxford were optional; and I took the opportunity of attending the lectures of famous scholars in subjects other than history. I still remember going to hear C.S. Lewis lecture on mythology in a packed theatre in the Schools. He was a very good actor, entering from the back of the hall with panache, gown billowing behind him, and beginning his lecture halfway down the aisle on his way to the lectern.

I must mention my membership of the Oxford Bach Choir. I still treasure the memory of singing in the chorus of Bach's Mass in B Minor under the direction of Sir Thomas Armstrong. Purists today would deplore the fact that the Mass was sung by a very large chorus. But I defy even the purest of today's music critics to deny the overpowering experience of hearing the majestic *Sanctus* of the B Minor sung by a large choir. From that point on, I came to appreciate how important art is for religion. It has the power to illumine and humanize what can so easily become an arid and rule-driven exercise.

Finally, lest I give the impression that Oxford was all about study and art, I ought to refer to my recreational activities. Being a priest and a friar in the 1950s meant that I could not indulge in many of the pursuits of normal university students. For one thing, having taken an undergraduate degree in theology and philosophy in Rome, I was older than the average Oxford undergraduate, although some students who were soldiers demobbed after the war, were roughly the same age as I was. I played some rugby during my freshman year. Then I decided to take up refereeing seriously. I had coached and travelled with school rugby teams and had discovered that the standard of school refereeing was rather low. I applied for a course that qualified me to referee English county matches. Though I never actually refereed any county game, I got a good deal of experience handling college games, some of which were supervised by judges of my standards as a referee. I passed the relevant tests and received my county badge. (I must say that rugby then was very different from today's professional game; referees then were a good deal less intrusive than they are today.)

After that interlude of rich and pleasant memories which helps to illustrate how important I found my entire Oxford experience, I must return to theology. I found that history made a notable difference to my theological thinking, and it helped to open me up to the need for structural reform in the church, and for different ways of doing theology. It also prepared me to think ecumenically. To put it mildly, neither historical perspective nor ecumenism had featured significantly in the neo-scholastic theology I had been taught in the 1940s, when error was deemed to have no rights; and, as possessors of the whole truth, we had nothing to learn, and everything to fear, from dialogue with the members of other churches.

Fortunately there were at that time Catholic theologians who, at considerable institutional risk to themselves, were engaging courageously in theologies that broke with the prevailing neo-scholasticism and were excitingly new to someone like me who had been a tame and incurious student in a Roman setting. We had been living in protective custody without knowing it. I had literally known no different theology from what I had been taught. We were not encouraged to read authors of any books that might have shown us alternatives to scholastic orthodoxy, and indeed we needed a dispensation to read books by theologians from other churches. The instruments of instruction were the 'manuals' (neo-scholastic textbooks), which were concerned more with preserving verbal orthodoxy than with the need for getting off the defensive and engaging hopefully and joyfully with the modern world.

Each topic in the manuals was headed by a 'thesis' which had to be defended by triumphant disposal of its 'adversaries', and by quotations from Scripture that were mostly innocent of modern biblical criticism and were unashamedly advanced as 'proof texts' of a thesis prescribed within the neo-scholastic system.

Matthew 16:18 ('...you are Peter, and upon this rock I will build my church...') performed heavy duty as the foundational text of ecclesiology, and it was appealed to in support of most developments of the papacy through the ages. Towards the end of the nineteenth century, just when the papacy was losing its temporal sway in Italy, the First Vatican Council had declared the pope to be infallible and to have immediate universal jurisdiction over the entire church. Pius IX went into a kind of self-imposed retirement, to become the all-powerful 'prisoner of the Vatican', enjoying a blend of sympathy and adulation.

The scholastic method that serviced the dogma of papal primacy and infallibility was deductive and *a priori*, and it served as a buttress for an authoritarian and dictatorial concept of church government. The 'proofs' from tradition were mostly of conciliar, and especially of papal, statements, interpreted literally, and usually without historical nuance. The system regarded truth as timeless, immutable and impervious to the ever-changing influence of history. The system was described as 'integralism', *i.e.*, a way of thinking in which no one point could be detached from the others without endangering the whole. The Second Vatican Council would dismantle integralism by its doctrine of 'the hierarchy of truths'. However, integralism still survives implicitly in curial attitudes.[4]

The whole method was impressively logical, in an Aristotelian sense, though the premises were narrow and inward looking. It lent itself to

---

4. It should be noted that the word 'integralism' is used differently in different contexts, consequently, consulting a theological dictionary or encyclopedia could be confusing. The meaning given to it by Joseph Lemius, the main draftsman of Pius X's encyclical, *Pascendi Dominici Gregis*, is the one I use here, namely, that in the system of doctrines comprising scholastic orthodoxy, no one point could be detached from the others without endangering the whole to which they belonged. The Modernists accepted this understanding of integralism and described it as 'extrinsicism': revelation is a package of divinely revealed truths to be believed by the mind because it is attested to by miracles and other exterior signs; human interior dispositions play no part in the process. It was this that the Modernists vigorously opposed.

learning by rote; and examinations were mostly oral and focused upon verbal correctness. The thinking required was largely a matter of having a good memory. 'Fresh' thought was generally derived from deducing logical consequences from accepted orthodoxies that were graded in rank by theological 'notes', assigning to each thesis an evaluation of its place in the hierarchy, not of truths, but of scholastically determined levels of importance.

Mariology was one of the very few theological areas in which doctrine could be developed with institutional safety, though it pointed in a direction that was excessively pietistic and impossible to square with Tradition properly understood. Yves Congar, the French Dominican theologian, would later teach the Second Vatican Council how to understand the term 'Tradition' in a sense that went back to the earliest days of the church. Congar astutely observed that the theology of Mary and the theology of the papacy marched in tandem. In an age taken up with dogmas that were settled beyond the reach of ordinary members of the church, thinking for oneself was discouraged. Faithful repetition and logical analysis of those dogmas constituted the principal task of Catholic theology and preaching. Unconditional obedience to the magisterium was what was principally required to make one a satisfactory Catholic theologian. Power and rigid control over the work of theologians became the practical basis of Catholic theology. The magisterium was – and in the estimation of traditionalists still is – the guarantor of theological orthodoxy.

The term 'magisterium' literally means 'teaching body', or even more literally, mastership. It is today firmly rooted in power and control. In contemporary Catholic usage the magisterium is understood to refer, in practice, only to the pope, with his curia, and the bishops. Great emphasis has been placed on papal and curial authority. By identifying the magisterium with Tradition, the rulers of the pre-conciliar church arrogated to themselves the exclusive power of thinking and acting in and for the church. Before the significant theological reforms effected or made possible by Vatican II, Scripture was not seen as a judge of developments in church doctrine and practice. Only Protestants, we were told, interpreted the Bible freely and without instruction from any authority.

In spite of the reforms of Vatican II, the new *Catechism of the Catholic Church* says: 'The task of interpreting the Word of God authentically has been entrusted solely to the Magisterium of the Church, that is, to the Pope and to the bishops in communion with him.' This is a forbiddingly authoritarian return to the age preceding Vatican II, when theologians and Scripture scholars were watched carefully and censored frequently. Today, Roman authorities are more taken up with systematic and moral theologians (who may envy their biblical colleagues for their relative freedom from institutional assault!)

It is no longer true that Catholics neglect the Bible, as Protestants, with some justification, used to claim. Priests and laity are perfectly free to read the Bible today; and since reading is necessarily an interpretative act, they cannot but think for themselves about it. Attention has now fallen on some legitimately disputed moral and disciplinary matters on which Rome is choosing to take its stand. Since there is very little in the New Testament about authority, the magisterium tries to supplement the omission by its own activities.

I mention these theological details as an explanation rather than as an excuse for my intellectual timidity. Fortunately, in France, Holland and Germany there were Catholic theologians and philosophers who were much more adventurous than I had been trained to be in Rome in the 1940s; and it was due to their courage and industry that scholars were available to introduce new, or forgotten old, ideas to the church in the council which Pope John XXIII unexpectedly called in 1959. The experience of the Second Vatican Council shook many of us out of the unexamined rectitude and the narrow horizons of our theological thinking.

A year after the closing of the council, I returned to Ireland to engage in full-time theological studies and teaching. I lectured first at the Milltown Institute of Theology and Philosophy, Dublin, and then at Trinity College, Dublin, the latter of which gave me the valuable experience of teaching theology in a secular and non-denominational setting, until I retired some 30 years later.

At Trinity College I had the good fortune to have as one of my colleagues a young German theologian, Werner Jeanrond,[5] who had come to Trinity from his doctoral studies in the USA, and is an expert in hermeneutics (the philosophy of interpretation). Coming to terms with

5. Professor Jeanrond subsequently taught theology in Sweden and Scotland, and is now a professor in the Faculty of Theology in Oxford University.

hermeneutics was extremely important in my theological development, and I am very grateful to Werner for his role in that development. At the invitation of Michael Hurley, S.J., I was also involved in the foundation of the Irish School of Ecumenics, where I lectured for more than 30 years until my retirement.

I wrote a book on Catholic Modernism,[6] the research for which brought me into close and detailed contact with an important reforming movement in the Catholic Church, which took place at the end of the nineteenth century and the beginning of the twentieth. My doctoral studies under the Anglican theologian, Anthony Hanson, were focused on Modernism, and I received my PhD from the University of Hull, where Anthony was Professor of Theology.

Modernism had been ruthlessly and comprehensively condemned by Rome in the days when neo-scholasticism was the touchstone of orthodoxy. Interestingly, and highly significantly, reliance on scholastic thought as a guarantor of orthodoxy has silently disappeared from contemporary Catholic theology. Considering that fidelity to neo-scholasticism had been deemed indispensable to Catholic orthodoxy as late as the pontificate of Pius XII, this disappearance is a striking indication of how officially prescribed theology can change radically without comment from the magisterium. In the Roman Catholic Church reform tends to be by amnesia, which enables its authorities to preserve the fiction of doctrinal immutability and the seamless continuity of church teaching.

Detailed historical and theological research into Modernism made me painfully aware of how intolerantly Rome had treated important thinkers in the church who were trying to release its theologians and biblical scholars from an outmoded way of doing theology and studying Scripture. In 1908 George Tyrrell, an Anglo-Irish Modernist, convert to Catholicism and member of the Society of Jesus, wrote a book called *Medievalism* which tackled the question of how neo-scholastic orthodoxy was strangling all attempts to bring Catholic theology up to date.[7] At the express command of Pope Pius X, Tyrrell was expelled from the Jesuits.

6. G. Daly, *Transcendence and Immanence: A Study in Catholic Modernism and Integralism* (Oxford, Clarendon Press, 1980).

7. G. Tyrrell, *Medievalism: A Reply to Cardinal Mercier* (modern reprint, London, 1994) with a Foreword by Gabriel Daly.

Considering the vehemence with which the Modernist critique of neo-scholasticism was condemned, it is truly remarkable how the magisterium, without comment, has tacitly dropped its earlier conviction that the neo-scholastic method is indispensable to Catholic orthodoxy. It is one of the most impressive illustrations of how the pretended continuity of official church teaching can be seen to be a cherished fiction. Pope John, in his opening address to the Second Vatican Council, observed that while the substance of the faith remains constant, the manner of its formulation can change. Traditional Catholic teaching before Vatican II would not have accepted that highly significant distinction.

This book is intended to offer a reflection on some theological subjects that arise when one considers the question of reform in the church. I have written it as a small contribution to meeting a problem that, at the moment, is confusing the unity that Jesus wished for his followers with a uniformity that suits the traditionalist authorities of the contemporary Roman Catholic Church.

The greater part of this book has been written during the pontificate of Pope Benedict XVI. I refer to him frequently as the contemporary exemplar of papal authority; and I do not subscribe to the idea that his retirement makes him or his ideas irrelevant to the new papacy. Since in their hope of change many Catholics see the new pope as an instrument of reform, some commentators even suggest that to continue to reflect on Benedict's influence is unfashionable and out of date; others take exception to the drawing of a contrast between Pope Benedict and Pope Francis. I make no secret of my conviction that it is correct, and indeed necessary, to make a substantial contrast between the two pontificates. A return to the ways of Benedict would cast a gloom over a church that is beginning to hope for change.

We do not know whether, or to what extent, Benedict continues to influence Francis. In a curious move, Francis has chosen to issue an encyclical, *Lumen Fidei*, which he states openly has been written mainly by Benedict; and it bears all the marks of German academic theological proficiency. He continues to lay stress on the continuity between Benedict's pontificate and his own. It remains to be seen how far Francis will depart openly from Benedict's attitudes and actions, some of which are incompatible with his own. At the moment, Francis' new style is hard to reconcile with his keenness to affirm his continuity with his predecessor. Only time will tell whether substance will follow style. It is one thing to welcome a change in papal style, it is quite another to believe that Francis will be able or willing to bring about the kind of reform that is needed in today's Catholic Church. His re-appointment of Gerhard Ludwig Müller to be Prefect of the Congregation for the Doctrine of the Faith is difficult to understand, given that they have contradictory views of church.

Opposition to Francis is growing stealthily among traditionalists whose ideology forbids them to disagree publicly with any pope. With many other Catholics, I continue to long for real change. To close down the CDF would take a great deal of courage because it is esteemed by some to be a bastion of orthodox belief. The Pope might hesitate to take such a radical step as this, but he could without any conflict with traditionalist convictions, command it to refrain from its assaults on people who do not share its mindset and are trying to make their faith relevant to the contemporary world.

While I am in an autobiographical vein, I ought to explain why this book, although it is in the main concerned with strictly theological matters, has been strongly influenced by the human consequences of the actions of the Roman Curia. I have consequently found it difficult to approach the topic of reform in the church with the detachment I would normally try to bring to a task such as this. I have witnessed the effect that the actions of an unreformed curial office have had on people whom I respect and admire for their efforts to make the Gospel live for modern men and women. This has made it extremely difficult for me to approach Vatican bureaucracy with restraint. Because of the anger I felt, I had to rewrite some of the first draft of this book in order to remove excessively adverse comment on Vatican officials. For what remains I ask the reader's indulgence.

I see no reason today for a body like the CDF to try to perform by force a task that can be carried out more credibly by academic debate in which scholars can be relied upon to dispute positions taken by other scholars. I am not trying, in the language of Yves Congar, to set up a para-magisterium to the curia. Discussion and debate are how ideas are normally clarified and, where necessary, challenged. Faith cannot be shaped by the exercise of mere power; *a fortiori* neither can the theology that supports it. By all means let Vatican theologians express their opinions in the market-place of ideas, where they can be examined, approved of or disputed by others who have an equal right to be heard. One can only hope that they may eventually come to appreciate the benefits of diversity in a pilgrim church.

2

Revelation and Reform

It sometimes seems that God does not wish to be found too easily. Our age is marked by the growth of atheism and agnosticism. There was a time when Roman Catholic theologians believed that God's existence could be confidently 'proved' by philosophical argument. Today, while not denying the validity of the classical proofs, theologians may observe that the bare declaration that God exists does not speak to the heart or engage the whole person. For that to happen, God must take the initiative by speaking to human beings, assuring them that they are loved with an eternal love that seeks reciprocation on their part. Divine revelation is therefore necessary, if God's purposes are to be realised.

Christians believe that the perfection of God's self-revelation occurred in the Middle East 2,000 years ago in a man who came from undistinguished stock, lived in an undistinguished part of his country, spent the greater part of his life as a craftsman, and in the final few years of a short life, left his trade to become a wandering preacher. It is hardly what one might have expected of God's unique self-revelation to human beings. The greater part of the life of Jesus and, most strikingly, the horror of his passion and death are not merely the setting for, but an essential constituent of, what God wishes to reveal to men and women about their creator.

Jesus from Nazareth was possessed by a conviction that God's reign was taking place in him, and that if his followers wished to find God, they must believe in him as God's communicating presence. He spoke to and about God as his Father, and in John's gospel he told one of his followers that to see him was to see the Father (John 14:9).

That is to make an impressive claim, which his followers are charged to believe and which their faith commits them to making. It is sometimes described as a 'scandalous particularity', which offended against the universal Greek philosophical values in the early ages of the church and continues to offend against modern sophistication. Preoccupation with the secondary matter of ecclesiastical authority can divert us from having to witness to it in today's world. We so easily face the world with the wrong scandal.

Answering a question put to him by some of the Jewish authorities about what the principal command of the Scriptures was, Jesus replied that the first and greatest commandment was that they must love God with all their heart, with all their soul and with all their mind. This first commandment was to be accompanied inseparably by a second one that resembled it, which was that they should love their neighbours as themselves. From these two commandments hang all the law and the prophets. (Matthew 22:34-40) It was a strikingly simple and direct message; and its simplicity is all too easily obscured by elaborate dogmas and arbitrary moral ordinances meted out to the world in the name of orthodoxy.

God had entered history in the guise of a modest craftsman whose followers were instructed to take this message to the ends of the earth. As St Paul was to tell the Christians of Corinth, the violent death of this craftsman-turned-preacher was at the heart of God's message to humanity, and it would be a scandal to Jews and folly to Gentiles. In speaking about God's 'folly', Paul was adopting startling language in order to bring out the counter-intuitive interpretation of the meaning of the cross, which he claimed was intended to confound worldly wisdom and to give to those who are called to discipleship an assurance that their salvation is to be found in Jesus Christ, who is the power and the wisdom of God (1 Corinthians 1:18-25). Instead of preaching the message confidently in full awareness of its challenge to worldly wisdom, Catholic authorities have tended to diminish it by wandering from its austere and challenging thrust and allowing it to be obscured by a preoccupation with institutional power.

The structures of the church need to be reformed, precisely so that its members may rediscover, in all its shining clarity, the primary meaning of the good news of the Christian Gospel. Our churchly preoccupations, many of them politically inspired, sometimes seem to be given more importance than attending in full measure to the good news with which we have been entrusted. Reforming the institutional church is therefore a truly *evangelical* task, and not merely a tinkering with structures so that the quality of church membership may be improved for our convenience and comfort.

It is in this context that we have to consider how the Catholic Church is being governed. As John Henry Newman remarked, Rome ought to be a name to lighten the heart at all times. Instead Rome[1] has become an admonitory agent, imposing beliefs that are distant from the main tenets of authentic Christianity.

If bureaucratic violence in the church were to be abandoned, we could learn to live with ideas and ideals that conflict with each other within the unity of the one church. We would be free to commend those we believe to be in keeping with the Gospel, and to live as amicably as possible with a vision of church that we do not share. Part of the problem of doing so is that some traditionalist views favour the punishment of those they like to describe as heretics. There is unfortunately an interpretation of orthodoxy that makes no allowance for diversity in matters that do not belong to the essence of Christianity.

The word 'orthodox' has the etymological meaning of 'right opinion'. In Catholic usage it has come to mean 'conformity with prescribed doctrine'. In early Christian usage it meant 'conformity with the officially recognised creeds'. In contemporary Roman Catholicism 'the teaching of the church', is probably the phrase most often used to convey the official Vatican concept of orthodoxy. It is located primarily in the magisterium, and it begs the question of the meaning of 'church'.

We must take exception to the exclusive extension of the term 'orthodox' to the teaching of those who are in power at any moment in the church and whose opinions are not always shared by other members of the church. The notion of orthodoxy should apply only to conformity with the creeds, *i.e.,* the central truths of Christianity. The word 'heresy' should not be used to describe opinions which differ from those held by official church leaders, but are nevertheless legitimate views within the compass of credal teaching. Thus, for example, Rome has a right to *hold* that women cannot be ordained to the priesthood; but does it have the right to censure those who disagree and, perhaps more importantly, the right to forbid discussion of the question? Discussion of, and even debate over, such questions is a necessary ingredient of the church's obligation

---

1. Throughout this book I use the word 'Rome' to refer to the pope and his curia. Since the curia is a sort of civil service which operates with the implicit authority of the pope, it is not always easy to determine whether some document or move comes directly from the pope, or from the curia acting with, or without, his presumed authority.

to search for the truth and to respect, not punish, legitimate differences of opinion in that search.

The present method of electing popes and appointing bishops is designed to keep the whole system in the hands of those who share a similar mentality. However, because this system of government can be reformed without any departure from the will of God in Christ Jesus, we can at least hope and strive for change. The new Pope offers real hope of that change.

There was a moment in the recent past when an event, which can be interpreted as occurring under the inspiration of the Holy Spirit, gave the church a pope, John XXIII, who called a reforming council and brought to his office an attitude that was inclusive, benign and, in short, Christlike. If the cardinals who elected him as a caretaker pope had known that he would call a reforming council, it is doubtful that they would have chosen him. I dwell on his memory at many points throughout this book, because it is a source of hope for those of us who are dispirited by what has been happening under the last two papal regimes. In the final chapter I couple the memory of John with the impression that Francis is making on the church. In these two men we have inspiring evidence that the papacy, in spite of its monarchical history, can be a source of inspiration, freedom and authenticity of faith today. History, so far from imprisoning us in the past, should be an agent for change when we realise that governmental structures that belong to an age that has passed may need to be reformed in the light of the Gospel today.

It is worth reflecting for a moment on the meaning of the word 'reform' in the context of the contemporary Roman Catholic Church. In its general sense, reform of an institution means an attempt to improve the culture and behaviour of its members, but particularly its structures of governance. In this book I speak of structural 'reform', as distinct from 'renewal', which is normally envisaged as taking place within the unchanged structures of the church. In the Catholic Church, as in most highly organised societies, the predominant governmental instinct has been to preserve the situation as it is at the present moment and to put the wellbeing of the institution before all other considerations. The *status quo* is defended with vigour and sometimes with a callous disregard for justice. Church officers almost instinctively resist any move to change things as they are. A sort of immobility affects the structures of the church, especially those that pertain to the papacy and its court. These structures are sometimes given permanence because of the curious conviction that Jesus himself has designed and prescribed them. The human element in the church is thus played down to the greatest extent possible, and the powers of the papacy and its court, as they have normally been exercised, are put forward as God-sanctioned. This is theocracy, and as a treacherous form of fundamentalism, it needs to be opposed in the name of the Gospel.

The phrase *Ecclesia semper reformanda (est)*, 'The church (is) always in need of reform', began its modern life in the seventeenth century Dutch Reformed Church and was enthusiastically adopted by the majority at the Second Vatican Council. In some respects it was an implicit ideal of the Reformation movement from its earliest days, but it became explicit as a result of continuing Protestant reflection on the meaning of what had been achieved by the Reformation from its beginnings.

As a result of the success of Martin Luther's condemnation of much that was going on in the church of his time, western Christianity became radically divided. Protestants increasingly appreciated the danger that they might come to think of the Reformation as a once-off event producing a reformed church that had cast off the trappings of Roman Catholicism and could now relax into its new status as a reformed church. The full version of the phrase is: *ecclesia reformata semper reformanda est*: the reformed church remains always in need of ongoing reform. Reform can never be *finally* achieved in a church that is composed of fractured human beings and knows itself as totally and permanently subject to God's judgement, and is consequently aware of its *continuing* need for divine mercy and forgiveness. 'Always' is the most significant word in the phrase 'The Church: always in need of reform'.

Catholic theology has resisted the Protestant notion that nature has been totally corrupted by sin. Instead, from the meeting of the Council of Trent onwards, it has preferred to speak of human nature, as wounded rather than corrupt. However, it has constantly asserted that grace presupposes nature as the arena of its action: grace is not an abstraction but a divine presence in everyday life. St Augustine has written that God who made us without our cooperation cannot save us without our cooperation. Grace does not operate as a compulsion but always respects human freedom, including the freedom to resist it.

Reform depends on context for its meaning, and it is the natural, especially human, element that supplies that context. The character and scope of reform differ from one church to another, usually for institutional reasons. Human beings, divided within themselves, inevitably produce social and political structures that are flawed. An excessively 'high' concept of church can produce an inflated theory of the sanctity of church authority, thus creating a situation in which the very notion of reform is seen as dangerously intrusive. The Second Vatican Council was emphatic in its rejection of that view and was quite explicit in recognising the need for reform. In its Decree on Ecumenism it has this to say:

> Christ summons the Church, as she goes on her pilgrim way, to that continual reformation of which she always has need, insofar as she is a human institution here on earth. (Art. 6)

In the light of this teaching of the council, it is difficult to understand Pope Benedict XVI's reluctance to speak of reform of the church. He dismisses the sociological reality of the church and substitutes a mystical interpretation for it. In an interview with Vittorio Messori in 1985, Cardinal Ratzinger said:

> If the church ... is viewed as a human construction, the product of our own efforts, even the contents of the faith end up assuming an arbitrary character.

And a little later:

> ... if [the structures of the church] are not willed by Christ, then it is no longer possible to conceive of the existence of the hierarchy as a service to the baptised established by the Lord himself ... [The church's] deep and permanent structure is not democratic but sacramental, consequently hierarchical.[2]

Such a statement that implies that democracy cannot be sacramental and that hierarchical structure is sacramental (and *therefore* not democratic) because Christ wills it. It is difficult not to see here a serious confusion of categories; the supernatural is made to exclude the human and

2. J. F. Thornton and S. B. Varenne (eds), *The Essential Pope Benedict: His Central Writings and Speeches,* (San Francisco, 2007), pp. 64 and 66.

political approach to ecclesiastical organisation, and the mystical is made to displace the social and political reality of church governance.[3]

As a result of the historical concentration of authority and power in the hands of the papacy and its court, structural reform has more than once been a point of tension in the history of Catholicism. Reform in the Roman Catholic Church is a sensitive issue, because the party in power may construe the desire for change as infidelity and disloyalty. Its spokesmen like to claim that disagreement with their point of view sows 'confusion' among the faithful. Fear of condemnation by, or even of disapproval of, the CDF can impair the drive towards real reform.

It is fairly obvious that the Catholic Church is in disarray in many parts of the world today. Decreasing membership in the Northern hemisphere, the scandal of clerical child abuse and its totally inadequate handling by the authorities, the despondency and low morale of clergy and the disillusionment of the laity, are all contributing to the felt need of reform throughout the Church. All these causes have been compounded by a feeling of helplessness resulting from the unwillingness of Rome and many bishops to listen to, and engage with, the problems that many Catholics face today. Pope Francis is showing clear signs of recognising the need for consulting the ordinary faithful, but it would seem that some bishops are embarrassed by the results of such consultation, which often reveal a situation very much at odds with official prescriptions. Up to the arrival of Pope Francis, the Vatican has been so busy denouncing the defects of those who disagree with them, that it never seemed to admit its own defects.

This book is by no means confined to comment on the Irish Catholic Church; but since I happen to be Irish, and live in Ireland, the institutions and culture of my country have shaped my experience; and authenticity demands that I recognize this fact and acknowledge it to readers of this book. Those who live in a different culture may claim that the problems I am considering here have no relevance for them. However, from what I read and hear, I suspect that many others, in the Northern hemisphere at least, are experiencing something similar to our Irish experience. Given the extent of secular cultural change occurring in a remarkably short time, the effect it has had on the Irish Catholic Church has been discon-

3. This argument was used by the CDF agianst Tony Flannery. See *infra* Chapter 7.

certing. There seem to be no straightforward answers to the problems it has raised and no officially sanctioned attempt to grapple honestly with them. Instead, we are often given well-worn official pronouncements that have the tired aura of lifeless ideas taken from the chest of approved orthodoxies. The institutional church, unwilling to admit its structural defects, fails to give satisfaction to its many critics, in spite of its belated and awkward attempts to admit its moral failure in the matter of clerical child abuse. Personal repentance plainly falls far short of what is needed.

There is evidence to suggest that the institutional church is structurally sick; and it will not recover until its authorities acknowledge that its present structures, and the behaviour of some of its authorities, have much to do with its sickness. Reliance on authority as the main instrument of church governance in the past has left many priests and bishops dysfunctional in their attempts to speak convincingly to people, except when they have the courage to speak from personal conviction.

The day has gone when morality could be credibly authority-based; and our church leaders seem to find it hard to approach the task of moral guidance with a fitting humility and respect for the consciences of those they are addressing. Because Catholic teaching has been presented in the mode of authority and obedience, our faithful are not listening to their leaders and they are rejecting any attempt to dictate to them how they should think and behave. Authentic Christian teaching needs to be commended, not commanded. It has to be offered with respect for freedom and received in the spirit of freedom. Conscience, not obedience, is the moral and psychological key to Christian living and behaving.

Vatican II was indeed a reforming council, but subsequent events have shown how easily the significance of the reform has been lost to sight by even well disposed members of the church. Reform needs to be sustained by continuing action; otherwise its inspiration and verve easily evaporate. The reforms of Vatican II have an importance that extends far beyond the 1960s. The trouble is that effective memories are hard to preserve over more than a limited time even for those who have had them personally; those who are too young to have had them, yet are beneficiaries of them, may wonder what all the fuss is about. They seem to have no idea of what institutional church life was like before the council. It had its praiseworthy moments, but these were outweighed by its structural and governmental defects.

The opponents of reform within the church openly regret what the council achieved, and they have campaigned against its spirit. They may be comforted by the thought that, with the passage of time, memories quickly grow dim. Amnesia serves as a comfortable alternative to having to face the burden of what the Spirit, who inspired the council, was saying to the church. Catholics have as great a need as Protestants to remember the force of the word 'always'. The Second Vatican Council was not simply an event that occurred in the 1960s and can now be forgotten.[4] Its moral and spiritual example is as relevant as its teaching; and the experience that it occasioned in many Catholics was as important as the documents it produced. Fifty years later we are faced with new problems and challenges that call for the reforming spirit and verve of the council perhaps more than its documents.

An appreciation of what the council meant for many Catholics demands some knowledge of the situation as it was before the council. In spite of our differences, as we commonly say in ecumenical dialogue, we have more in common than we may be prepared to admit. What we need is respect for the differences and a realization that a wounded world can benefit from the attentions of a wounded church.

As T.S. Eliot vividly put it: 'The whole earth is our hospital ...' – which is a poet's way of expressing a profound truth of Christianity. We have been sent out to bring the good news of salvation to the whole world. It is a case of the wounded trying to heal the wounded while recognizing the existence of their own wounds. However, we may find that internal structures constitute an obstacle to that mission. If that is true, it follows that structural reform becomes an essential part of our bringing the good news to the world; in short it is an evangelical task in which revelation necessarily entails reform.

I am uneasily aware that to concern oneself with church reform may come from a very Eurocentric view of things. I wish therefore to consider how cultures interrelate and how Christian theology has to contextualise itself in different cultures, if the word of God is to speak with relevance and force. There are two methodological ways of proceeding: one is to

---

4. See *infra* Chapter 9 for further treatment of this theme.

have a concept of faith that is localised in the historical circumstances of Galilee in the time of Jesus; this view may appeal to biblical fundamentalists who make no allowance for the passage of time or for the implications of changing cultures. The other approach is to practise the kind of faith that is rooted in the highly abstract doctrines of fourth and fifth century patristic and conciliar teaching; this view may appeal to Christians who have a propositional idea of revelation and a corresponding concept of faith as assent to these propositions; this method was employed by most neo-scholastic theologians. Both of these views suffer from a similar defect: neither of them relates their faith to their own socio-political circumstances.

It is widely accepted today that Christian theology needs to be contextual; that is, that it must relate abstract concepts to actual persons, places and events, and that it can face the challenge of 'translating' one culture into another. The natures of Christ take on genuine spiritual life only when they are related to the concrete circumstances of the birth, life, teachings and death of Jesus of Nazareth. Both the life of the historical Jesus of Nazareth and the doctrinal definitions of the councils of Nicaea and Chalcedon need to be related to subsequent cultures that change with the passage of time, if the Gospel is to address the changing circumstances of history. Otherwise, Christianity is imprisoned in a museum. Latin America and African America provide vivid contexts in which Christian faith has to be practised.

Some African American theologians like to say that say Jesus is black. The tense is important, since it is the present not the past that furnishes the moral context. The actual colour of Jesus' skin is not the point at issue. However, these American theologians are seeking to contextualise their Christian faith in their own actual social and political situation, where in some states black people are discriminated against and denied equality with white people. The message of the Gospel of salvation has to be related to their social and political circumstances, and the context in which the work of Christ takes on effective meaning for them is the actual world of racial discrimination. When the Gospel speaks to them, it speaks to a world of racial inequity which is in total dissonance with the ideals and teaching of Jesus. For these theologians the Gospel must be translated into the cultural circumstances in which they are living.

Evangelical preachers who taught them to look to heaven for relief from their sufferings inspired many of their ancestors, in the days when slavery was rife. This produced a culture dominated by otherworldly longings, which they expressed in some beautiful 'spirituals', or songs that were a blend of European hymns and African cultures that were shaped by the experience of slavery and racial inequality. Their religion located all their desires in a transcendent world where they would be comforted and freed from their bondage.

A fine artistic illustration of how different cultures can blend with each other and show how widely different situations can inspire a deep universal human experience is the English composer Michael Tippett's secular oratorio, *A Child of Our Time*, which was begun on the day that Britain declared war on Germany in 1939. The Nazi pogrom against the Jews had already started and the shock of the notorious *Kristallnacht* (November 1938), when Jewish homes, synagogues and businesses were wrecked all over Germany and Austria, and thousands of Jews were sent to concentration camps, was still fresh in peoples' memories.

Because Tippett believed that Christian and Jewish hymns were too limited in scope and context for his purpose, he wanted to compose a work that would resonate with every human tragic situation that witnessed to 'man's inhumanity to man'. Consequently he stressed the secular character of his work. The appalling story of the Nazi pogrom against the Jews, and of one boy's cruel fate in it, provided him with a narrative that encompassed all human tragedy. Nevertheless, he took Bach's great Passions as his model, but instead of chorales he inserted nineteenth century Negro spirituals. It was a brilliant idea in spite of the fact that they were hymns. He argued that the American spirituals, which were the direct product of oppression, have a human universality about them that most religious hymns do not. Clearly, Tippett, an unbeliever himself, did not have much regard for conventional European hymns, many of which are expressions of personal, and usually otherworldly, piety. It can hardly be denied that black American spirituals emphasise otherworldly longings, yet Tippett chose five of them to suggest a universal and this-worldly human reference. Unlike Bach's chorales, which stand apart as congregational interludes in the passion narratives, Tippett, using a device that is possible only in music, made his spirituals arise directly out of the musical texture of the terrible 1930s story, and this gave them a context similar to the story. (There is a magical moment when at the end of Part 1 the dramatic narrative melts[5] naturally into the spiritual, *Steal away to Jesus*, and at the end of the oratorio *Deep River* gives a feeling of hope and healing, or as Tippett himself put it, a feeling of winter turning to spring.) The art of music achieves an effect which mere theological analysis could never achieve. Nevertheless, good theology can arise out of pondering the effect of art upon the mind and heart.

We have here a fascinating challenge: how can Christian revelation and the human response to it be both contextual and universal? Christianity is not an abstraction; if its ideals are to be realised, it needs a concrete living world where men and women interact with one another. The work of Jesus Christ can be effective only in the context of what is actually taking place in the lives of faith-inspired men and women. The first modern practitioners of this sort of contextualised theology were the Liberation theologians of South America. They knew that their political interpretation of the Gospel would invite opposition from the guardians of orthodoxy. The Holy Office, under the leadership of Joseph Ratzinger, not being affected by the concerns of socio-political life in Latin America, simply condemned Liberation Theology as Marxist. Ratzinger could not be more explicit: 'An analysis of the phenomenon of liberation theology reveals that it constitutes a fundamental threat to the faith of the church.' [6]

In the fourth and fifth centuries the problem was how to correlate the divinity and humanity of Christ. In the twentieth century the problem was how to come to religious terms with a culture in which the rich were exploiting the poor, while in many cases practising a highly conservative form of public and private religion. The Liberation theologians proclaimed that they could not preach the Gospel without struggling to remedy the appalling socio-economic situation in their countries. They were creating a contextual theology that did not accord with the mindset of the Holy Office, and, on the basis of abstract ideologies, this led to their being condemned as Marxists. Pope Francis, in spite of his early unease with Liberation theology, is now a champion of Gustavo Guttiérez whose

5. I owe this illuminating metaphor to Ian Kemp, a biographer of Tippett.

6. J. F. Thornton and S. B. Varenne (eds.), *The Essential Pope Benedict: His Central Writings and Speeches*, (San Francisco, 2007), p. 217.

famous pronouncement on 'the fundamental option for the poor' now has a distinguished place in theological history.[7] Francis' problem is how to avoid direct conflict with Pope John Paul II, Pope Benedict XVI and the CDF on all this. The European mindset that has characterised them will have to change if they are to be responsive to Pope Francis' vision. In this, as in other matters, Francis is trying to change attitudes while avoiding open conflict.

Peter McVerry, S.J., who has done so much to change attitudes to the poor and the homeless in Dublin, concludes his contribution to a book on Pope Francis with these words:

> Of course, poverty and injustice have always been concerns for the Church, as evidenced by many social encyclicals. What Pope Francis has done is to put the poor, the problems of inequality and structural injustice at the heart of the Church's mission, and therefore at the heart of Christian spirituality and living.[8]

7. It may come as something of a surprise to discover that the slightly menacing figure of Gerhard Ludwig Müller is a pupil and friend of Gustavo Guttierez.

8. John Littleton and Eamon Maher (Eds.) *The Francis Factor: A New Departure*, The Columba Press, (Dublin 2014), p. 92.

3

Metanoia: Paul, Augustine and Luther

Reform of the Catholic Church's structures may well depend on a change of mindset. How this comes about can vary. I take here the example of three distinguished Christians who underwent a radical change of mind and heart and who in consequence have contributed greatly to the shape of church life. The apostle Paul was an evangelist and theologian who gave the infant church direction and theological ideas that have proved unceasingly stimulating and durable down to our own times. Augustine, by his conversion and subsequent intellectual life, left the church a library of profound works that are of continuing importance. Martin Luther challenged many of the religious attitudes and values of the late Middle Ages, having undergone a dramatic personal crisis of the spirit. All three men underwent a major change of mind and heart that can be described as having all the properties of metanoia, though the circumstances of each were very different. What, then, are we to understand by the word 'metanoia'?

The second century Christian lawyer, Tertullian, pointed out that the Greek word *metanoeo* was incorrectly translated into Latin as *paenitentiam agite,* which in turn later came into English (for example in the King James Bible) as 'repent'. According to Tertullian, 'in Greek, *metanoia* is not a confession of sins but a change of mind'.[1] Thus Tertullian, in a pithy remark, made a point that nineteenth and twentieth century biblical scholars have written about at length. The King James version, of course, heavily influenced the English language, and even today, 'repentance', as the English for *metanoia,* continues to appear in many modern English versions of the Bible.

This is no mere trivial dispute about words. The New Testament was

1. Edward J Anton, *Repentance: A Cosmic Shift of Mind and Heart* (Discipleship Publications, 2005), pp. 32-33.

written in Greek; and since the word *metanoia* [2] plays a very significant part in the teaching of Jesus, it matters that Christians should understand it correctly.

Biblical Greek scholars have claimed that there is no English word that accurately renders *metanoia*, which should be translated not as the word 'repentance' but by a phrase, 'having a change of mind and heart'. One could repent of having done something wrong, without being convinced that the situation now requires not merely being sorry for having done wrong, but appreciating that only a complete change in one's way of seeing things will meet the demands of the present circumstances.

Repentance necessarily bears upon *past* wrongdoing, whereas metanoia concerns the present and the future. It will normally be brought about by a situation that comes to be seen, not merely as reprehensible, but as demanding a complete change of mindset that entails abandoning a former way of looking at the world, which we now appreciate as no longer capable of doing justice to how we have now come to see the world and our behaviour in it.

Repentance does not necessarily call for a radical change of the structures of one's life and religion, such as, for example abandoning one faith and replacing it with another. If I fail in the observance of the laws and moral requirements of my faith or church I can repent *within* the ambience of my faith or church, and have no need to alter the moral or religious structures of my life. Although metanoia can be occasioned by past wrongdoing or by failure to do what is right, it can also be brought about by a situation that was formerly interpreted as correct, and even virtuously so. Like Paul, one could be an observant Jew – free from moral guilt – yet be called to a whole new perspective on life in general and religion in particular.

It is harder to be converted from a good and conscientious life than from a life of plain wrongdoing. This was particularly so for the immediate followers of Jesus, who heard him say: 'Do not think that I have come to abolish the law or the prophets; I have come not to abolish but to fulfil them.' (Matthew 5:17) This pronouncement sets up a tension between the conservative instinct to think and act according to the Law and the

2. I use the word 'metanoia' as a transliterated English word, except where I am refer-ring to the Greek original.

prophets, and the injunction to have a change of mind and heart. Matthew attempts to meet this problem by establishing a firm connection between the teaching of Jesus and the precepts of the Law. Nevertheless, he is intent on showing that Jesus is 'fulfilling' the Law, not abandoning it. He has Jesus employing deliberately hyperbolic language to defend himself from the accusation that he was encouraging infidelity to the Law, of which, he said, not one letter or stroke of the pen is to be removed until the Law is fulfilled. Jesus said to the crowds and to his disciples: 'The scribes and the Pharisees sit on Moses' seat; therefore, do whatever they teach you and follow it; but do not do as they do, for they do not practice what they teach.' (Matthew 23:1-3) On another occasion he tells his disciples: 'unless your righteousness exceeds that of the scribes and Pharisees, you will never enter the kingdom of heaven'. (Matthew 5:20) The Law must be obeyed, and its official custodians must be listened to, but it must be properly interpreted, not distorted by casuistry and crafty evasions.

A pressing question arose after the death of Jesus, when the infant church had to make a weighty decision concerning the admission of Gentiles to their number, and the Law had to be seen to be superseded by faith in Christ. In this crucial instance, a change of mind and heart became unavoidable, as Paul's argument with Peter made convincingly clear.[3] As the American theologian, Sandra Schneiders, remarks, no later proposal for change in the structure of the church would ever prove to be as radical as this.[4] It was not a conversion from wrongdoing to virtue; it was a reckoning with a situation that demanded a practical decision to re-direct one's life. Fortunately Saul [5] of Tarsus, with his pastoral experience in evangelizing the Gentiles, was on hand to supply a theological argument in favour of the decision.

The conversion of Paul is the most dramatic event in the history of Christianity. It involved both repentance and metanoia, understood as a radical change of mind. He was a Jew, a Pharisee and a zealous opponent

3. It is not easy to collate Paul's account in the Letter to the Galatians (Galatians 5:17) with Luke's in Acts (15).

4. S. Schneiders, *Beyond Patching: Faith and Feminism in the Catholic Church* (New Jersey, 2004), chapter 2.

5. 'Saul' and 'Paul' were used interchangeably, though St Augustine in his *Confessions* wrote that he 'changed his name from Saul to Paul' to mark his conversion. (*Confessions*, Bk 8, ch. 4)

of the new faith. He took an active part in the martyrdom of Stephen (Acts 6:8-8:1). He quite genuinely hated Christians for religious reasons. Some years later in his Letter to the Galatians he was forthright about his former life.

> You have heard, no doubt, of my earlier life in Judaism. I was violently persecuting the church of God and was trying to destroy it. I advanced in Judaism beyond many among my people of the same age, for I was far more zealous for the traditions of my ancestors. (Galatians 1:13-14)

In the language of today, his deep Jewish faith had some of the characteristics of sectarianism. His hostile attitude to the followers of Jesus was changed by a vision in which Jesus asked him why he was persecuting him. The question led to the shattering of Paul's hostile attitude to the followers of Jesus and the abandonment of his former faith, at least as far as attacking Christians was concerned. His conversion had all the features of *both* repentance for his treatment of the Christians *and* a change of mind and heart. He went on to become one of the outstanding exemplars of the power of grace – with the ability to reflect theologically on what had happened to him.

After Paul, the next most influential convert to Christianity was arguably Augustine of Hippo who wrote his *Confessions* towards the end of the fourth century in his first years as a bishop. In the *Confessions* he gives a detailed, introspective and emotion-filled account of his conversion to Christianity and addresses it to God in an extended prayer. It was a conversion of some complexity, reaching an animated climax in the garden of a villa, in the presence of a close friend, Alypius, who did not know what to make of all that was happening. Today we might identify it as something like a nervous breakdown. Whether this is true or not, Augustine's conversion is a major event in the history of the Christian Church.

A popular view of Augustine is that he was puritanical about sex. On the contrary, he was a slave to its power, having taken up with it promiscuously in adolescence, but, later in his life, falling in love with a lower-class woman who bore him a son, Adeodatus. His dismissal of her was not done for religious reasons; it was a social move prompted by his mother, Monica, a religious but also a worldly-wise woman who wanted to see her son married to a reputable wife of his own social class. He describes his forced parting from his lover briefly in anguished and moving language:

> The woman with whom I had been living was torn from my side, because she was regarded as an obstacle to my marriage. My heart was ripped open and bled, because I loved her deeply.[6]

Sadly, he never reveals her name, though he does name Adeodatus, the son they had together. She returned to Africa, a casualty in his spiritual odyssey, 'vowing to you never to give herself to another man'.[7] It is regrettable that he tells us so little about this fascinating and nameless woman. I like to imagine the three of them now together in the loving splendour of the God whom Augustine had sought down the years with such commitment and fervour.

Augustine's conversion process had begun much earlier than its climax in the garden. He was intellectually converted well before the emotional crisis he describes so vividly in the eighth book of his *Confessions*. He had passed through several different philosophies in his search for a truth that would satisfy his desire for transcendent meaning. His problems were focused more on the will than the intellect. In the *Confessions* he disposes of the Manichees almost casually as he pursues his real interest, namely, the divided will that prevented him from becoming a baptised and settled Christian. He was ready for Baptism long before he found himself capable of willing one thing – his full conversion to Christ. In the *Confessions* he recalls with amused wit his prayer for chastity in his younger days when he 'used to say [to God], "Grant me chastity and self-control but, please, not just yet".' [8]

It is worth paying attention to the psychological situation he describes so vividly in Book 8 of the *Confessions*. After much dedicated and persistent study, he became intellectually convinced that he ought to be baptised. However, he knew what this would mean for his peace of mind. If he did not marry, as Monica wished, he would be bound to a life of chastity. He had intense images of what this would mean for his life-style. So far from being a prude, he found himself imagining the sensual details of a sexually satisfying life. He became fascinated by the sheer power his sexual

---

6. Augustine, *Confessions*, Bk 6, ch. 15, from the O'Rourke translation (DLT, 2013), p. 246.
7. Augustine, Confessions, Bk 6, ch 15.
8. Ibid, Bk 8, ch. 7.

desires had over him. His great spiritual autobiography begins on the note of desire, with his most famous and characteristic prayer:

> You stir in us the desire to praise you. Our delight is to praise you. For you have made us that we long for you, and our heart is restless until it rests in you.[9]

He relates his desire of God to his sexual desire which he sees as a confining influence on his search for God. I like to think that this, not his reputed 'pessimism' or the sharp distinction between his two cities, is the note by which typically 'Augustinian' theology should be identified. Even as late as the 1920s, post-Modernist orthodoxy was uncomfortable with Augustine's emphasis on desire and the will as the highway to God. Somehow, his preoccupation with desire for God jarred with neo-scholastic emphasis on the role of the intellect in the act of faith as construed by the Fathers of Vatican II. Book 8 of the *Confessions* depicts a man who has reached beyond the intellectual aspects of the mystery of God and is engrossed in the role of desire and the will in the journey into God. He is trying to comprehend why, despite his mental clarity about the things of God and his human obligation to love and serve God, he is still fatally and embarrassingly restrained from arriving at union with God.

Paul, as Augustine well knew, had been here before him:

> For we know that the law is spiritual; but I am of the flesh, sold into slavery under sin. I do not understand my own actions. For I do not do what I want, but I do the very thing I hate. (Romans 7:14-15)

Augustine, however, does not simply attribute his situation to sin and leave it at that. Although he was later to base the doctrine of original sin on a literal interpretation of the early chapters of the Book of Genesis, in the *Confessions* he shares Paul's puzzlement over his divided will. Paul's conclusion had virtually personalized sin as another self: 'Now if I do what I do not want, it is no longer I that do it, but sin that dwells within me.' (Romans 7:20)

In his struggle with the Pelagians, Augustine would later distinguish between personal and original sin, the latter being a sin of nature in-

---

9. Ibid., Bk. 1, ch. 1, O'Rourke, p. 3.

herited from our first parents by the mere fact of being human. Human beings enter this life stained with ancestral sin, which remains with them as 'concupiscence' – an open invitation to personal sin. This came to be described as 'Augustinian pessimism'. Here in the *Confessions*, however, Augustine remains preoccupied with what had taken place in the journey towards his conversion, and especially with what had happened so dramatically in the garden.

This is Augustine of the unsatisfied heart. He has confessed to God how he sought God outside himself whereas God was nearer to him than he was to himself. There are many similar remarks in his writings.

One feature in his conversion that is particularly striking is the effect on him of the example of others. A fellow African, Ponticianus, a high-ranking imperial courtier, and a fervent Christian, who was visiting him and his friend, Alypius, noticed a book on the table, and opening it, was delighted to find that it was the letters of Paul. They got talking about religion and Ponticianus mentioned Antony the Egyptian monk who had undergone a radical conversion experience that had changed his life. Neither Augustine nor Alypius had heard about Antony, so their guest warmed to the chance of telling them about him and other desert fathers. Augustine was riveted and shamed by what he heard.

> My inner self was divided against itself. In the storm that raged there, a storm that I had raised in the innermost place in my heart, I rushed to Alypius. My face showed the tumult in my mind, as I cried out, 'what is wrong with us?' What is this story saying to us? These people who have little education rise up and take heaven by storm, while we, with our knowledge but without any heart, flounder in the grip of our sexual desires. Are we ashamed to follow their lead? Should we not be more ashamed not to follow? [10]

This marks the final stages of the birth of metanoia in him, with all the drama that characterised Paul's conversion. There is, of course, implied repentance in it, but it is primarily an expostulation of shame, and a feeling of powerlessness and shaming failure. The rest of the story is equally dramatic. In a storm of passion he dashed out of the house and

10. *Confessions*, Bk 8, ch. 8.

into the small garden attached to it. Only his own words are adequate to the situation.

> What the outcome would be, you, Lord, knew. All the while I was losing my mind on the way to sanity. I was dying a death that was bringing me to life. I was aware of the evil that held me. I was unaware of the good thing that was about to be born in me.[11]

This is metanoia in slow motion, building up to a climax that is almost anti-climactic, because of the intensity of what precedes it. He knows that we know how it will end, but he delays the telling of it, because it still remains a vivid memory for him and he still remembers that he felt at the time that he was 'falling to pieces'. The process of his metanoia was long drawn-out and penitential, and he now sees it as divinely willed.

> This was the conflict going on in my heart, a conflict in the depths of my heart with myself and against myself. Alypius stayed at my side, and silently waited for an end to this extraordinary turmoil.[12]

The remainder of the story is well known, and although it is the denouement of the drama, it is a facsimile of Antony's biblical awakening. Augustine hears some children nearby sing out, 'Take up and read' ('*tolle lege, tolle lege*'), and so he took up the book of Paul's letters, opened it at random and came across some words about abandoning carousing, drunkenness and sexual immorality, together with an exhortation to put on the Lord Jesus Christ; and at that moment 'it was as if a light of certainty flooded my heart and the dark shadows of doubt were dispelled'.[13] The long metanoia was now complete, and the words of St Paul broke into his life as a most powerful grace, releasing him from the bondage of a disordered love. He later developed the doctrine of original sin, thus giving the Western church a heresy of its own which the Eastern church never understood.

It is a doctrine that is in considerable difficulties today, owing to its dependence on a literal interpretation of the first chapters of the book of Genesis.

11. Ibid.
12. Ibid., Bk. 8, ch. 11.
13. Ibid., ch. 12.

One of the great admirers of Augustine was a sixteenth century German Augustinian friar, Martin Luther, who was influenced less by the Augustine of the restless heart, and more by the Augustine who attributed every good deed to grace and regarded every non-graced act as a sin. From his own experience Augustine had concluded that the unaided human will is incapable of doing good and pleasing God. In his book, *The City of God*, he gave a political twist to this faith-conviction: 'Accordingly, two cities have been formed by two loves: the earthly by the love of self, even to the contempt of God; the heavenly by the love of God, even to the contempt of self.' [14]

It was this aspect of Augustine's thought that fired Luther, who took it further, stating that human beings were totally corrupted by sin – a corruption that could be healed only by the unmerited gift of God's grace. The Council of Trent would later state the Catholic teaching that human nature was 'wounded', not corrupted, by sin.

Luther described the moment of his change of mind and heart long after the event itself, and we must allow for a certain exaggeration in his description of the miseries of his life as a friar. He put his life into a background of unrelieved spiritual distress. He wrote of the ordeal which resulted from radical anxiety over his standing with God. He tells us that he performed numerous acts of penance, was scrupulous about his prayers, yet he never felt accepted by God in spite of all his efforts to be a good friar. As a result of all his self-torture he came to hate God whom he saw as a heartless and cold judge. The degree of his unhappiness has been disputed, but there can be no doubt about its existence. Then, one day, he was reading Paul's Letter to the Romans and he came across these words:

> For in it [the Gospel], the righteousness of God is revealed through faith for faith; as it is written, The one who is righteous will live by faith. (1:17)

Suddenly, light and joy filled his mind, and a heavy burden was lifted from his heart. The Pauline text was telling him that it is faith through grace that makes one pleasing to God: righteousness comes not by good works such as penances, self-denial, and indulgences, but by faith. There

14. Augustine, *The City of God*, Book XIV, Chap, 28

is nothing we can do to make ourselves pleasing to God. Luther's experience of being justified by faith was 'as though I had been born again.' Thus the doctrine of justification by faith alone was born and would soon become the corner stone of the Protestant Reformation.

We must distinguish between Luther's personal feelings and the effect that his 'twice-born' experience had on others. This was metanoia, not repentance. He was not repenting of a misspent life: he was regretting an arid and joyless one. However, his experience chimed with the times. This metanoia was not merely personal, it seeded what Hans Küng has called a change of paradigm for the church, a new way of looking at the meaning and scope of religion.[15] The Lutheran paradigm-change occurred in an age of faith. In scarcely more than a century, with the advent of the Enlightenment, the paradigm would change, as a result of the advance of science and secularised culture, when Christianity, Protestant and Catholic, had to relate itself to modernity and secularism, and when one man's personal religious crisis would mean little or nothing to the secular mind. Küng points out that though the Reformation must be attributed to many theologians, 'Luther is and remains the figure who embodies the Reformation programme more than any other.' [16] 'Luther found a direct existential approach to the Apostle Paul's doctrine of justification in a way which no one, even Augustine, had achieved in the previous 1500 years.' [17]

Luther's interpretation of Romans 1:17 can be seen as a reader response hermeneutic; but it can also be plausibly argued that he was actually rediscovering Paul's intended meaning. If this were found to be true, there would be no good reason why a Roman Catholic today should not be able to respond positively to Luther's interpretation of justification, in a more personal way than the Agreed Statement on Justification between Lutherans and Catholics, which tends to be rather abstract. In a less ecumenical age, every effort was made to find theological reasons to make a sharp distinction between the Catholic and Protestant understanding of faith,

15. The notion of paradigm shift was introduced by Thomas Kuhn in his influential book *The Structure of Scientific Revolutions* (1962), a change in the basic assumptions, or paradigms, within the ruling theory of science. Though Kuhn himself restricted the notion to science, Hans Küng in his book, *Christianity: The Religious Situation of Our Time* (London, 1995) used it as a structure for his entire book.

16. *Christianity*, p. 525.

17. Ibid., p. 534.

justification and the relation of both to morality. Küng makes an important observation about the relationship between Luther's personal conversion experience, and the paradigm shift that occurred as a result of it.

> Much as Luther came to know the private pangs of conscience of a tormented monk and aimed at the conversion of the individual, his theology of justification went far beyond the creation of privatistic peace for the soul. His theology of justification forms the basis for a public appeal to the church for reform in the spirit of the gospel, a reform which is aimed not so much at the reformulation of a doctrine as at the renewal of church life in all areas.[18]

I am not concerned here with the subsequent history of the rise and spread of Protestantism, but Küng's point that Luther's theology of justification led directly to a general call for reform in the church is closely relevant to the topic of metanoia in a social as well as personal sense. A change of mind and heart in a charismatic person can lead to others feeling the need to join in a social and institutional reform. Martin Luther was such a person. The pinning of the 95 theses to the door of the Castle Church in Wittenberg was not intended as a gesture of rebellion, but it stated Luther's views on the sale of indulgences and they chimed with widespread popular hostility to the preaching of indulgences as a means of raising funds for the building of St Peter's basilica in Rome. 'What infuriated him about indulgences was that every assumption behind the indulgence system conflicted with justification by faith.'[19] There are German Catholics today who cannot look at St Peter's without the bitter memory of what its funding meant in the history of their church in Germany.

If we consider what these three instances tell us about the need for a change of mind and heart as a preliminary or continuation to a Christian life, we can see that each has a different slant on life.

Paul's example has an institutional perspective: he can no longer remain the sort of Jew who persecutes the followers of Jesus. To this extent, he repents of his behaviour to Christians. He does not repent of being a Jew and a Pharisee.

---

18. Ibid. pp. 537-8.
19. Diarmaid MacCulloch, *Reformation: Europe's House Divided, 1490-1700* (London, 2003) p. 122.

In chapter 11 of his Letter to the Romans he shows that he resents the cocky attitude of Gentile Christians to Jews. 'I ask then, has God rejected his people? By no means! I myself am an Israelite, a descendant of Abraham … God has not rejected his people whom he foreknew.' (Romans 11:1-2) Metanoia for him meant seeing all the implications of his conversion to Christ. He was uncomfortably ambivalent about his continuing Jewish affiliation. It takes all his skill as a theologian to show that God still cared for his people Israel.

What has Augustine's change of mind to say to today's church? How emotions can be an obstacle to adherence to Christ, certainly. However, very few people would be faced with the dramatic situation that faced Augustine in the fourth century. Perhaps the effect on Augustine of the example of others, such as Antony and the Desert Fathers, might serve as a reminder of how our behaviour can effect the lives of others. Roman curial behaviour, as Pope Francis has reminded us, can set a regrettable example to others and create an atmosphere of negativity, bureaucratic rigidity and a lack of true care for others.

Martin Luther's example is perhaps most relevant to the church of today. He drew from his personal conversion experience the impulse to look at the church of his age and to see there an absence of fidelity to the Gospel. The church of his time was too little aware of the message of the New Testament and too preoccupied with its own status and power. Moreover, it had failed to condemn a widespread obsession with practices like possession of relics, indulgences to release the dead from purgatory, or to increase the coffers of the rich and powerful. His teaching on justification by grace through faith provided a sound theological foundation for reform of church life. This could have been the remedy for many ills in the church of his time, but instead Pope Leo X ordered him to recant the content of his 95 theses. At the Diet of Worms Luther refused to recant, and accordingly he was excommunicated, and his insights ignored. A chance for radical reform was thrown away.

What, then, of the Catholic Church today? There can be little doubt that Pope Francis has issued a call for metanoia, especially to bishops and priests, and most of all to the Vatican Curia. One of Francis' favourite words is 'attitude'. Reform begins, for him, with a change of attitude, where necessary. He himself sets a very clear example of what he means.

Some of the curia may respond with a reluctant acquiescence, hoping for a new pontificate when they can revert to their old ways. Francis is looking for a complete and willing change of attitude. He wants pastors, not clerics intent on laying down the law and treating the church as a kingdom or corporation. Coming closer to home, one wonders how the Catholic bishops of Ireland might respond to Francis' call. Most of them were appointed during the pontificates of two conservative popes. This has meant that their outlook has been cautious and unadventurous, allowing Rome to do their thinking for them, as Yves Congar wrote in his *Journal* about bishops in general. The present pontificate is inviting them to think for themselves and speak in a collegial manner without fear of reprisal.

Members of the Association of Catholic Priests of Ireland would greatly appreciate an opportunity to discuss the pastoral matters that all members of the church have in common. The bishops would not be expected necessarily to agree with what they would hear, only to listen sympathetically, rather than regard them as troublemakers. As fathers in God, the bishops would be more concerned with brotherly interest than with protecting a system of rules and regulations. All orthodox members of the church recognise the importance of bishops and would value a brotherly relationship with them, sharing in the difficulties of the episcopal office in an age of serious pastoral problems.

There is a division of attitudes in the church, sometimes referred to as conservative and liberal. We need to acknowledge the legitimacy of both mindsets, avoiding the use by either side of institutional condemnation or interference. Each has a contribution to make to the health of the church. Could we not agree to disagree on matters that do not belong to the essence of Catholic beliefs, and perhaps to recognise that the inspiration of the Holy Spirit may be found in an amicable clash of opinions within the unity of God's people? It might take a change of mind and heart not to confuse unity with uniformity, but rather to welcome legitimate diversity in the one church. Metanoia in our age might consist in showing to the world that disagreements do not necessarily imply hostility. Reform in the Christian church nearly always entails greater awareness of, and fidelity to, the demands of the Gospel, which in turn may call for a change of mind and heart.

4

The Council, Diversity
and Collegiality

For many of us who lived through the period of Vatican II, memory of
it remains a vivid, unceasingly relevant and exciting experience that can
still be pondered and relished. We think and speak of it with the sort of
enthusiasm that our young colleagues today seem scarcely able to understand or appreciate. It is our main symbol of contemporary reform
in the church; and that is why we appeal to it today for inspiration in an
atmosphere of repression.

As Wordsworth said of the early French Revolution: 'Bliss it was in that
dawn to be alive, but to be young was very heaven!' To apply a poet's reflection on the French Revolution to a reforming council of the Catholic
Church may seem a little *outré*, but it is testament to an exciting experience
that belonged to an age that has passed and no longer casts the same spell
over the young. Many of us who have lived to see a reaction against the
spirit of an age that was full of hope and challenge wonder at what has
happened in so short a time since the Second Vatican Council closed in
1965 and wonder also how so life-giving an experience can lose its glow so
quickly. The election of Pope Francis has given new light and heat to the
embers of a fire that was dying, but the dampening forces of negativity,
stricture and joylessness remain as a threat to the new hope. The controversy over giving the Eucharist to people in irregular marital situations
is proving to be a miniaturized version of the contests of Vatican II. We
cannot afford to seek a false consensus between two views of church that
are mutually contradictory. There are moments in the life of the church
in which a false eirenicism has to be resisted, and confrontation becomes
a conscientious necessity.

When we look at the church as it developed since Vatican II, we see
certain gains achieved by the council and perduring down to today; but
we can also see a reaction against the achievements and a return to attitudes we thought had been banished at and after the council. Many of

today's young priests, for example, seem to feel the need to take refuge in their clerical status and in a managerial approach to the sacraments. Like all young people, of course they quite properly feel the need to react against their elders. The trouble is that many of their elders are more adventurous than they are, and in rejecting the concerns of their elders, they are rejecting the promise held out by the Second Vatican Council – which, it should be stressed, was an experience before it came to be a set of documents.[1]

For four years in the 1960s we rejoiced in the experience of a church that was occupying itself with badly needed reform and change. It was refreshing to many of us, but it was seriously disturbing to some powerful members of the Roman Curia. The council had been called into being by a pope who, though conservative in his beliefs and spirituality, had no time for the authoritarianism and the condemnations which had marked earlier church councils and which would return shortly to mark papal and curial activities. What Pope John showed so beneficently was that it was possible to be conservative in one's beliefs without being authoritarian or rebarbative in one's actions. He was instinctively inclusive and warm in his thoughts and actions, and thus he provided an example that fellow Catholics could look up to and follow with enthusiasm. Today's tradition-alists have every right to *hold* reactionary opinions; they have no right to impose them on others, in the name of a false conception of orthodoxy and authority.

In his opening speech Pope John told the council that it should not concern itself with definitions and anathemas, as earlier councils had done, but should look with compassion at a suffering world; for he made it quite clear that he spoke not merely to his fellow Catholics, but to the whole world. People everywhere, whether they were Catholics or not, warmed to his compassion and to his sheer humanity. He showed that a pope could speak in a caring way without condemning his brethren or reflecting morosely on the modern world. He was a Christ-like figure, and by his very presence he evangelized his fellow Catholics and impressed those of other faith traditions and non-believers alike. Unhappily, his successors have sometimes proved unwilling, or psychologically unable, to follow his

1. See Chapter 9, *infra*, on the reception of Vatican II.

example. He was beatified with Pius IX and canonized with John Paul II. It was as if canonizing Pope John on his own might have seemed to the curial mind to be too politically and theologically adventurous.

The key to understanding what is happening in the contemporary Catholic Church is, it seems to me, the realization that men of one mentality have secured supremacy in the church and are treating with hostility those who do not share it. It looks upon them as dissidents, disobedient to church authority, and worthy only of censure. It totally fails to see them as brothers and sisters who deserve to be listened to and respected, if not agreed with. This official attitude can be found in people of like mind throughout the Catholic Church, and, because of the use of coercion, it makes the church a cold place to live in.

Serious differences of mentality have all the appearance of unquestionable division, and history shows that radical divisions, if left untreated through lack of consultation and discussion, can lead to the institutionalising of difference, as happened in the sixteenth century Reformation. The ecumenical movement today is trying to heal the breach that resulted from the Reformation. Differences of opinion and mentality are normal in any freely organized society, secular or religious. Search for the truth, which constitutes the nature of a Christian faith seeking to understand itself in the light of Scripture and Tradition, and in careful and discriminating reflection on all that is happening in the modern world (which Vatican II called 'the signs of the times'), must occupy itself with a unity that includes legitimate diversity. Failure to appreciate that unity is not the same as uniformity inevitably leads to the sort of situation that has existed in the Catholic Church; and faithful Catholics have a right to protest against it with impunity. As I write, a pope has resigned and another has taken his place. It is still too early to know whether the new pontificate will bring about the kind of reform that is so badly needed. There can be little doubt that Pope Francis has already shown signs of wishing to bring about a different sort of church; but there are limits to what one man can do when facing a culture of intransigent and privileged conservatism.

We need to be clear about the implications of division of opinion in the church. The dominant division is, for want of an agreed terminology, between liberals and conservatives. Attempts to heal the rift between them are commendable, but they are often cosmetic, because the rift is due to two radically different and irreconcilable concepts of church. The language and theological concepts of each party are incompatible and mutually exclusive. Without tolerant discussion and willingness to disagree amicably there can be no progress, since consensus is logically impossible. If one side relies on force instead of argument, the outcome will be bruising and frustrating. Reform may therefore have to begin with a disarming of powerful prelates and a recognition that lawful diversity is not merely permissible but beneficial to the health of the church.

There is only one prospect of a peaceful reconciliation, and that is a willingness to accept and live amicably with diversity of views in the church. This means seeing diversity as an enrichment rather than an impoverishment of church life in matters that are not essential to Christian faith. The Gospel is eloquent on the need for a loving co-existence. Engagement with the ecumenical movement teaches us that genuine unity can coexist with differences of conviction, emphasis and opinion.

The term 'magisterium' is often employed in a manner that emphasises the views of those who are in power in the church. We should, however, note that the term originally meant the right to teach with authority, *e.g.*, in a medieval university, and in an age when popes readily consulted university scholars rather than a bureaucracy of like-minded men. Today it has become virtually applicable only to the pope, his curia and the bishops in general council. When we hear it used, the context is usually censorious and intended to draw attention to the over-riding role of authority.

For centuries Rome has perceived the magisterium as the admonitory instrument of church government, and its authority is sometimes invoked in a manner that is intended to bring closure to topics that are still, and will remain, matters of legitimate discussion. It is thoroughly regrettable that matters of discipline are in effect being turned into matters of literally unquestionable dogma. This is theologically gauche and morally unacceptable; and Catholics have a right to say so fearlessly, and to resist it for the good of their church. We need to practise ecumenism *within* the church quite as much as with Christians of other churches. When members of other churches look at what is happening in the Roman Catholic Church, they can be discouraged in their ecumenical efforts towards unity. How can one seek communion with a body in which a doctrinal and moral dictatorship prevails and freedom of conscience is so lightly discounted?

In fewer than 50 years in Ireland, we have passed from being a docile, obedient and unthinkingly conservative Roman Catholic Church, to one of widespread questioning, though not necessarily repudiation, of the accepted beliefs and practices of the past. The media can hardly be blamed for dwelling on the misfortunes of the Catholic Church, or for pouncing on the latest statistics that show a fall-off in numbers attending Mass or participating in the other sacraments. If they lack depth in their analysis of what is happening, that is only because such analysis does not sell papers or make for exciting television or radio. This is why I believe that the journalistic and theological approaches to the church should blend, each having an effect on the other.

Most of the bishops the pope appoints have been chosen for their ideological reliability and for their willingness not to rock the boat. If they don't share papal ideas, they are usually careful to keep their views to themselves, such is the extent of fear in the church under recent papal regimes. Blind institutional obedience, however, may prevent a conscientious response to situations that call for pastoral care. People who, for example, have gone through a divorce need non-judgemental pastoral care, not prohibitions against approaching the sacraments. It is altogether possible to prescribe matrimonial permanence, while caring with pastoral empathy for those who, for different reasons, may find themselves unable to comply with the prescription. Sacramental restrictions are not a way to approach the situation with the mind of Christ. The urge to make human tragedy an occasion for the display of institutional power is unworthy of those who profess allegiance to the Word of God. Using the sacraments as weapons of reprisal is thoroughly unchristian. The church should be a sanctuary of healing, and not a place where condemnation has been the instinctive response to perceived doctrinal or moral failure.

Emphasis on obedience as the supreme virtue is a tactic promoted by an authority that brooks no dissent. In religious orders and congregations the vow of obedience used to take practical precedence over the other vows, and the slogan 'the voice of the superior is the voice of God' could result in tyranny in superiors and infantilism in 'subjects'. Moral and disciplinary teaching should be imparted with a proper respect for the dignity and freedom of the recipients of the teaching. Sometimes an honest question may be a better way of proceeding than an over-confident affirmation.

People sense the lack of authenticity in attitudes that are shaped by party-whip conformity, whether in church or state. Mere obedience to authority, without inner conviction, is no assurance of true Christian faith or of teaching that is adequate to it. Blind obedience, if prescribed by religious teachers, offers people a stone when they ask for bread (Matthew 7:9).

Perhaps the worst effect of enforced conformity is that it weakens conscience, with the result that we may no longer convey the impression that we really believe what we proclaim, as distinct from repeating received orthodoxies. Rome proclaims that it believes in the primacy of conscience; but it adds ominously that it must be an 'informed' conscience. This sounds fine until we realize that in the eyes of the magisterium an informed conscience means, in practice, one that conforms to *its* way of thinking. In point of fact, however, an informed conscience is one that has carefully considered *all* the evidence.

If we are trying to understand what has happened to Roman Catholicism during the last few decades, we need to consider social as well as religious factors. I must here acknowledge, without examining in depth, such powerful influences as television, the internet, foreign travel, and perhaps especially, the loss of automatic respect for authority of all kinds, in particular, for church authority. The world we live in provides the context in which religious faith must be practised and pondered; and context is indispensable to effective living and preaching of the Gospel. The distinguished Protestant theologian, Karl Barth, envisaged true evangelists as advancing on their task with the Bible in one hand and the newspaper in the other.

I must leave to sociologists of religion the task of weighing the influence of secular society upon religion and *vice versa*. To the sociologically untrained eye, what has happened in the last few years is remarkable, perhaps disturbing and not always easy to interpret. From being notably conservative only a few years ago, many members of the Irish Roman Catholic Church have become much more questioning in their approach to religion and their church. They no longer accept doctrinal and moral directions based exclusively on the word of authority, which is what they have often been officially given. This marks an advance from infantile to adult thinking; and it has taken place in a very short time.

Parents have seen it in their children, and teachers have noted it in their pupils. There comes a moment in the life of a child when the answer to 'Why?' can no longer be 'Because I say so'. Something analogous happens in the church. How can adult Christians witness to their faith under restrictions imposed by authority? A sentence in the New Testament comes to mind in this context: 'Always be prepared to make a defence to anyone who calls you to account for the hope that is in you, yet do it with gentleness and respect.' (1 Peter 3:15).

It is lamentable when we are forced to make a defence of our faith while an intransigent magisterium insists that moral questions in modern life can be adequately answered by listening to an autocratic and sometimes reactionary church authority. Infantilism is not required for a truly Christian response to the Gospel. When Jesus said that we must receive the kingdom of God as little children (Mark 10:15), he did not mean that we must revert to the naivety and inexperience of childhood. He was recommending the child's capacity for wonder and willingness to enter the kingdom with simple trust, openness and without prejudice or worldly wisdom (Matthew 19:13-15).

Changes in attitudes to authority that have occurred in everyday secular life, have had a notable effect on religion. Although it may be temporarily disquieting, the secular challenge to Church authority, on deeper reflection, offers an opportunity to make Christian faith a more honest and more truly interior activity, than mere external conformity did in the past, when there was passive acceptance of the status quo, and little vision of what could be.

To take weekly attendance at Mass as an accurate barometer of faith is misguided. Falling away from frequent Mass-going is not of itself an adequate indicator of Christian unbelieving, and it can in fact co-exist with a genuinely Christian outlook. Whether we like it or not, church-going is no longer universally seen as the natural expression of one's religious convictions. Empty churches are disturbing to those who minister in them, but they witness to a phenomenon that calls for honest and courageous consideration. I am far from believing that the drift from regular attendance at Mass need not trouble us; but that drift happens to be the case, and it presents us with some unavoidable questions that the managerial mind may find disconcerting.

During Vatican II there was much appreciation of the fact that the council gave impressively preferential treatment to liturgy. This was, in some respects, a rather rarefied response to the perceived needs of the church; and it gave little thought to the fact that the significance and relevance of liturgy is a fairly sophisticated matter, and one, moreover, that is vulnerable to preciousness and affectation. In practice, to give it meaning and vitality, liturgy requires previous evangelization together with some appreciation of how symbols function. Attendance at Mass *can* be a purely social act, and there is evidence that it has been so in Ireland in the past age of apparently untroubled belief and conformity, when it would have been socially unusual *not* to go to Mass on Sundays.

I fully accept the important role that newspapers, radio and television play in a free society; but we perhaps too easily allow the media to shape our idea of where the church is today. Statistical surveys and opinion polls rarely offer any explanation of *why* things are as they are. Questions like 'Are you a religious person?' in opinion polls mean nothing, unless the term 'religion' is carefully defined. When asked if they are 'religious', people often take the question to mean if they are flamboyantly pietistic, and, not surprisingly, they hastily deny that they are.

We may also overlook the fact that that the media normally discuss only the external, and especially the political, characteristics of belief and church membership. Back in the 1960s the editor of the Italian newspaper, *Il Tempo*, openly admitted that the approach of his newspaper to church affairs (Vatican II was sitting at the time), was unashamedly political. He made no secret of, or apology for, not being interested in theology or spirituality, which he did not consider newsworthy.[2] Most media today take much the same line, without perhaps saying so as explicitly and honestly as the editor of *Il Tempo*.

At the time of Vatican II, however, the Irish media had correspondents who happened to be knowledgeable, faithful, if critical, members of the church; and they took a more than political look at what was happening to the church in council. For journalists this was unusual, and the Irish church was fortunate to have them, for there was little wise guidance from Irish participants in the council, some of whom assured their people that

2. Yves Congar, *My Journal of the Council* (Dublin / Adelaide / Collegeville MN; Dominican Publications / ATF Press / The Liturgical Press, 2012), p. 485.

nothing would happen to disturb the even tenor of their lives.

The recent revelations of clerical crimes against children have, of course, produced a massive disillusionment with the Roman Catholic Church throughout the world. Irish Catholics were unprepared for the fallout from the clerical abuse of children, for they had been primed to think of their priests and bishops as beyond reproach.

Even more disturbing than the crimes themselves has been the failure of some leaders in institutional realms of the church to deal in a properly human, legal and Christian manner with the appalling effect of clerical crime against children or to gauge the effect it has had on the majority of non-offending priests and religious. The older among us have long been conditioned to put the church as institution first, and to look to canon law, rather than to civil law, for instruction on how to react to situations touching the church. We are learning today that this kind of deference to church authority is wrong, and we can no longer practise it. As a result of it, victims of abuse were not listened to, because listening to them would have threatened institutional interests; and that had to be avoided at all costs. The clerical child abuse situation, and, above all, the official response to it, has become a painful moral learning experience for the entire Catholic Church. It was public opinion and the media, not internal church sources, which affirmed passionately that the rights of children take precedence over institutional discomfort and embarrassment. Freedom of the press can be an important instrument in helping to bring about reform in the church.

The institutional instinct, especially in the ruling circles of the church, to put the good name of the church ahead of seriously coming to terms with the significance of the crime of clerical abuse of children gave wide-spread scandal, and has been universally and fervently condemned. The Vatican appears to have been unprepared for the criticism that was leveled at it, and from Ireland of all places!

As a result of clerical crimes against children, and of the scandalous response of leaders to what was happening, the church is having to learn a painful lesson that extends far beyond the external consequences commented on in the media. The authorities are being invited to revisit, however reluctantly, their whole theology of church.

Rome, however, has seen off many attempts prompting it to do so. To proclaim, both in liturgy and theology, that the church is sinful must be seen to be more than a merely formal and edifying gesture. There must be a real existential recognition that it is a body always in need of reform. The problem lies not merely in the crime of paedophilia itself, bad as that is. People were as shocked by the tactics of superiors in dealing with it so casually, as by the crimes themselves.

Canonization and beatification have become political acts; and it is like-minded men who decide that a pope practised a life of heroic virtue and that the requisite number of miracles can be attributed to him. Pope John Paul II linked Pope John's beatification with the beatification of his antithesis, Pope Pius IX, in a clearly political act designed to appeal to both wings of the church. In turn, Rome decided to canonise Pope John XXIII with Pope John Paul II. The attempt to achieve a balance between these two opposed attitudes to the church is misguided; the aim must be to persuade the supporters of each view to live together in harmony and tolerance, in spite of their differences and disputes.

I am in no way questioning the personal virtue of these popes (only God can judge that); but those of them who have victimised, or allowed their underlings to victimise, irreproachable men and women who are trying to lead lives of true and relevant pastoral concern is for many people a scandal demanding repentance and a change of heart. If they were only private persons with deeply pessimistic ideas about the modern world, one might regret their pessimism, but it would be their unquestioned right to hold such ideas.

A major achievement of Vatican II was its teaching on collegiality. Much time and study have been spent on the precise meaning of collegiality. One of the best recent attempts to do so is by Mary McAleese in her study, *Quo Vadis: Collegiality in the Code of Canon Law*.[3] In this book McAleese subjects the notion of collegiality to a clinical examination with the precision one would expect from the former Reid Professor of Criminal Law, Criminology and Penology in Trinity College, Dublin. She also brings with her all the experience of being President of Ireland. She is here devoting her time to Catholic canon law with notable distinction.

Theologians have much to learn from this book, in which she points

---

3. Mary McAleese, Quo Vadis: *Collegiality in the Code of Canon Law,* Dublin, The Columba Press, 2012.

out how imprecise the word 'collegiality' is. She shows that while the pre-conciliar Code of Canon Law was quite precise in its prescriptions on how the bishops of the church relate to the pope, Vatican II, together with the new Code of Canon Law (1983), failed to achieve the same precision in spite of conciliar reforming zeal.

A theologian might venture to suggest that at Vatican II the concept of collegiality was too weak and undefined to make untroubled progress against the ingrained autocracy and absolutism of the papacy. The weight of the First Vatican Council lay heavily upon theology and practice in the Catholic Church, until the Second Vatican Council partially lifted it. In an age of increasing democracy in the world at large, the papacy has been imprisoned in the spirit of the old monarchism and in its absolutist approach to governance. If those at present in power in the Roman Curia succeed in their repressive tactics, it will be immensely difficult to achieve what Vatican II envisaged.

The Christian Churches, Catholic, Anglican and Orthodox, can be relied on to provide panoply and ceremonial when circumstances call for them, and they are a fitting means of proclaiming the glory of God. Ceremonial, when done well, can deepen prayer and give aesthetic expression to the glory of God. The problem arises only when the ceremonial is linked to a celebration of human rather than divine power. As Yves Congar remarked, a papal ceremony in St Peter's in Rome has had a tendency to suggest the glorification of the pope rather than the majesty of God.[4]

There are signs that an increasing number of Catholics want to see reform of the manner in which the church is being governed. 'The word "collegiality" captured something of an incipient impulse towards greater inclusivity and respect for the voice and views of the individual.'[5] The people of God want to be heard by the church's government. McAleese makes the point that the church is living in a world that has changed rapidly in recent years. If it is to speak with authority to that world, it will need to appreciate that monarchical government has become an anachronism in modern Western society, and there is no good reason why the church should maintain it. She writes: 'The church which is still in the process of adapting to the Council after fifty years, exists in a world which has shown

4. *My Journal of the Council*, p. 318.
5. *Quo Vadis*, p. 158.

an amazing capacity to adapt much more rapidly to things infinitely more complex than collegiality.'[6]

She quotes with approval from the 2005 report of the Faith and Order Commission of the World Council of Churches: 'Speaking collegially can mean reflecting back to the community the legitimate diversity that exists within the life of the church.'[7] That is precisely the whole point of a concern for contemporary reform. We need to hear a great deal more from the Vatican about legitimate diversity in church life; for we have been living under regimes that rejected or willfully ignored it. Struggling for official recognition of that legitimate diversity will entail a sustained battle that will not be for the faint-hearted.

McAleese claims that Vatican II never really defined the term 'collegiality' with any clarity. Arguably, the council was unable to do so, because it was tackling the thorniest problem in Catholic theology. A clear definition might have looked like a defiance of all that Catholicism was taken to stand for, namely papal supremacy. In non-legal terms the matter at issue was whether papal monarchical power should be reduced by greater attention to the collegial status of the bishops. This is admittedly a decidedly clerical preoccupation, but it is at least a step in the right direction.

> While LG [*Lumen Gentium*, Constitution on the Church] acknowledges the centrality of the People of God and states that the entire faithful share in 'the one priesthood of Christ' (LG 10) the words associated with 'collegiality' fade from the text of LG once it has finished talking about the episcopacy. By the time it moves on to the priests, deacons, religious and the laity such words are entirely absent.[8]

This is precisely the problem with the word 'collegiality'. It was intended by Vatican II to perform a task that was too weighty for it. People had a general idea of what it stood for, but the pope wanted it expressed in canon law; and this transference from council to canon law forced it to become more precise than the council documents had been. The council, by its redefinition of the church as the People of God, had raised hopes of giving the laity a greater say in how the church is to be governed. However, canon

6. Ibid, p. 157.
7. Ibid, p. 35.
8. Ibid, p. 65.

law focused attention on the relationship between pope and bishops, and this said little about lower clergy, and still less about the laity. As McAleese points out perceptively, even *Lumen Gentium* itself failed to do this.

The weight of history lay against it, especially the defeat of conciliarism in the sixteenth century. The Council of Constance (1414-1418) proclaimed that a council was superior to the pope. The Great Western Schism – when there were three claimants to the papacy all of whom fiercely proclaimed his legitimacy – had occasioned the conciliar movement. The council deposed the three claimants and elected Martin V as the new pope. Since the papacy had proved unable to remedy the situation, it appeared clear that only a council could do so. The Schism inevitably raised the question of the relationship between councils and popes; and the Council of Constance was forthright in its declaration that a council had its authority immediately from Christ. It was emphatic that its declarations were not limited to the ending of the Schism, but were intended to apply to all future councils.

There was intense conservative opposition to conciliarism, and the Fifth Lateran Council (1512-17), on the eve of the Reformation, reaffirmed papal supremacy over councils and condemned the conciliar movement. In the nineteenth century the First Vatican Council, by its definition of papal primacy and infallibility, completed the doctrinal restoration of papal authority and power. The comprehensive defeat of conciliarism posed an onerous challenge for Vatican II's progressives in their struggle for collegiality; and it continues to do so. The reestablishing of papal supremacy had entailed the condemnation of one council by another – which constitutes rather serious historical evidence against the much-asserted Roman claim to continuity of papal and magisterial teaching.

The Council of Constance had decreed that the reigning pope should call councils regularly. However, it proved all too easy for popes to be tardy in doing so, thereby demonstrating the weakness of any reform of the institution in which the initiative lies exclusively with the pope. The blunt fact is that any successful reform of the governmental system in the Catholic Church will depend on two changes: First, canon law will have to lay down precise times for the meeting of councils, or properly representative synods that are free of papal and curial control. Second, bishops will have to be elected locally rather than being appointed by the pope and his curia. Rome will retain the right to approve or object to an elected candidate, but it will not initiate the procedure.

This second point is the only way in which legitimate diversity can be achieved at governmental levels in the church. The present system of papal appointment of bishops, adopted originally as a defence against Austrian, Prussian and French intervention in church matters, has in practice ensured that only bishops with views similar to those of the Roman Curia are appointed. It seems certain that Rome will fight pertinaciously to retain its prerogative of appointing bishops, since merely approving their appointment would amount to serious curtailment of its present hegemonic powers which lie at the heart of what needs to be reformed.

Perhaps the lack of precision in Vatican II's understanding of collegiality could be beneficial for contemporary reform. The council, in drawing attention to the church as the people of God, clearly intended its reforms to extend to more than merely the relationship between the pope and the bishops. If the doctrine of collegiality were tightly defined as bearing upon only the pope and the bishops, clericalism would prevail, and there would be a failure of the ideal of giving God's people a real say in how their church is to be run. This matter has become clearer and more insistent today than it was in the 1960s.

We have to realise that Vatican II cannot be expected to give us answers to all our pastoral and institutional problems today. What it did was to create an appetite for reform and to point the way towards it. The last 50 years have seen a proliferation of further questions and problems, and, short of calling another general council, there seems at present to be no mechanism to deal with them.

Synods have shown themselves to be too vulnerable to papal and curial control. The best that those in favour of reform can do is to keep the matter alive by calling insistently for reforming action. Since the number of bishops throughout the church has increased greatly, a council made up of all of them would be unwieldy. Perhaps the Synod, *in a reformed guise*, will have to undertake the duty formerly performed by a council.

In the last session of Vatican II, its documents received final approval and the council concluded in an atmosphere of satisfaction, joy and hope for the future. Something really important for the church had been achieved after four years of hard work, intense debate, open conflict and the experience of having to fight for a cause with energy and, above all, with freedom. Criticism of how the church was being run could now be expressed in a way that would not have been possible before the council had met. The trouble is that in 1965 the council concluded, leaving an unfinished task, which its curial opponents have been successful in frustrating. The existence of an over-centralised church could give the impression that in the many uncertainties and problems of life in the modern world the church's advice to its members would seem to be, in the manner of Victorian mothers to their daughters on the eve of marriage, to lie still and think of the Vatican.

5

Church as Gathering, Church as Institution

We can illustrate the relationship between the church as gathering and the church as institution with a general observation on the development of any human society. People can assemble for a variety of reasons. Their gathering may be spontaneous and unplanned, or it can be politically motivated. In either case as soon as it decides that it is a collective entity that must plan for the future, it has to organise itself. The result is an institution that, in its earliest days, may remain in touch with its originating ideals as a gathering. However, bureaucracies are an inevitable result of organisation. As time advances, the institution may take on a life of its own and allow an ever widening gap to occur between its present self-understanding and the ideals of the original gathering: for example, a political movement can become a party that is self-sufficient and no longer feels the need to attend to the original reasons for its existence. It may in time split into increasingly divergent mentalities and then into separate parties. Some political parties seem to lose all contact with their original inspiration and run themselves as autonomous institutions that are there for their own sake and not out of any debt to historical origins.

We can apply these considerations to the Christian church, which began as an informal gathering of men and women who listened to, followed and gave allegiance to, a man from Galilee called Jesus. As matters turned out, this gathering brought into existence a movement that was destined to spread across the world proclaiming the message of salvation. The controlling principle of the Christian Church is that, unlike many other institutions, *it can never, with impunity, lose sustained contact with its historical origins.* Those origins, recorded in the New Testament, remain as a constant judge of institutions that bear the name 'Christian'. Protestants have been more sensitive to the judgemental role of Scripture than Catholics, who have customarily given that role to church authority. A statement recently made by the Faith and Order division of the World Council of Churches gives eloquent expression to a truth shared by all Christians:

> The Church was intended by God, not for its own sake, but to serve the divine plan for the transformation of the world. Thus, service (diakonia) belongs to the very being of the Church. [1]

A major problem that faces some of us in the Catholic Church is that it often seems to be run for its own sake. It is historically clear that Christianity has its origins in Jesus and his followers. To say that he was the founder of a hierarchical church may suggest that he had in mind the church as it is today, which would, of course, be anachronistic and historically impossible. Traditionalists seemingly believe that by saying that Jesus was the founder of the 'hierarchical church' it follows that Jesus would necessarily approve of church structures as they are today. If Jesus of Nazareth were to see the twenty-first century institutional Catholic Church, he might wonder what on earth had happened since he taught in Galilee. The mode of procedure in their ecclesiology is that you begin with the church *as it is structured today* and then return to the gospels to find supporting 'proofs' for their institutional claims. This simply puts the cart before the horse, and it is how the neo-scholastic method worked. It began from the modern church and went back two thousand years, artificially projecting onto the church in the time of our Lord and of the apostles the structures that are there today. Its ontological mindset was stronger than its sense of history.

It was customary in that theology to argue that Jesus, being God, must know everything and foresee everything, as if that were possible for any human being, divine or not. Although the church had battled resolutely and with institutional success against the theories of Gnosticism, Docetism and Monophysitism, in practice Christ's divinity was allowed to obscure Jesus' humanity. Even earlier, a high doctrine of Jesus had its beginnings in John's Gospel, especially in its Prologue. As a result of this trend, when greater attention was given to Christ's divinity, and with it an increasing emphasis on church organisation, a divine sheen settled upon all church

---

1. *The Church: Towards a Common Vision*, Faith and Order Paper No. 214, World Council of Churches, 2013, art. 58, p. 33. This Paper is greatly indebted to the Lima Document of 1982 on Baptism, Eucharist and Ministry.

offices and structures, casting a veil over the sheerly human character of how it is governed.

How, it asked, could such a divinely willed organisation be in need of reform? The intentions of God are not open to being challenged and changed. This kind of argument appears to have returned to dominate Vatican thinking under the last two popes. It seems that one was not permitted to advance a model of the church in Catholic theology different from the one which proclaims the doctrine that Christ is the 'head' of the church; that the apostles are a 'college'; that the pope is the successor of Peter; that the bishops are successors of the apostles. The structure is a legitimate, if anachronistic, model for interpreting what happened after the death of Jesus. Today, however, precisely because those who want to justify their authoritarianism use it, it needs to be challenged by the people of God who want to see a church which behaves in a manner that is closer to Gospel values.

We currently have a clerical church that continues to exclude its laity, and notably its women, from playing their part in its organisation. There are a number of intimidating weapons in its armoury, such as excommunication, censorship of writing and teaching and, in the case of members of religious orders, dismissal from their order – all of them difficult to square with the Gospel. In the case of religious congregations, the normal procedure adopted by the Congregation for the Doctrine of the Faith is to instruct the order to deal with the matter. It would be a courageous superior who stood up to this kind of pressure.[2]

I should, perhaps, make it clear that I am in no way advocating the abolition of church institutions. That would not be a resolution of our contemporary problems. It may very well be that an age is ending, and new organisational structures will have to be found, if the Gospel is to be preached effectively to modern men and women. Care will need to be taken that the new situation does not suffer from the same defects as the present one. Gatherings that grow in size and complexity always need organisation. One must hope that, in the case of the Christian church, the necessary structures will be found and that they will be responsive to the ideals of the Gospel that Christians have been given to practise and preach.

2. I examine this matter further and discuss the cases of some of its victims *infra* in Chapter 7.

The phrase 'organized religion' may prove attractive to those who want to attack religion; but disorganized religion poses a serious threat to rationality and even peace. The problem is not the existence of authority but the way that it functions. Some of the worst kinds of violence and terrorism today are religiously motivated. Those who want to be Christians but are disenchanted by the attitudes and actions of an institution that has its historical origins in the first preaching of the Gospel, have an arduous task before them. They have to decide whether to set up a new institution, exit from, or strive to change, the old one. Many of us are convinced that the struggle for change is preferable to flight. Reform does not entail the disappearance of the papacy; it does, however, entail a change in the way it has functioned during the last two pontificates, and especially in the way its bureaucrats behave.

Pope John Paul II, in his Encyclical, *Ut Unum Sint*, shows that he is aware of the problem that the papacy poses for other churches:

> I am convinced that I have a particular responsibility in this regard, above all in acknowledging the ecumenical aspirations of the majority of the Christian Communities and in heeding the request made of me to find a way of exercising the primacy which, while in no way renouncing what is essential to its mission, is nonetheless open to a new situation. (art. 95)

Exaggerated emphasis on the institution easily obscures the life-giving link with its origins and with its evangelical mission. The 'good news' which Jesus of Nazareth gave to his followers can never, without loss to its inspiration, allow itself to be shorn of its original life-giving properties because of the way in which its members came to be organized later. As in any institution, there will always be politics in the church. Papal conclaves, for instance, are not passive recipients of divine inspiration: the Holy Spirit works through the flawed character of the electing cardinals with their different political convictions. The process should neither be sacralised nor cut off from Gospel values by pretence of dominical authority or of a directly transcendent intervention by the Holy Spirit. God's grace is given within the untidy circumstances of normal human life. It should not be left to secular journalists to point out the political reality of what is going on. The inspiration of faith is quite congruent with political reality. Jesus preached the good news of salvation within the structures of Judaism, of which he was openly critical. He practised his Judaism in a free enough way by criticizing what he saw as being out of harmony with his understanding of the reign of God.

He was a Jew who accepted the laws of his nation and religion; but he practised and preached obedience to them in a manner that interpreted them in the light of his controlling idea of God's reign. The authorities of his Jewish religion disliked much of his open and inclusive teaching and, in consequence, they pursued him and finally brought about his death as an apostate. He accepted, and lived within, the structures of contemporary Judaism, but he was openly critical of the way in which they were understood and interpreted, often in a casuistic manner.

Organisations may become acutely sensitive to anything that seems to challenge their authority or their notions of orthodoxy. One has only to remember how, during the meeting of the Second Vatican Council, the 'conservative' minority opposed, often bitterly, the initiatives of the 'progressive' majority. Conservatives can sometimes deny to others the legitimate freedom to think differently or to pursue a progressive course of action that they deem to be a threat to Christian uniformity or to orthodoxy as they understand it.

A major concern of religious conservatism is often with the good name of the institution, rather than with continuation and renewal of the ideals of its historical origins. This not only prevents reform; it limits the idea of development of doctrine to restrictively drawn boundaries of orthodoxy, thereby excluding the possibility of real reform. This happened to the Roman Catholic Church in the nineteenth and twentieth centuries, when its authorities adopted a programme of opposition to modernity. In the nineteenth century they seem to have compensated for their loss of the Papal States by defining the doctrine of papal primacy and infallibility as a compensation and, to some extent, as a, perhaps unconscious, way of saving face. In the twentieth century they condemned the Modernists, who sought to speak about their faith in a way that modern men and women could understand; and this involved opposition to the tyranny of mandatory scholasticism.

The notion of infallibility, which was intended to apply only to the papacy, and then only under clearly defined and limiting conditions, was gradually extended silently and practically to virtually every papal statement and to the self-understanding of the Roman Curia. It became known as 'creeping infallibility' and was as if proximity to the pope allowed some of his authority to rub off onto his immediate servants, giving them a strong vested interest in promoting his authority, often at the expense of collegiality with his fellow bishops. The papal curia soon became, and remains, the main instrument of repression in the Church and, as such, is a body seriously in need of reform.

Rome kept Catholic theologians safely occupied by pointing them in directions that would not run counter to the accepted orthodoxy. Canon law became increasingly important in church governance. In the realm of doctrine, Mariology became a favourite topic for development. In Mariology theologians were less likely to pose a threat to authority, and its more enthusiastic proponents could be mildly restrained from what the authorities thought of tolerantly as excess of zeal. The infallible definitions of Mary's Immaculate Conception and Assumption into heaven were products of this serious limitation of theological scope. Mariology provided a safe alternative to facing the problems of modernity. It also allowed the popes to parade their exclusive authority and their pre-eminent status in the church, thus exemplifying Congar's point about the close connection between mariology and the nineteenth and twentieth century papacy.

The next stage was, in the view of some, to be a definition of Mary's state of being a 'co-redemptrix' with her son, and of her status as 'mediatrix' of all graces. The occurrence of a church council put a stop to these pietistic excesses by showing that Catholic theology could break free of the neo-scholastic hegemony that had imprisoned it since the Council of Trent and especially since the late nineteenth century.

Pope John XXIII's calling of a council came as a severe shock to some prominent defenders of the *status quo*, who quite correctly appreciated the threat to them of a council faced with the task of implementing the Pope's vision of *aggiornamento*. They had grown accustomed to condemning most ideas and philosophies that had come to prominence during and after the Enlightenment, and this often brought the church into needless conflict with modern intellectual challenges.

An evocation of the dangers of 'Modernism' could be heard in certain circles of the church down to the calling of Vatican II, and even later. This

anachronistic warning was a throwback to the existence of a Catholic movement in the late nineteenth and early twentieth centuries that attempted
to make Roman Catholic beliefs more intelligible to the modern mind,
above all by abandoning its reliance on scholastic thought as a flagship
of orthodoxy. Modernism, which had protested vigorously against the
turning of scholasticism into a tool of intellectual control, was successfully condemned, indeed ruthlessly obliterated, in the first decade of the
twentieth century, and the condemnation was made to serve as a warning
to intellectual circles in the church that they must keep away from 'dangerous' contact with the modern world and must remain within the confines
of scholastic thought which had become an instrument of regulation.[3]

Pius XII's Encyclical, *Humani Generis*, in 1950, was one of the last official
papal statements explicitly prescribing the continuing need for fidelity
to scholastic orthodoxy. The urge to condemn 'Modernism' showed itself alive and well in conservative thinking and it provided a convenient
target to attack; though anti-Modernism generally died out after a few
early protests at Vatican II. However, the word 'modernist' still remains
as a term of abuse in the vocabulary of some Catholic ultra-conservatives.

The great thirteenth century Dominican theologian, Thomas Aquinas,
had been made the talisman of orthodox doctrine in the church and has
consequently had to be conceived afresh today as an important historical
force rather than as the author of an artificially produced and perennially
valid theological orthodoxy.[4] Thomistic theology has had to be rescued
from its imprisonment in the straightjacket of mandatory orthodoxy.
The notion of a perennially valid philosophy has had to be abandoned
in favour of the free interplay of different philosophies, and the change
has left the guardians of orthodoxy without a convenient ideology to back
their institutional procedures. On the other hand, Aquinas can now be
studied historically as the brilliant thirteenth century thinker that he was,

---

3. In a theological context, 'dangerous' is a highly subjective term.
4. See Fergus Kerr's *After Aquinas: Versions of Thomism* (Wiley, 2008). In an illuminating
article, 'A Symphony of Theological Renewal' (*The Tablet*, 17 November, 2012, pp. 16-17).
Tracey Rowland discusses the various attempts that were made to interpret Aquinas in the
light of the elemental change brought about in philosophy by Kant and Heidegger. Karl
Rahner's transcendental Thomism was probably the most influential movement in the years
following Vatican II. Rowland refers to the traditionalist appeal to an uninterpreted Aquinas
as 'fundamentalist Thomism'.

instead of as an embodiment of perennially valid orthodoxy.

This restrictive vision had resulted in the accumulation of problems that were calling for urgent consideration. Consequently, the waters of modernity built up an ever-increasing pressure on the dam of an artificial concept of orthodoxy. Pope John XXIII's calling of a council breached the dam and released the waters of modernity into a Church that was largely unprepared for the crisis that followed. It was a beneficial crisis, and it should have served as a warning about what happens when you keep putting off necessary reform.

The warning demands attention today, as we have witnessed a renewed attempt to rebuild the dam, not by a return to neo-scholasticism, the principal philosophical support of pre-conciliar orthodoxy, but by recourse to the selection of the passages in Vatican II documents that had been included mainly to pacify the integralist minority, in spite of contradicting the intended thrust of the document. Significantly, today's arena of control is in moral rather than in dogmatic theology. Today the dam of enforced orthodoxy is made of more brittle materials than its neo-scholastic predecessor in the nineteenth century. It bases itself on disciplinary issues rather than on traditional doctrinal theory, thus unintentionally weakening its right to pronounce its teachings to be Catholic orthodoxy.

Christianity began as a spontaneous gathering inspired by the charismatic personality and leadership of Jesus of Nazareth. Jesus was a Jew who was often critical of the Jewish establishment, which, however, had a tradition of allowing for internal voices that criticised what was happening to established religion in their time. The men who sometimes fulminated against the establishment were known as 'prophets'. What mattered was that the prophet spoke as the voice of God. Prophets normally addressed people, and especially their leaders, and told them bluntly and sometimes with colourful imagery that they were being unfaithful to the covenants made by God with Abraham and Moses. Since they claimed to be speaking in the name of God and were often critical of the establishment, prophets were disliked, feared and sometimes killed by the authorities and were always open to the charge of being false prophets. Contemporaries of Jesus, not knowing how to describe him, often resorted to the title of 'prophet', since he embodied the criteria of traditional prophecy. The beginnings of Christianity witnessed a gradual separation from Judaism, as the new and growing body of Christians defined themselves as followers of Jesus and ceased to obey the requirements of Jewish law.

The first followers of Jesus were conscious of belonging institutionally to Judaism, which had its own regulations, religious ethos, and culturally shaped attitudes. After the death of Jesus his disciples were faced with an urgent practical difficulty, when Gentiles sought entry into the gathering of his followers. It led to the challenge that a Jewish convert to Christianity named Paul made to Peter, the acknowledged leader of the apostles. This famous challenge was occasioned by the ever more urgent practical problem that was now facing the followers of Jesus. The unavoidable question that faced them was: what was to be done about Gentile converts to Christianity: did they have to become institutional Jews by practising circumcision and dietary observances in order to become followers of Jesus? Paul wrote bluntly and with intensity about it to his converts in Galatia:

> When Cephas came to Antioch, I opposed him to his face, because he stood condemned. For before certain men came from James, he used to eat with the Gentiles. But when they arrived, he began to draw back and separate himself from the Gentiles because he was afraid of those who belonged to the circumcision group. The other Jews joined him in his hypocrisy, so that by their hypocrisy even Barnabas was led astray. When I saw that they were not acting in line with the truth of the gospel, I said to Cephas in front of them all, 'You are a Jew, yet you live like a Gentile and not like a Jew. How is it, then, that you force Gentiles to follow Jewish customs?' (Galatians 2:11-14)

What is most relevant to the theme of reform here is less Paul's theological skill, than the fact that the crisis was not settled by recourse to Peter's authority. Paul knew that Peter was the senior member of the apostles and that Jesus had treated him as such; but Peter made no attempt to invoke his authority in response to Paul's challenge on a matter of utmost concern to the early church.

I am not suggesting that there is a direct precedent to be drawn from the Peter/Paul event. Nonetheless, it remains a striking example of the use of theological argument rather than having recourse to authority in order to settle perhaps the most serious crisis in the history of the Christian church. However, even with due allowance for the circumstantial difference between New Testament times and our own, there is surely still something of importance to be learnt from it.

In 1985 an Extraordinary Synod took place in Rome. The Extraordinary Synod had been originally designed by Pope Paul VI as a way of continuing the work of Vatican II, but Paul made it very clear that the Synod was to be called by the pope and supervised by him. It soon ceased to be an instrument for the continuation of collegiality. Avery Dulles remarked on the cult of secrecy which marred the Synod of 1985 and which has been a lamentable feature of so many authoritarian church activities. The curia had, by this time, regained control of the machinery of government in the church and was making its presence felt.

Dulles uses the theologically accurate if inelegant word 'supernaturalistic' to describe the attitude of the group that had recovered the initiative lost during the council. The term 'supernaturalism' has the great benefit of treating the situation in theological rather than simply in political terms. The supernaturalists see the church as 'an island of grace in a world given over to sin'. They are careful to avoid outright rejection of Vatican II, but they manage to suggest that the council was naive in its openness to the world. To anyone fired by Pope John XXIII's vision, it is a seriously reactionary standpoint. The conservative view is disproportionately influential because the people who hold it have power and authority on their side, and they depend upon that power as the best guarantee of what they see as internal church unity, which they deliberately confuse with uniformity.

The 'progressive' attitude of the council, which Dulles describes as 'incarnational and this-worldly', prescribes a much more optimistic and communitarian approach to the practice of faith in the modern world. There is no reason why it cannot be recovered; but recovery will call for resolute opposition to coercive authority that avoids free discussion in the prosecution of its aims.

Though those values are familiar to most Christians, they can never be rehearsed too often. Jesus preached the Kingdom of God as embodying values to be aimed at by his followers. There has been much scholarly discussion of what Jesus meant by his invocation of the term 'kingdom'. First of all, it may be better translated as 'reign', or even 'reigning', rather than as 'kingdom'. 'Reign' is a more active word than 'kingdom', which, by identification of church with kingdom, can claim for itself the aura of divine approval.

Catholic ecclesiology often conveniently identified 'kingdom' with 'church', and this enabled 'supernaturalists' to use the identification as if it imparted divine approval to the all too human manifestations in the historical church. It was also a useful tool to oppose necessary reform. Metaphors like 'the bride of Christ', though biblical in origin, when applied to the modern church can give it a divine sheen protecting it from all attempts at reform. This is why Christians must constantly return to the New Testament for inspiration, and especially for correction of too exalted a notion of authority in the institutional church and too worldly a method of governance.

A useful aid for recapturing the spirit of the historical Jesus is provided by José Antonio Pagola in his book, *Jesus: An Historical Approximation.*[5] In this fine book Pagola conveys something of the atmosphere that surrounded Jesus as he made his way through the villages of Galilee, announcing to his listeners the coming of God's reign amongst them and singling out the poor and the suffering for special attention, often inviting the rejects of society to sit with him at table. Pagola puts it well: 'Jesus in Galilee was not teaching a religious doctrine for his listeners to learn and follow. He was proclaiming an event, so they could accept it joyfully and faithfully.'[6]

It was not the sort of programme for life that could be easily handed on to his followers in the centuries to come. It was too spontaneous and too informal a way of life to be translated easily into the grandiose structures that were to become the norm for the institutional Church in later ages. Only a convinced supernaturalist could pretend that the splendid buildings, erected in Jesus' name by his followers, could be a fit memorial to the Son of Man who had nowhere to lay his head. (They can, of course, be defended from an aesthetic point of view and as a major contribution to culture and civilisation. Many of the visitors to the Sistine Chapel do not go there for religious reasons.)

I make this point not to deride the institution to which I belong, and which finds it hard to speak credibly in the name of Jesus to the modern world. I wish simply to draw attention to the intrinsic contradiction of celebrating Jesus' presence and action in that world through institutional

5. José Antonio Pagola, *Jesus: An Historical Approximation* (Convivium Press, Miami, 2009).
6. Ibid p. 99.

means that rely upon power expressed through strictures and punitive acts as signs of its fidelity to God in Christ. A resolute belief in the practice of repentance, and in divinely granted forgiveness arising out of the doctrine of redemption, is the basis for the work of the Christian Church in any age. That is the central message of the Gospel, and Paul expresses it tersely and authoritatively: 'God was in Christ reconciling the world to himself'. (2 Corinthians 5:19) The early church was forced by historical and cultural circumstances to abandon Pauline simplicity, and adopt much more complicated modes of expressing its theological convictions..

Jesus held out the highest ideals to be pursued by his disciples in every age and place, but he did so with the assurance of trust in God's forgiveness as an ongoing remedy for the shortcomings of human life in the everyday world. It is not a message likely to be cordially received by those who rely on the efficacy of regulation and arbitrary condemnations to produce an artificial uniformity, rather than by admitting, and permitting, legitimate diversity as the proper way to respond to the ideals put before us by the Gospel, which was given in freedom and the spirit of largesse, and was intended to be received in freedom and joy. It is what Pope Francis means by his constant references to 'mercy', which he sees as a constituent of the very being of God.

Clearly there would have to be development of the institution of the Christian church, if only because it is impossible to replicate in the fourth, sixteenth or twenty-first centuries the conditions in which Jesus himself lived and taught. The following of Jesus Christ in later ages would entail the arduous task of living and teaching in accord with the ideals held out by Jesus, but without reproduction of the precise social and political conditions in which Jesus lived and taught. There would have to be an interpretation of biblical life and an application of the Gospel to new circumstances, which is what we mean when we describe Christianity as an historical faith.

'History' has two distinct though complementary meanings: (1) the factual existence of past events, coupled inseparably with (2) the process of interpreting those events. The only avenue to the existence of past events is by documents and therefore through an inevitably interpretative process. To argue, without reference to its historical and literary context, that the Bible says this or that, cannot constitute an argument in support of a present-day moral or doctrinal claim. This, however, is usually what fundamentalists do. They cite biblical, papal or conciliar texts without reference to their context in particular circumstances that may in fact have little relevance to the situation for which they are arguing.

Thus it is futile to look to the Bible for immediate and uninterpreted guidance on, for example, a complicated contemporary financial or economic matter, unless one is prepared to engage in an argument that is fully aware of both the historical circumstances of the biblical text and of contemporary economics. Quoting, for example, a text displaying hostile attitudes to the practice of usury is probably of little immediate relevance to modern financial situations, unless one is able to engage in a highly sophisticated process of interpretation of both the biblical text and the modern financial situation. Simplistic attempts to solve contemporary problems by reference to a literally interpreted biblical text serve only to obfuscate contemporary moral and disciplinary questions in the church, especially when they are raised to the status of binding dogma.

Theologically, the relationship between the Jesus of history and the Christ of faith is always difficult to discuss in general terms, because of conflicting theories about the historical Jesus and his message. The matter has been subject to close attention in Protestant theology since the beginning of the nineteenth century, and in Catholic theology since Vatican II. There have been several 'quests' for the historical Jesus ('Jesus as he actually was', as some uncritical people have put it), but they tend to remain in scholarly hands and indeed could have the effect of emptying churches if preached unskillfully. The wise, academically nurtured, preacher will recognize that what goes on in theological academies may shock or simply bore ordinary church members, if given in undigested form and not carefully adapted to a pastoral context. The best a preacher can do is to make his congregation aware that there are genuine difficulties to be faced, if one tries to come to grips with the life and teaching of Jesus and the historical problems of the gospels. Thus the story of the marriage feast at Cana is easily assumed to be a literal account of what really happened. A preacher who tells his congregation that the marriage feast 'never really happened' can disturb his listeners needlessly, unless he knows that they appreciate the literary character of John's Gospel.

Nevertheless, in spite of these difficulties, a convincing picture of who

Jesus was can emerge from a prayerful and thoughtful reading of the gospels; and this picture can be fruitfully applied both to prayer and to service of one's fellow human beings. It can also be used to bring the Gospel to bear on the institutional Church in any age. We do need, however, to approach our faith with a humble and enquiring mind that is always ready and willing to face questions about the interpretation of our sacred texts. We may not understand the philosophical impossibility of the search for 'Jesus as he actually was', but we can recognize that our church is always subject to the judgement of Scripture, and that means that it is always in need of reform, and that we are always subjected to the uncertainties of interpretation. 'Jesus as he actually was' usually turns out to mean 'Jesus as I would like him to have been'.

If we are gathered in the name of Jesus, we need to recognize that he resists all attempts pin him down in precise doctrinal statements about his nature(s). In many ways the picture of Jesus will always remain deeply mysterious. The German Protestant theologian and polymath, Albert Schweitzer, closes his great book, *The Quest of the Historical Jesus* with words that are memorably simple:

> He comes to us as One unknown, without a name - as of old, by the lake-side, He came to those men who knew Him not. He speaks to us the same word: "Follow thou me!" and sets us to the tasks which He has to fulfill for our time. He commands. And to those who obey Him, whether they be wise or simple, He will reveal Himself in the toils, the conflicts, the sufferings which they shall pass through in His fellowship, and, as an ineffable mystery, they shall learn in their own experience Who He is. [7]

That really says it all.

---

7. Albert Schweitzer, *The Quest of the Historical Jesus: A Critical Study of Its Progress from Reimarus to Wrede*, trans. W. Montgomerey, third edition (New York: Macmillan, 1956), p. 403.

6

Church as Community
of Believers

In the fascinating story within a story, 'The Grand Inquisitor', which constitutes a chapter of Dostoyevsky's novel, *The Brothers Karamazov*, the reader is taken by surprise to discover that the Inquisitor – the man responsible for examining the doctrinal orthodoxy of others – has himself long since ceased to be a believer. He is quite prepared to imprison and burn people for heresy though he himself has lost his faith. The shock to the reader comes not so much from seeing a churchman corrupted by power and using that power in the manner of secular tyrants, but from discovering that he lacks the only quality which would offer some sort of excuse, however immoral, for his politically inspired despotism.

There are many possible reasons why people belong to religious bodies of one kind or another; but membership of the Christian Church has no religious meaning or justification, if it is not motivated by faith in God who manifests himself and his word through Jesus of Nazareth. This is why novelists and playwrights have exploited the dramatic possibilities inherent in a priest's loss of his faith. In such a loss we have a tragedy for someone who does not wish to leave the priesthood but whose entire lifestyle could be reduced to a nonsense by the absence of faith. We have, of course, to allow for the case of someone who devotes his priestly life to social and socio-political work, but even here, there would inevitably be transcendent moments that called for a strictly faith-inspired response that was no longer possible for him. The church is a community of believers and not merely a bastion of beliefs considered as an ideology. We need to pay careful attention to the distinction between faith and subscription to beliefs.

Protestant theology has attached importance to this distinction. When Martin Luther proclaimed that we are saved not by works but by faith, he intended faith to refer to the *act* of believing not to mere assent given to the content of faith. (Theologians brought up in the scholastic tradition may remember the distinction between *fides qua* and *fides quae,* which was the Latin equivalent of faith and belief.) Faith and belief are to be distinguished but not sundered from one another. One cannot have faith without an object, or more accurately, a subject towards which it is directed; but the subject or object must not be allowed to obscure the act which is the moral and spiritual agent of the process.

Theoretically, of course, the distinction is implicit in Catholic theology; but in practice, Catholicism has placed emphasis on content, often at the expense of act. Justification by grace through faith became a prominently divisive issue between Lutherans and Catholics after the Reformation. Both sides have often, for sectarian reasons, misrepresented and distorted each other's positions on this.

Clearly, faith cannot be practised in the abstract: it must, of course, have content; but emphasis on the act rather than on its content became the guiding light of the Reformation. It remains a difference of emphasis between Protestantism and Roman Catholicism today. Many Lutherans believe that Catholics seek salvation through good works rather than through faith. Many Catholics believe that Lutherans, by placing such heavy emphasis on faith, dispense with good works. Each distorts the views of the other.

Nevertheless, there is ecumenical agreement today between Catholics and Lutherans – at least on paper. The Joint Declaration on the Doctrine of Justification, signed by both The Lutheran World Federation and The Roman Catholic Church on 31 October 1999, states that 'consensus in basic truths of the doctrine of justification exists between Lutherans and Catholics.' We too easily relax comfortably into the knowledge that there is theoretical agreement between the two; in practice, however, it remains a persistent difference between them, in that faith, unlike beliefs, is not vulnerable to control. A united Christian church needs a balance between both attitudes.

There is another, and much more challenging problem to consider in this context. Placing emphasis on the content of faith at the expense of the act makes it possible for the body designated the magisterium to adopt a position of control and dominance; and this is a problem in serious need of attention. The magisterium can do nothing about the quality of faith as an act, since only God can read the human mind and heart; but it can condemn the verbal expression of those who, legitimately or not, differ from it.

Faith cannot be commanded by will power or by authority. How it comes and how it goes is unfathomable. The connection between faith and morality is virtually impossible to determine. There is no external way of telling the difference between believers and non-believers in terms of intelligence, psychology or morality. Not long ago some neo-scholastic theologians used to hold that loss of faith is always culpable. Today many of us would reject that idea as being presumptuously moralistic. The urge to moralize and be judgemental can be very strong in authoritarian Catholicism. I am not denying that loss of faith can indeed occur as a result of moral waywardness. It can, however, also occur because of an unhappy experience such as, for example, a broken marriage, a bereavement or a grave setback in social, financial or psychological circumstances.

People without religious faith can live lives of morally irreproachable character; while people of beliefs can have low moral standards or can practise them defectively. Whether a person has or does not have religious faith is deeply mysterious, in the sense that there seems to be no satisfactory explanation for their condition. They may find that they can no longer accept, for example, the existence of an after-life as popularly presented. One can, however, confuse an inability to imagine something with a loss of faith in it. In this respect the only remedy may be to call to mind the teaching of a theologian like Thomas Aquinas, that what we do not know about God greatly exceeds what we do know. We easily fall into the sort of anthropomorphism that treats God as a sort of superior human being, another object, however exalted, in the universe, thus overlooking the qualitative difference between God and nature, including us human beings. On the other hand, people without faith may evince moral standards and performance that many believers would recognize without hesitation as godly. This is a reminder that the Spirit breathes where it wills, and that grace can occur in what we may arrogantly think of as the most unlikely of persons, places and things. 'For who has known the mind of the Lord, or who has been his counsellor?' (Romans 11:34)

When someone says 'I no longer believe in God', it is pertinent to ask 'What sort of God do you not believe in?' I remember the case of a man who said that one day, when he was 15, he suddenly realized that he no longer believed in the existence of God, and, he said, 'The relief was tremendous!' From this remark one can conclude that his idea of God warranted rejection; the pity is that he did not replace it with a better one. Voltaire's cynical but stimulating remark that 'God created man in his own image and likeness, and man returned the compliment', is a reminder of a profound truth: to say that we believe, or disbelieve, in God tells us little until we describe what sort of God we believe, or disbelieve, in.

The German philosopher, Friederich Nietzsche, is a major figure in the creation of modernity. It is important to note his main preoccupation in denying the existence of God. In his book, *The Gay Science*, he has a madman rush into a group of sophisticated people and announce 'God is dead: we have killed him ... we are all his murderers'. In Nietzsche's view the advance of science has destroyed our need of God. We are now free to become what we want to be. Humans not merely can, but must, now aspire to being gods and declare themselves captains of their own ships. The idea of God, and especially of his manifestation in Christianity, has, in the opinion of Nietzsche, made slaves of humans. We have rebelled against the very idea of God, because we have found that it infantilises us. In this way of thinking, in an age of enlightenment, without the restraints of Christian faith, there is no limit to what we can become. Nietzsche's rejection of God is largely due to his notion of God as a limitation on our freedom.

Sigmund Freud expanded on Nietzsche's proclamation of the death of God by delving into the subconscious mind and finding there that religion is a neurosis and can be explained by our earliest infantile experiences and longings. He respected religion and its place in human historical development, but he saw it as a force keeping humankind in tutelage. He believed that modernity, and especially science, has now demonstrated that religion is a neurotic illusion. Where Kant had declared that we cannot know the world as it is in itself, Freud asserted that reason itself is subject to the limitations imposed on it by the subconscious mind.

Both Nietzsche and Freud were born into strongly religious backgrounds and were less concerned with God as a conceptual problem than with God as a restraint placed on human freedom. We have to concede that there are certain kinds of religion that do induce neuroses and serious restraints on human freedom; and although Nietzsche and Freud had a deep and knowledgeable conception of the religion they rejected, other atheists often take deformed kinds of religion as their targets.

In March 1963 the Anglican bishop of Woolwich, John Robinson, published an article in *The Observer* newspaper. Headed 'Our Image of God Must Go', it summarized the thesis of his book, *Honest to God*. Both the article and the book caused a storm of outraged criticism from traditionalists of every stripe. The 1960s was a period of general theological excitement, and Robinson was reflecting the spirit of the age.[1] The heading that *The Observer* gave to the article contains a truth of permanent importance that deserves careful consideration in any age. Our image of God must be carefully distinguished from the actual being of God. As John Calvin wrote, the human mind is 'a factory of idols'. The problem is that, although we have no alternative to approaching God through our image of him, that image is always in need of review, lest it become an idol.

The wise believer will recognize that in the assembly of believers there will be a multiplicity of images of God, ranging from the sophisticated to the crudely anthropomorphic. With regard to the latter, thoughtful Christians may regret crude images of God, but they need to remember that God's grace may be as active in popular religion as in its more intellectually refined kinds. Education and good catechesis can make a difference to the quality of belief; but for Christians the memory of Jesus and of his teaching remains salutary, salvific and permanently instructive, no matter how sophisticated the believer. Jesus took pity on people who struck him as being like 'sheep without a shepherd', in spite of the institutions and prescriptions of their religion. He proclaimed the reign of God to them in homely stories and gracious acts that took no notice of who the person was or whether they were inside or outside the official institution. That reign was to be found not in palaces or temples, but at tables where Jesus enjoyed a meal with the outcasts of society.

The word 'church' ought to suggest a free community of believers whose members associate with each other joyfully and non-judgementally, and with the world in general, in order to co-operate in bringing about the

---

1. A major influence on the age was the German-American theologian, Paul Tillich. In Chapter 13, *infra*, I discuss Tillich's thesis on how Catholic substance should relate to Protestant principle.

reign of God. That was the aspiration of Jesus of Nazareth in the Israel of his time. In practice, however, owing to a long history of accommodation to the political ways of the world, the true message of the Gospel has sometimes been obscured. A grim history witnesses to the fact that Christ's followers, when institutionally organized, have all too often been ready, indeed eager, to employ the power-structures of the world to promote their aims. Wars, or violence of any kind, where religion is the motive, contradict the very essence of Christian faith. In short, without explicitly subscribing to the dictum that the end justifies the means, Christ's followers have sometimes given little conscious attention to the means they employ to bring about what they see as good ends. Successful control of its members, together with a belligerently contrived uniformity by the institution, can be all too conveniently identified with God's will. Theocracy can be a mask for power-seeking religious people. It uses God as a means of control.

An institution can fail in faith by employing means that implicitly contradict the ends for which it exists. In spite of the fact that authority is not a major concern in the New Testament, ecclesiastical preoccupation with authority is allowed to overshadow other more important concerns. There must indeed be authority in all institutions; but Christian institutions are not always especially attentive to the manner of its exercise. Nevertheless, by this shall the disciples of Christ be recognized: that they love, and not oppress, one another.

The all too human urge to put the institution before the demands of the Gospel is a dismal failure in the practice of Christianity. Institutional organization of any social body with a plan for the future is inevitable, but in the case of the church, Christian leaders need to be constantly aware that power tends to corrupt, even in religious assemblies. Religion does not make power any less potentially hurtful than the oppressive action of secular authority. In fact, when the power-mongering is religiously inspired, hypocrisy is added to an already immoral situation.

There are small groups of Christians who, sometimes to the general applause of onlookers, try to dispense with complex organization and a doctrinal system of developed beliefs. Considering the damage that may have been done by Christians who have created a complex organisation for the expression of their beliefs, one can understand those who seek to avoid such complexity. Most Christians, nevertheless have felt that they must organize themselves for effective action in the world, and their doctrines into a coherent system. The challenge is how to ensure that the institution does not vaunt its authority at the expense of the spiritual and conscientious freedom of its members.

Preoccupation with the authority of the messenger can suggest a lack of confidence in the power of the message. The introduction of an alienating note into the message is in dissonance with the joyful thrust of the Gospel itself. The trouble is that concentration on the question of authority, papal, episcopal or communitarian, distracts from other far more important matters that are clamouring for attention in the modern world. A preoccupation with self-reference can also be a problem for other churches; but the Catholic Church places an exceptional emphasis on authority.

Catholics can remain imprisoned by a nineteenth century preoccupation with papal authority that sought compensation for the loss of the Papal States to Garibaldi and the Italian revolutionaries. In the following century the Lateran Treaty of 1929 saved face for both the papacy and for the fascist dictator, Benito Mussolini, by setting up the tiny politically independent Vatican State, which could employ clerical diplomats to serve in states throughout the world. This has meant that the Vatican, through its network of papal diplomats, could reassert its centralizing power throughout the church and win for itself a recognized position in international politics.

Recovering Luther's powerful insight into the relationship between faith and beliefs could well be at the core of the reform which has become so necessary in today's Catholic Church. It cannot be achieved without careful regard for the manner in which authority is exercised. The opponents of those who are looking for reform may be correct when they accuse 'liberals' of being Protestants. Unless we are using the word 'Protestant' as a term of abuse, and are blind to the truth in Protestantism, the ecumenical movement has taught us to listen to what Protestants are saying. The Reformation in the sixteenth century failed to extend itself to all Christians, and instead caused a tragic institutional division that ecumenists today are trying to repair. The more painful sources of that division have yet to be faced.

The heavy weight which Rome places upon the importance of its own statements and tactics is at the root of the injustices it inflicts upon those who seek a better, or at least a legitimately different, way of being a Catholic Christian today. The Second Vatican Council gave conciliar expression to the doctrine of collegiality, but, under pressure from the minority, it was immediately accompanied by a fresh proclamation of papal power.

Lest, however, we think of collegiality as a purely domestic issue, it is worth listening to Lukas Vischer who was Director of the Faith and Order Commission of the World Council of Churches, and a theologian from the Reformed tradition. As a distinguished ecumenist he, of course, writes with discretion and fraternal understanding. Nevertheless, he is clearly convinced that neglect of the concept of collegiality is at the heart of much that separates the Roman Catholic Church from the other Christian Churches. No amount of ecumenical tact can excuse an honest observer from expressing very grave reservations about what has been happening in the Catholic Church.

> The readiness of the papacy for discussions and meetings has indeed created a new atmosphere, but the manner in which the papal ministry is actively exercised does not offer any basis for real agreement.[2]

Vischer cannot but point to the discrepancy between the theory as found in the agreed statements of various inter-church dialogues and the actual practice of the papacy and its curia.

Even in the sphere of theory, as Vischer astutely observes, the texts of Vatican II 'left room for divergent interpretations', and therefore can be received in divergent senses. He reduces these views, in practice, to two by asking pointedly whether the unity of the Church is 'made visible primarily by one man or by the communion of the college'.[3] Both views, he notes, can appeal for support to the teaching of Vatican II. This is a sober and perceptive assessment by a committed ecumenist. He concludes with this incisive observation:

> The real breakthrough in the ecumenical movement will come, therefore, not through reception of the debate on collegiality, but

---

2. G. Alberigo, J. P. Jossua, and J. A. Komonchak (eds.), *The Reception of Vatican II* (Tunbridge Wells, 1987), p. 241.
3. Ibid p. 243.

only through reception of the entire history of the conciliar idea in the Church.[4]

Several Anglican and Protestant commentators have made the point that we need to distinguish between official ecumenism and grassroots ecumenism, the latter of which is in good shape and is forging ahead, sometimes into ventures that are viewed with disapproval by authority. Official ecumenism in the Catholic Church strikes many members and observers as excessively and needlessly restrictive. Eucharistic hospitality, for example, is, on the whole, frowned upon by authority, which displays an attitude that resists the instincts and expectations of many of the people of God and treats the Eucharist as an instrument of segregation.

The word 'lay' has, perhaps inevitably, though regrettably, taken on the meaning of 'non-clerical'. Strictly speaking, it should describe the entire people of God, including, without upgrading or detaching, the clergy. There is an increasing call for greater involvement of the laity, especially women, in church activities and governance. Since the clergy have traditionally carried out most of these activities, greater lay involvement will necessarily entail less clerical exclusivity. Unhappily, the call for lay involvement sometimes seems to be due less to theological conviction than to being simply a consequence of the shortage of priests, notably in the northern hemisphere. This pragmatism may do something collaterally to promote the cause of lay involvement; but it is a poor substitute for sound theological conviction.

Clerical reform in the Roman Catholic Church will necessarily involve breaking with the Tridentine model of the priest as a sacred person, segregated from the world and basically charged with an exclusive sacramental apostolate. As Pope Frances has observed in his interview with Antonio Spadaro, 'The people of God want pastors, not clergy acting like bureaucrats or government officials.'

There is also the political consideration that a clerical church is more easily controlled from the top through its institutional structures than lay people would be. These structures are not conducive to the practice of what has been preached in theory, especially at Vatican II. We need to remember that in 1965 the Council left the implementation of its ideals to

4. Ibid. p. 248.

the very organization that was most in need of reform, and most resistant to it, namely the Vatican Curia; and within the curia the CDF, which has reigned supreme.

Lay initiatives in worship may bring a new freshness to the celebration; but this can worry those Catholics for whom conformity to rules is more important than prayerful and committed performance. Admittedly there are folk who, for example, want to bring popular songs into the liturgy, but wiser heads can usually guide them without the need for more officious action. Desire for the Latin Mass may be due not so much to the stately flow of a dead language as to the comfort of unchanging formality. Too much liturgical regulation can stifle the spirit of prayer.

Mandatory clerical celibacy and the refusal to ordain women are potent symbols of the contradiction between the missionary ideal of the council and the persisting unreformed structures of the church. Any structure that sets the priest apart from the laity, and gives him duties that are exclusive of the laity, in practice denies the laity, especially women, an active role in church affairs. Priests have little enough power to make any significant changes in the church; the laity have still less. We belong to a hierarchical church whose structures stand proud against effective reform. An increase in the number of bishops worldwide would make it difficult to organise a General Council. The synodical idea would seem to be preferable, if it can be removed from its present papal control and become representative of the entire people of God.

The bishops may be constrained from entering into real dialogue with the faithful, lest they be forced to listen to, and perhaps even to agree with, views that are unacceptable to their masters in Rome. Roman Catholics have allowed themselves to be defined as Catholics by almost exclusive reference to the Bishop of Rome, together with some sexual and repro-ductive issues; and thereby they have acquiesced in a self-definition that has not alone been distorted into a taboo, but has diverted attention away from matters that are far more important for Christian truth and unity. The Bishop of Rome can be a focal point of unity and openness to fellow Christians, or he can be the cause of division and strife, if he allows his underlings to attack men and women who wish to live by a vision and values that are opposed to attitudes and a theology that oppresses theirs.

We are redeemed by faith, and not by theology. Once we have taken this salient fact into careful consideration, we must immediately go on to assert that an intelligent faith must necessarily issue in a supporting theology. If sophistication and learning are not necessary properties of faith, neither are they an obstacle to it. Inverted spiritual snobbery of the kind that seeks to disparage the spirit of enquiry in the practice of faith is just as false and obnoxious as the snobbery that exaggerates the spiritual value of learning. For some men and women the stark choice is between an intelligent and critically aware faith, and no faith at all. Failure to appreciate and respond to the spiritual needs of these believers, or potential believers, amounts to a pastoral betrayal of the church's evangelical mission to teach and care.

The danger of the neo-scholastic system was that it lent itself to an extrinsic and authoritarian mode of church governance. Its integralism promoted the view that revelation is a sequence of divine teachings delivered to the church to be received as a whole and assented to in an act of reverential mental obedience (the Latin word for it was '*obsequium*'). Once this was done, the faithful Catholic could leave all the thinking to the magisterium, which, from Leo XIII's pontificate until the meeting of Vatican II, discouraged the 'learning church' from doing any thinking for itself. In a managerial church, obedience to the teaching of the Roman Curia, coupled with a spiritual life based on a rather shallow devotionalism, tended to take the place of genuine theological thinking of the sort that could appreciate the difference between Gospel values and a pious devotion to the latest Marian appearance . By this I do not mean to patronise popular devotions, but to comment mainly on the lack of clerical leadership in teaching and preaching.

The situation in Ireland before, during and after the Second Vatican Council, provides a fairly apposite example of what I mean. Led by its bishops, Catholic Ireland, after the achievement of national independence, was not a place where new theological ideas had circulated with much excitement or at any depth before the council. The Irish bishops had made little contribution to conciliar debates; and on the whole they were not at ease with the new theology. An article that Vincent Twomey, S.V.D., contributed to *The Irish Catholic* mentions the case of an Irish bishop who, when asked how he got on at the Second Vatican Council, is reported to have replied: 'Well, it was really all a bit of a waste of time.

They talked about nothing but theology.' [5] We cannot say to what extent this comment reflected the general attitude of the Irish bishops who attended the council; but living theology had not played a notable part in the life of most Irish clerics. The then Archbishop of Dublin, John Charles Mc.Quaid, felt able to reassure his people at the end of the council that 'No change will worry the tranquility of your Christian lives'.

The mode of teaching is as important as its content. This educational principle has a moral as well as a psychological reference, especially in a religious context. Much Catholic catechesis has been traditionally directed towards children. While the catechesis of children is altogether necessary, in the Catholic Church it has traditionally been promoted at the expense of adult education in faith. Today, however, something is being done to correct this imbalance. In the 1960s the *Dutch Catechism* was an effective instrument for reflecting the reforming initiatives of Vatican II. The latest Roman Catechism marks a return to conservative inspiration and is playing a significant part in the contemporary post-conciliar revanchist enterprise.

Church leaders who are trying to respond to the inspiration of the Holy Spirit, and the reforming energy initiated by Vatican II, need the support of all Christ's followers. Bishops, for example, have the unenviable task of furthering renewal while maintaining unity and fidelity to what is proclaimed by Rome to be unchangeable in Christian Tradition. Today they have to live with the problem of increasingly aggressive and querulous neo-conservatives who report them to Rome for any perceived deviation from traditionalist ideas. One must hope that the Roman Curia is able and willing to discriminate between pathological cranks and the legitimately worried. At the moment, the CDF takes them seriously, protects their anonymity, and uses them as an excuse to intervene in matters of local concern. In an increasingly pluriform church, priests, especially in their capacity as preachers, have a difficult and delicate task. It has become nearly impossible to speak to everyone's spiritual (including intellectual and aesthetic) needs. Whether Rome likes it or not, the Catholic Church is no longer the monolith that it was deemed to be before the council. An average congregation differs not merely in intellectual and aesthetic education and taste, but also in theological sensibilities, which may range

5. Vincent Twomey, 'The Second Vatican Council and the Irish Church', *The Irish Catholic*, October 11, 2012, pp. 12-13.

from extreme conservatism to advanced radicalism.

Blunt 'common sense' does not qualify a preacher to sail blithely and self-indulgently into complex theological and moral issues that call for accurate information, sensitivity to the need for careful qualification, and immense compassion towards those who are wrestling with these issues. There are sectarian priests who will not give communion to anyone who has not been to confession in the previous three weeks! No priest has the right or the authority to lay down shibboleths like that. To do so is to bring the church into disrepute, since the individual is sometimes identified with the church.

Institutions are convenient scapegoats, because the flaws of institutions are only too obvious. It is inevitable that 'the church' is blamed for the faults of its members. It is particularly regrettable, however, when the church is identified with one point of view. If the Bishop of Rome allows himself to be identified with the church, those of his fellow Catholics who legitimately disagree with him, on matters that are not essential to the faith, are thereby denied their rightful claim to orthodox membership of their Church – which is a grave injustice.

Faith is practised, less by railing against the failures of the institution, serious as these may be, than by pressing on despite the obstacles to reform of these failures. If there were no obstacles, and causes could be pursued without let or hindrance, perhaps the very pursuit would develop its own hardness of heart. Struggling with opposition or apathy can actually strengthen an initiative. Our chains can be the source of our strength, as long as bodies like the CDF do not render its critics impotent by an unscrupulous resort to crude power. Christian faith is transformed into hope, and Christian hope is largely a matter of waiting upon God, if possible with humour, while working patiently to bring about needed change.

I have been stressing the thought that Christian faith and morality are as concerned with means as with ends. It is this thought that single-minded and intolerant fundamentalists so easily overlook. For them it does not matter who gets hurt in the process, since the end, in their view, is good. This may be a fondly imagined orthodoxy, but it is emphatically not Christianity, which teaches that what we do must be matched by awareness of the need to do it with the mind of Christ.

A community of Christian faith has to be a community of healing. In

Eliot's apt phrase, the whole earth is our hospital. Pope Francis is particularly eloquent on this theme:

> The thing the church needs most today is the ability to heal wounds and to warm the hearts of the faithful; it needs nearness, proximity. I see the church as a field hospital after battle. It is useless to ask a seriously injured person if he has high cholesterol and about the level of his blood sugars! You have to heal his wounds. Then we can talk about everything else. Heal the wounds, heal the wounds.... And you have to start from the ground up.[6]

To live in the world as a Christian is to recognize that we are wounded people dealing with other wounded people. The process of healing therefore has to begin within the church itself before it can be effective in society at large. The church has to demonstrate how healing is brought about by being frank about its own need of healing. Since the world's wounds are to be found in the church itself, there is where the healing must begin. The point remains insistent: the message given by Jesus is inseparable from the manner in which he chose to give it. 'Do you think that I cannot appeal to my Father, and he will at once send me more than twelve legions of angels?' Jesus asked one of his more impatient and bellicose followers (Matthew 26:53). In the centuries that followed, his followers have dispatched many legions – with few angels in them. Jesus looked not for ruthless determination to bring about the reign of God, but for faith in himself as God's Word. Determination has to sink itself into quiet hope, with equal attention given to the means that it chooses to employ as to its end.

According to John the Evangelist, when, in the course of his passion, Jesus stood before Pilate, the governor was momentarily intrigued: 'So you are a king?' he asked. Jesus replied, '"You say that I am a king. For this I was born, and for this I have come into the world: to bear witness to the truth. Everyone who is of the truth hears my voice." Pilate then said to him, "What is truth?"' (John 18:37-38). Truth, finally and comprehensively expressed in the guise of a Galilean craftsman and preacher, stood before him; and he chose to ask a tired and disillusioned philosophical question

---

6. *America* magazine, September 19, 2013.

before walking out. Pilate, the military diplomat concerned with career advancement, knew that truth had little to do with his way of life. For him power was all: who wielded it, who was subject to it, and who could at a whim take it away. Truth, if allowed too close, might threaten the values by which Pilate lived, and endanger his relationship with those who had put him where he was. Truth was therefore a dangerous irrelevance. If conscience stirred, it could always be stilled by the washing of one's hands.

When, with consummate artistry, Dostoyevsky places his Christ-figure before the Grand Inquisitor, all the atmosphere of Pilate's palace can be felt. Once again the Prisoner is silent, as the ecclesiastical chief of police explains vehemently to him that the church knows far better than he, the Prisoner, could ever do, how to keep people happy with bread and circuses, with answers to unasked questions and with the suppression of unanswerable ones. The Prisoner had promised to set them free - most unwisely in the Inquisitor's view; for who wants freedom when they can have their decisions made for them by others who know better?

The Prisoner's answer was to kiss his captor, who then dismissed him with the injunction never to return. And what of the old man? enquires Alyosha of his brother, Ivan, who has related the story. He has not changed his views, answers Ivan; but the kiss still glows in his heart.

7

Faithful Criticism: Towards a More Compassionate Church

In January 1870, during the First Vatican Council, John Henry Newman wrote to Bishop William Ullathorne:

> Rome ought to be a name to lighten the heart at all times, and a Council's proper office is, when some great heresy or other evil impends, to inspire the faithful with hope and confidence; but now we have the greatest meeting which ever has been, and that at Rome, infusing into us ... little else than fear and dismay.

Later in the same letter he continued:

> Why should an aggressive insolent faction be allowed to 'make the heart of the just to mourn, whom the Lord hath not made sorrowful?' Why can't we be left alone, when we have pursued peace, and thought no evil? [1]

Ian Ker, in his book on Newman, describes this letter as 'perhaps the most indignant he ever wrote'. [2]

Newman is in some ways a bridge between the conservative and progressive wings of the Catholic Church. He is unquestionably orthodox in his Catholicism, including his loyalty to the papacy and acceptance of papal infallibility; yet he can be critical of Roman authority, as we see in this letter, which is a perfect exemplar of faithful criticism (from a man, incidentally, soon to be canonised). He already believes what the First Vatican Council is thrusting unnecessarily upon the whole church, and he sees no reason for this gratuitous display of power, which can only alien-

---

1. The letter is printed in J. Sugg (ed.), *A Packet of Letters : A Selection from the Correspondence of John Henry Newman* (Oxford, 1983), pp. 180-182. The quotation is from Ezekiel 13:22 in the Douay-Rheims Bible: 'Because with lies you have made the heart of the just to mourn, whom I have not made sorrowful.'

2. Ian T Ker, *John Henry Newman: A Biography* (Oxford, 2009).

ate faithful Catholics who are uneasy about what is happening in Rome. He blames 'an aggressive insolent faction' in the church for prompting Rome to brandish its authority in so demonstrative a fashion. It is worth remembering that many of the opponents of the definition of papal infallibility chose to slip quietly away from Rome before the definition. The conservative minority at Vatican II were treated much more gently and tolerantly.

A controlling theme of this book is that, in terms of power, one mentality has become exclusive of all others in the bureaucracy of the Catholic Church. This way of thinking has resulted in the denial of justice to those who cannot share it.

Love and compassion ought to be the signs by which Christians are known, whether in a lowly or an exalted position in the institution. Truth and justice demand the admission that opposing opinions and attitudes have a right to be held and heard in the church, when they cannot be shown to be genuinely unorthodox according to generally accepted theological criteria. Church leaders are as free as anyone else to have their own opinions. Personal opinions, however, do not give anyone, however exalted, the right to impose those opinions on others, or to take offensive institutional action against faithful dissenters. Truth is established by discussion and argument, not by the proclamations of authority; yet Rome has refused to conduct a caring discussion about some matters that are in legitimate dispute in the contemporary church. In many respects the Roman Catholic Church's curial administration has remained firmly lodged in nineteenth century attitudes.

What, then, are we to make of the different wings that all too plainly exist in the church today, only one of which claims the power to put forward its views as exclusive orthodoxy? It is true that other Christian churches also have their institutional problems and disputes; but other churches do not display the same obsession with authority, and unquestioning obedience to it, that Roman Catholic government does. The magisterium, by dint of its oppressive power, may instill fear in the church, but it is difficult to see what *pastoral* function it has. As Newman says: Rome ought to be a name to lighten the heart at all times. Under Pope Francis it could, if he can reform the curia successfully and with some permanence.

In January, 2014 the Pope addressed the Congregation for the Doctrine of the Faith telling them that they ought not

> to understand the doctrine in an ideological sense or to reduce it to an ensemble of abstract and crystallized theories. In reality, doctrine has the sole purpose of serving the life of the People of God and it seeks to ensure our faith of a sure foundation.[3]

These words give a partial picture of what has been happening for centuries, but especially, during the last few years. One must hope that Francis will keep a sharp eye on the curia in general but on the Congregation for the Doctrine of the Faith (CDF) in particular, and will insist that it restore the good name of those it has, in many cases, attacked so unjustly and so unprofessionally. However, it would be prudent to entertain the disquieting possibility that the curia, and especially the CDF, could return to its old ways after Francis has gone, just as it did after Vatican II.

As matters have been recently, those who teach and write are, of course, more vulnerable to institutional attack. They cannot carry out their apostolate in the same way as frontline pastors can. Some of them are both frontline pastors and authors. To write is to give hostages to fortune or, worse, to the CDF. Academics and communicators are vulnerable to bureaucratic assault: they can be removed from office in establishments that are under church control. This tends to induce self-censorship, which may be as injurious to the pursuit of truth as bureaucratic censorship. Silence and inaction can be taken for approval of a system of government that is oppressive and careless of justice. Yet silence and inaction may be the only recourse open to those who wish to remain in their posts.

There is a faction in the church that is urging the papacy to take ever more stringent measures against men and women who are trying to make the Christian message heard in the world of today. Newman, as we have seen, called it 'the aggressive insolent faction', and it tries to achieve its misguided purposes by institutional action. We must always make a careful and sharp distinction between the *holding* of traditionalist opinions and the effort to *impose* them on others by punitive action. The former must be tolerated, however wrong-headed we may think it to be. We have every right to oppose the latter tooth and nail, without making any concessions

3. Austen Ivereigh, *The Great Reformer: Francis and the Making of a Radical Pope* (London, 2014), p. 374.

to it in the name of liberality or broadness of view.

Since Rome has been prone to indulge ultra-conservatives, while treating 'liberals' with hostility and suspicion, progressive Catholics have every right to protest against the sheer unfairness of allowing one clique an audience while giving the other a cold shoulder. This protest is not a matter of seeking special treatment for one theological opinion over another; it is merely for the freedom to hold and promote its views without persecution.

I have been greatly encouraged by something that Yves Congar wrote during the Second Vatican Council:

> Experience and history have taught me that one must ALWAYS protest when one feels in conscience or by conviction that there are grounds for doing so.[4]

This, it seems to me, applies not merely to distinguished theologians like Congar, but also to all who work, however modestly, in the same field as he did.

I am convinced that there is a serious pastoral neglect of fellow Catholics who are disillusioned by the way in which the church has been governed in recent years. I have written this book in the hope of giving them some assurance that they are not alone, and that their disapproval of what the last two popes and their curias have been doing is in no way disloyal.

It would mean a great deal, primarily to priests and members of religious orders, but also to many of the laity, if at least one or two bishops would come to the defence of priests and sisters who are attacked by the CDF. Under the last two popes it could have led to dismissal from the active episcopate; to expect any bishop to risk such a punishment might have been asking too much. Under the present pope things might be very different. Much will depend on whether Pope Francis will be prepared to discipline the CDF and come to the rescue of priests and members of religious orders under attack.

Throughout this book I repeatedly point out that unity does not entail uniformity. In a body such as the Christian Church, there are bound to be different interpretations of, and responses to, so great a mystery as the life, teaching, death and resurrection of Jesus Christ. None of us is

---

4. Yves Congar, *My Journal of the Council* (Dublin, 2012), p. 12. Congar has put 'ALWAYS' in upper case – his usual method of emphasis.

required to respond to that mystery by demanding, or accepting the need for, theological and moral uniformity. On the contrary, we *are* bound to accept and live amicably with the legitimate differences that occur naturally in any body such as the Christian Church. Even in discussion of doctrines that are defined, different theological treatments that respect what is of faith, are legitimate and are, indeed, a normal way of trying to penetrate more deeply and more relevantly into the mysteries of our faith. We can, for instance, be faithful to the church's doctrine of Christ without having to use fourth century language.

As Pope John XXIII stated in his opening address to the Second Vatican Council, there is a difference between the substance of faith and the manner of its formulation. Faith remains constant while theologies change. In fact, it is the change in theologies that protects the constancy of faith and gives it fresh relevance in every age. If genuine errors occur, there will be no shortage of other theologians ready to point them out and attempt to refute them. In a climate of oppression and fear, however, there will be a disinclination among many theologians to make life worse for anyone who is under attack by governing bodies for whom condemnation has taken the place of rational discussion, and whose own theology may be in serious need of reconstruction.

The Second Vatican Council tried to make serious adjustments to the relationship between the papacy and the rest of the church. This was, and remains, a sensitive task, because of the taboos that have arisen around the papacy since the nineteenth century. A pointed question raised by Congar was whether the pope should be seen as being *within* or *above* the Church. The doctrine of collegiality, which made possible a reformed view of papal primacy, was debated with passionate intensity during Vatican II. For a time it mistakenly seemed that the battle for it had been finally and definitively won.

There has for long been a strong Catholic compulsion to place the pope above criticism. This was not so during the Middle Ages, often called the period of faith – and alleged obscurantism. Roman Catholics, since the nineteenth century, have grown so accustomed to honouring the *person* of the pope, that he has acquired the status of being beyond criticism; indeed some zealots may construe criticism of him as an offence against his sacredness. (The fact that popes have taken to canonizing each other intensifies this attitude.) Pope Francis has given hope to a constituency in the church that has been assailed or neglected; and some traditionalists obviously resent the attitude of the new pope; but they, especially bishops, will be careful to express their resentment very obliquely. Some of them will wait in the expectation that the old ways will soon return.

We need to remember that the most empirical of the pope's titles is geographical: namely that he is Bishop of Rome, even when he decides, usually for political reasons, to reside elsewhere (such as in Avignon in France from 1378 to 1417). Other titles and prerogatives have been acquired in the course of history, down to his status as monarch and temporal ruler of the Vatican state. Some of them have been disingenuously attributed to the intention of Jesus himself. We have allowed an all too human awe for the office to overshadow the Christian obligations of its holder. It is sobering to recall that in the recent past, Catholic opposition to the church's claim to *temporal* power was regarded as an offence against orthodoxy. This is another illustration of how a former orthodoxy can be dropped without comment by those who once promoted it.

The Second Vatican Council sought gently to draw the Bishop of Rome into the church from where he saw himself, and allowed others to see him, as being above the church. The question must now, however, be asked: did he, during the last pontificates, return to his former station above the church; and has the vision of a reformed church, so cherished by the council, been set aside, leaving those who lived through the days of renewed hope, lost, angry and perhaps demoralized?

Joseph Ratzinger, a German professor of theology and future pope, who was initially a seemingly willing participant in the work of a reforming council shortly afterwards changed his attitude radically. Throughout this book I oppose several of Ratzinger's opinions. I respect his scholarship, but I regret some of the issues to which he has put that scholarship. There was a time when his views were different from those of his later career. What he wrote in his book, *Introduction to Christianity* in 1968, when he was still a theologian inspired by the achievements of Vatican II, remains impressive in the candour of its critique of a church more interested in control than in acting as a conduit for God's loving care.

Taking a line not dissimilar from the attitude of Pope Francis, Ratzinger says that for many people today, the Church has become the main obstacle to belief. They can no longer see in it anything but the human struggle for power, the petty spectacle of those who, with their claim to administer official Christianity, seem to stand most in the way of the true spirit of Christianity.[5]

These severe and perceptive words could pass for a damaging critique of the views and actions of their author when he became pope. Though he was careful not to say explicitly what his own opinion was, it is plain that he was sympathetic to the sentiments expressed. At the very least he expressed an awareness of what many ordinary people were thinking. Could anything be more apposite as a description of the power-bearing offices in the Catholic Church, and of the measures they are inflicting on those members of it who are trying to put into practice the early Joseph Ratzinger's vision of a church that recognizes its own sinfulness and gives careful consideration to the startling observation that 'it has become the main obstacle to belief'?

Today we have to listen with shame to the often-convincing criticism of the Catholic Church by outsiders who are able to see and draw attention to its irrelevance in the modern world and to the injustices perpetrated by some of its senior officers. Our official superiors often seem unable or unwilling to criticize the faults of our church from the inside. We leave it to secular newspapers to point out the faults and defects of the institution; and we sometimes attribute their criticisms to anti-Catholic prejudice, thus conveniently avoiding the need for repentance and change. Because some of the secular press are praising Pope Francis, it does not follow that believing Catholics should react against this by emphasising the virtues of his predecessors. The reasons for contrasting Francis with Benedict should be pastoral and theological not partisan.

All institutions have a tendency to close ranks when under attack. A sacralised institution rarely admits to its faults, or else it does so with reluctance and understatement. Its denial of guilt, largely implicit, can demoralise its members as they face a critical and sometimes hostile world while lacking the understanding and support of its leaders. Indeed in some cases its members find themselves under heartless attack by the authorities of their own church. The CDF plans its attacks on members

5. Joseph Ratzinger, *Introduction to Christianity* (London, 1969), p. 263.

of religious orders in the knowledge that superiors will usually be anxious to avoid offending curial sensitivities.

In the developed countries large numbers are turning away from Catholicism, Christianity and religion in general. Most of the Christian churches are dismayed by the rejection of, or disregard for, the faith that they profess and cherish. Catholic Church leaders usually attribute this falling away to the moral defects of the modern world. Before the arrival of Pope Francis there was not a scintilla of self-questioning as a response to this crisis. What is badly needed is an honest attempt to see ourselves as others see us. What do people see when they look at the government of the Catholic Church? They see an institution which governs through diktat, which has, until the arrival of Pope Francis, retained its princely style and which refuses women any significant place in its structures. History has bestowed on the papacy an external magnificence that is difficult to reconcile with the ideals put before us by Jesus of Nazareth. Although the pope himself may not care for the splendour of his surroundings, his curia make effective use of this magnificence to further their institutional supremacy. All this finery is as nothing when put alongside the way in which the government of the institution behaves. It constantly gives the impression of believing that the monarchical model of government is essential to its existence. It is heartening that Pope Francis has turned away from this model.

There is no shortage of truly dismaying examples of Rome's behaviour. One thinks of the Leadership Conference of Women Religious in the United States, and how they were pursued by Cardinal Gerhard Ludwig Müller and the CDF. One thinks also of the priests in Ireland, some of whom have been severely censured for their efforts to bring their Christian faith to bear on the world of today. Numerous individual authors have been treated with scant regard for their human rights. What, for example, is Rome afraid of in the matter of female ordination, that it can take such egregious steps to oppose it? Feminists would reply simply that it is a plain manifestation of misogyny; and it is hard to disagree with their diagnosis. Theological or biblical reasons put forward to justify the Roman interdiction on women's ordination are unconvincing, to put it mildly. To say that because Jesus did not ordain women, women can never be ordained, is often offered as an argument why we should not do so.

There are many things that Jesus did not do that we today do without a thought or scruple. One needs to be very short of decent arguments to have to rely on this one.

I consider here some cases of religious priests whom I know to be faithful members of the church and who have been trying to reach people by means that are fresh and designed to bring Gospel values to men and women of today. How the Congregation for the Doctrine of the Faith has treated them defies justice and Christian values. I happen to know most of the Irish priests who have been so unjustly assailed by the CDF. My interest in what has happened to them is not simply academic; it is personal and, I must admit, angry, and I ask the reader's indulgence if that anger comes through in what I write. I cannot understand why the Roman Curia has been allowed to continue perpetrating these acts of violence, in the interests of a spurious orthodoxy.

I give here a short outline of what happens when complaints are made to Rome, where the response has been frequently intolerant and oppressive. The normal procedure begins with a complaint made to Rome by some person, lay, clerical or episcopal, about an alleged error or act that does not conform to the expectations of the traditionalist mind. If the alleged offender, as is often the case, is a member of a religious order or congregation, the task of the curia (usually the CDF, which has doctrinal authority over the other dicasteries) is made less complicated by using the structure of the religious institution to execute its injunctions, thus escaping from the human consequences of its actions. The curial dicastery, usually the CDF, informs the superior general of the order or congregation of the complaint and instructs him or her to act appropriately. The general superior passes on the curial instruction to the local or provincial superior, or else deals with the matter personally. The identity of the complainant is never revealed, and secrecy is enforced as far as possible. Transparency, so often mentioned by today's media, is scandalously absent in the procedure. The superiors of the order or congregation do not have to agree with the Roman authorities that the alleged offender is at fault; nevertheless they are placed under heavy pressure to do something in response to the CDF's diagnosis of the situation. They may be bemused by what is happening and may act only out of the felt need to be submissive to the CDF. They belong, after all, to the establishment, even when their attitudes and behaviour are normally free of authoritarianism. When they fail to stand up to the unjust tactics of the CDF, they become the most vulnerable link in the chain of authority by allowing the CDF to claim that it is the religious superior rather than the curial Congregation who is responsible for what has happened to the accused. This cowardly and dishonest procedure offends against elementary human rights and normal civilised legal procedure as well as being an assault on personal dignity.

The victim is sometimes left in limbo (in the non-theological sense: 'an uncertain period of awaiting a decision or resolution') which, for a priest, is particularly distressing, since it removes him from the exercise of his ministry, damages his good name and gives him no opportunity of replying to his accusers or of knowing who they or his judges are.[6]

Let me at this point instance the example of four Irish priests who have come under attack from the CDF. I am not approaching the matter from a purely academic and detached standpoint; I cannot help feeling indignant about how some good priests have been treated by men who should welcome what they are doing instead of attacking them for lack of fidelity to an outmoded way of thinking and acting.

Old age or bad health is no protection against persecution. I think with dismay about what has happened to Seán Fagan, S.M., a friend and former colleague who has devoted his life to pastoral work by writing, lecturing and counseling, and who has been unjustly assailed by the CDF, in spite of the fact that he is old and in constant arthritic pain. In addition, the family of the accused may be adversely affected by the attack made on their relative; and this may be the reason why the accused unselfishly complies with the prejudiced injunctions.

The case of Tony Flannery is fairly well known, owing to his courage in exposing the actions of his victimisers. His book, *A Question of Conscience,* gives a personal account of the CDF's pursuit of him. As a founder of the Association of Catholic Priests he has been in the Vatican's sights and has been the subject of close investigation. I focus here on an article he wrote for the journal *Reality,* because it reveals that the CDF is not merely

6. For an example of the tactics adopted by the CDF see Tony Flannery, *A Question of Conscience*, (Dublin, 2013). Flannery has courageously refused to accept the injunction to secrecy imposed on him by the CDF. His book is a valuable record of what happens to victims of the Congregation.

tyrannical; it can be theologically inept. In the course of his article he writes, 'Whatever Jesus intended, I don't think anyone can credibly claim that he intended the type of system we now have in the church.' 'I no longer believe that the priesthood, as we currently have it in the Church, originated with Jesus.' His views here are both theologically and histori-cally unexceptionable. His attackers have simply failed to reckon with his qualification, 'as we currently have it in the Church'. Their view seems to be that everything we have in the church today can be attributed to the authority of Jesus – which is palpably untrue.

Another victim of the CDF is Brian D'Arcy, C.P., who for years has writ-ten a column in a Sunday tabloid, thereby reaching many people who may not normally encounter church ministration. He is deeply involved in the pastoral care of people who see him 'as an authentic voice of compassion and positive criticism'. The CDF has attacked him for being 'a source of great scandal to the faithful' and, incredibly, has pronounced 'a formal canonical warning to cease being critical of the Vatican'! The effect of all this has been to damage his health and almost drive him to abandon the priesthood. In an act of remarkable faith he has so far resisted the temptation to leave, and he continues his apostolate of reaching people whom authoritarian bodies like the Roman Curia pastorally neglect.[7]

My last case is that of Iggy O'Donovan, a confrere and friend, who has ministered with great success in the Augustinian church in Drogheda for many years. He has been credited with reaching people who might oth-erwise have left the church. On one occasion at a Baptism he allowed the parents of a child to pour the water on the child's head. Astonishingly, he was denounced to the archbishop of the diocese and to Rome. The CDF went into action and contacted O'Donovan's religious superiors accusing him of causing 'confusion and scandal'. The general and regional supe-riors of the order were instructed to do something about Iggy's alleged malfeasance. In consequence he was removed from Drogheda, where he had done so much good.

All these examples demonstrate the serious defects of the CDF, both moral and theological. The punishments inflicted on good men and dedicated priests are similarly indefensible from a Christian and humane

7. See an interview with D'Arcy by Martin O'Brien in *The Irish Catholic*, March 20, 2014, p. 12.

point of view. The utter lack of care about the effect that their acts have on their victims is callous, to say nothing of their unchristian character.

These moral defects are damning enough, but their theological motive is worth examining. The CDF simply assumes that all that happens in the central administration of the Catholic Church is above reproach and needs no justification. No theologically valid reason for this assumption is ever given. The 'formal canonical warning to cease being critical of the Vatican' given to Brian D'Arcy would be risible, if it were not so injurious to the victim. It assumes that the Congregation is without fault, thus putting it beyond reform, whereas it happens to be the ecclesiastical institution most in need of reform.

There is in all this a total disregard for historical development and a seeming unawareness that the beliefs and practices of the church are always subject to judgement in the light of Gospel values. The church is sinful as well as holy - a thought that the CDF never seems to entertain. What I am protesting against is not primarily the attitude or the unaccountable theology of the Congregation (which can be freely disputed on academic grounds); it is the baseless assumption that its agents have a sacred duty to oppress those who oppose their outdated theology.

The members of the CDF have no grounds for claiming that they have a solemn prerogative to regard their theology as the only orthodoxy; and they most certainly do not have any God-given right to take action against fellow Catholics who have been trying to respond to the Gospel in the modern world.

As Yves Congar remarks in his *Journal of the Council*, the church has yet to find the language to speak convincingly to the world of today. It is hardly going to do so by treating its own members harshly and unjustly for adopting ways of approaching the ministry that are, though patently well within the bounds of orthodoxy, different from its own. Rome seems to see all too clearly the need for reform in the world, while never including itself in that need. Without such inclusion, reform will remain superficial and inauthentic. If it is true that the institutional Catholic Church is a major obstacle to belief today, then the programme for reform must necessarily include a critical examination of how the church is being governed, of its organisational structures and of the tactics that it is employing in the pursuit of its aims. Pope Francis in his Apostolic Exhortation, *Evangelii*

Gaudium, places impressive emphasis on joy and positivity – qualities not often evident in curial activities. He is also unambiguous about the need for structural conversion:

> The papacy and the central structures of the universal Church also need to hear the call to pastoral conversion.[8]

For too long we have allowed curial power to ride roughshod over faithful members of the church. If we do not speak out against what has happened only recently, Roman authority will continue to mete out the worst excesses of its customary tyranny. I make my criticisms from *within* the church that I care about, and not as a disillusioned former member of it.

I believe that the gratuitous problems of living in today's Catholic Church have to be faced honestly, and always in the hope that authority may appreciate, if not the gravity of the problems themselves, then at least the fact that some, perhaps many, Catholic Christians are trying to remain faithful in spite of serious temptation to give up the struggle. When a church is described as Catholic, it cannot allow itself to dwindle into a sect of like-minded and intolerant people.

There is regrettably no pastoral programme designed to meet the difficulties of those who disapprove of what is happening in the church today. It is, of course, much less trouble to condemn or neglect them than to be pastorally or intellectually concerned about them. The principal reason for this neglect is that, in the absence of a general council of the church, the effort involved in drawing up such a pastoral programme, and then implementing it, would threaten the security of those who have withdrawn to the safety of a secluded supernatural refuge where 'enemies' and perhaps 'heretics' are easily identified and condemned, and where legal and moral standards are idiosyncratic.

Avery Dulles, the well-known American theologian who was made a cardinal by John Paul II, has described the attitude of the traditionalist camp in the Catholic Church as 'supernaturalist', in the sense that it seeks to withdraw from the world into a segregated island unaffected by, and hostile to, the world. This attitude is to some extent a reaction against the alleged 'excesses' committed in the period following Vatican II, when

---

8. *Evangelii Gaudium: The Joy of the Gospel: Apostolic Exhortation of the Holy Father Francis* (Dublin, 2013), p. 25.

some traditionalists felt that Catholic engagement with the secular world had made the church too 'natural'. Engagement has today given way to withdrawal, and an ivory tower has been built that has enabled church authorities to live a life segregated from the world they were sent to evangelise by dialogue and respectful listening.

Engagement and withdrawal, however, are two inescapable poles in the Christian experience of discipleship. They need to act as correctives, each of the other. The Christian Church requires both views for its health. The victory of one over the other, especially if it is attained by main force, makes for a distorted vision of the Christian mission. The tension between them is a healthy experience in Christian life and should be accepted and lived with as such. Reform may sometimes consist in a readjustment of the balance between them. Emphatic engagement may neglect the need for prayer, contemplation and otherworldly concerns, while emphatic supernaturalism makes the church top-heavy, theocratic and out of touch with reality.

A psychological excuse for withdrawal from the problems of practising one's Christian faith authentically in the world of today may indeed be understandable; but from a moral and pastoral viewpoint such withdrawal is pusillanimous and biblically indefensible. Psychologists have much to say about the felt need of some people to control others; and one certainly cannot deny the presence of that psychological impulse in institutional church circles. In any civilized society there are limits to power, however legitimate that power may claim to be, and there is no good reason why the church should be an exception to these limits. At the moment, a paralyzing subservience to ecclesiastical power prevails over conscience and good sense. The system is designed to bring about conformity and uniformity. Its major weakness from a traditionalist viewpoint is that it is vulnerable to the election of free-spirited popes like Angelo Roncalli, and Jorge Bergoglio, who act in an unexpected way that threatens the security of the Roman Curia.

Pope Benedict's disapproval of concern with institutional reform is unacceptable, because its appeal to some sort of mystical notion of church that has no empirical reference, serves as an escape from the concrete actuality of life in the church. One reason why there is not a wider and more concerted opposition to Rome's victimization of non-conformists, is that the secular world cannot be expected to appreciate what ecclesiastical censure can mean to a loyal Catholic. As we shall see, some young clerics today even portray themselves as virtuously indifferent to Roman oppression of their brothers and sisters.

If something analogous were to happen in secular life, there would be an outcry, and probably a call to protest and to bring pressure to bear on the offenders. Since, however, religion is being increasingly privatized in secular society in the West, there is no protest against what is regarded as not being one's business. This leaves faithful members of the church to act for themselves when they are under attack by their own brothers.

A commonly expressed view is that if you disagree with enforced conservatism, you should simply leave the church. This is just the sort of remark that might be made to a recalcitrant member of a social club, and it may be understandable from a secular viewpoint; but it totally fails to appreciate what membership of a church can mean to a genuinely religious person. Membership of a church is radically different from membership of a club. One cannot take seriously the superficial notion, sometimes heard from officious and superficial Catholics, that the Church of Christ may be compared to a club with rules that must be observed under pain of expulsion. Such a view fails to understand how one can be loyal to the church without approving of its leaders or their attitudes, or especially of their theology. One has every right to remain in the church and struggle for its reform; and a little episcopal understanding and encouragement would not come amiss. In the last analysis it is a matter of conscience whether to leave or to stay; leaving, however, may help the 'aggressive insolent faction' to resist reform.

In Ireland, only two generations ago, when the Catholic Church exercised inordinate influence on secular society, criticism of it was mainly literary rather than political, and as such it reached only a literary elite, some of whom were of an anticlerical mind. Only very few courageous politicians spoke out against ecclesiastical interference in secular affairs; and they were often regarded as cranks not to be taken too seriously. It really was a 'church-ridden' society. Today, by way of reaction, politicians respond with alacrity to the least hint of ecclesiastical interference. We are paying the price for the sins of the past, even when we may not have been personally guilty of them.

The age of 'Catholic Ireland' is a much-discredited memory for many now; and churchmen are very careful today not to draw down on themselves the fury of the public, together with denunciation by the media, for seeming to pontificate on political matters in the name of religion or church teaching. Irish politicians today, aware of the timid subservience of their predecessors, are hypersensitive about any attempt by bishops to exert influence in the public arena; and since most questions of public morality have a political dimension, this can inhibit Catholic leaders from speaking out on matters that are legitimately their concern. This is the price that is being paid for past arrogance and for recent dereliction of duty in the matter of clerical child abuse. It is all very well to claim the undeniable right of the church to comment publicly on social and political affairs; but in contemporary Ireland, clerical commentators need to remember that in the not-too-distant past such comment often took a dictatorial shape, resulting in an ambience of fear, timidity and suppressed anger.

Today there is recognition that much about the church was wrong in the new Irish State; however, the Catholic Church rarely makes public apologies for anything. 'Catholic Ireland' of recent memory enjoyed a flourishing number of priests and members of religious congregations, and this meant that the institutional church took on tasks for which the state made no provision. Today, however, shrinking of the clerical body and increased rejection of organised religion, means that these tasks are carried out by secular men and women.

Public secular discrediting of the church may be distressing for the believer, but it can provide an occasion for repentance and reform, both personal and institutional. Although Rome, with the exception of Pope Francis, has shown no sign of giving a lead in this respect, local experience of anti-clericalism, loss of power and diminution of public esteem, however unpleasant, can prompt sentiments conducive to genuine Christianity. It can drive the discouraged Catholic back to the cleansing power of the Gospel. On the other hand, it can also, unfortunately, result in a circling of the wagons by those who see themselves as being under siege from a secularized and hostile world.

The fronts on which Rome has chosen to take an autocratic stand have their own importance, but they are peripheral to the main body of Christian doctrine. Ordination of women and sexual orientation, are important topics in their own right, to be sure; but they can hardly be said to have primary doctrinal significance in the Christian scheme of things. These topics are controversial; yet Rome has given them an institutional significance that is intended to justify the egregious tactics it has been employing in its resistance to the call for change. Powerful traditionalists present their own opinions as 'the teaching of the Church'.

This is not the place to consider these issues in any depth. Here I simply wonder why Rome has decided to instance such matters as female ordination, homosexuality and contraception as pivotal in the magisterium's exercise of its authority. Is it because it can no longer find a convincing philosophical underlay, like neo-scholasticism; or is it because the Vatican is unwilling to admit any divagation from former statements of the magisterium, lest this might weaken its authority? The latter was the main reason why Paul VI chose to reaffirm the papacy's opposition to contraception, in spite of the counsel of his advisers. Paul, however, never made *Humanae Vitae* an explicit test case of Catholic orthodoxy, as so many traditionalists are doing today, often for reasons of political churchmanship. The magisterium needs to recognise that it is influenced by cultural and political, as well as by doctrinal, considerations.

Declaring an issue such as female ordination to be beyond discussion by faithful Catholics is a preposterous abuse of authority. These matters are crying out for discussion and debate. The role of women in the Church is a live issue for many faithful Catholics today, and it is going to be freely discussed, whether or not Rome approves.

Sexual orientation has become an area on which Rome has unwisely chosen to take an authoritarian stand. Why it refuses to allow open and free discussion is fear of theological defeat. The last pope was a professional theologian used to the cut and thrust of academic life. Condemnation and the prohibition of free discussion convey the impression of hard-heartedness and bigotry, and, in the matter of sexual orientation, it can serve to intensify a homophobia that is all too evident throughout the world; yet Rome has chosen attitudes towards homosexuality and gay marriage as a test of deference to the magisterium!

This intransigence is a major factor in the disillusionment of many Catholics today. It slams the door in the face of people who are seeking to be heard and understood in the present-day church. Some of them pay a heavy price for speaking truth to power. We never hear the Vatican make a concession to their sincerity or to their right to be at least heard according to the norms of a civilized modern court. On the contrary, they are treated like criminals, with no recognition of their right to a good name in their church. Often they are not judged or punished; they are deliberately isolated and treated with passive aggression. Their isolation is a deliberate tactic to make them feel unloved and unwelcome in their own church; yet the followers of Marcel Lefevbre are approached with solicitude for their return to the Catholic Church. Faithful Catholics are assailed and even ejected from their church while hyper-conservative schismatics are cajoled to return to it.

Although there is always a danger of paranoia under an oppressive regime, it would seem that curial conviction has been growing that the old ways can be restored, not by argument, but by raw coercion. It worked before, for example against the Modernists in the early twentieth century; and there appears, in the view of traditionalist authoritarians, to be no reason why it should not work again today. It was tried against some defenceless theologians in the 1940s and 50s who went on, in spite of Rome's attempts to discredit them, to be seen as luminaries in the church at Vatican II. The Roman bureaucrats appear to have learnt nothing from their mistakes. Centuries of unquestioned power have made them seem invincible. They exercise the type of power that underwrites the views of ultra-traditionalist minds which easily find reasons to justify their actions. Those Christians who are intent on helping to reform the church have no choice but to oppose centres of domination like the CDF. The Christian church cannot allow itself to be a forum for the unrestrained triumph of power over conscience, if it is to retain some semblance of the ideals of its founder and the vision of the present Pope.

In the period immediately following Vatican II, liberal ideas and ideals flourished in the Catholic Church. It was undoubtedly a disagreeable time for ultra-conservatives, who felt sidelined and excluded; but they were never coerced to change their views by anyone. Since then, however, there has been a slow but inexorable dilution of the ideals of that time, and a return to the authoritarian ways of the past. Sometimes it seems that Catholic authorities are not comfortable away from the imposition of restrictive practices. With the possible exception of Pope John Paul I, popes of a similar mentality to John XXIII did not succeed him until the election of Pope Francis.

It would be a mistake to believe that the change that has taken place a few years after the council is merely a natural swing from progressive ideas and ideals to more conservative ones. It is something more serious. The contest between conservative and progressive forces within Catholicism is in no way an evenly balanced or a fair one at present, since all the power lies with the conservatives. Authoritarian tactics did not produce the change that took place at and immediately after Vatican II; it came about through the free circulation of liberating ideas and ideals. That is the main difference between the two mentalities. If the free circulation of ideas had been responsible for the later conservative swing, there might rightly be strong opposition to it, but there could be no valid liberal complaint about the manner of what was happening. However, that swing is being produced by force and by institutional control, not by the free circulation of ideas, and it puts the matter far beyond the simple and healthy conflict of ideas.[9] The Synod on Marriage and the Family has become the arena in which the classical contest between conservatives and liberals is being fought, as it was at Vatican II.

What has been happening is not a case of conservatism replacing progressivism as a natural and unforced change. The change has been brought about by recourse to raw power and the politically determined choice of 'safe' men to fill the offices of government. One can only regret that official conservatism does not seem able to promote its cause by the use of free argument without relying on institutional coercion. Liberals in the church would be equally guilty (as well as inconsistent, of course, with their principles), if they had power and were prepared to use it in pursuit of their aims.

When Popes John XXIII and John Paul II were canonized at the same ceremony, the intention apparently was to appeal to two opposing wings of the church. Many of the large crowd, gathered for the ceremony in St Peter's Square and beyond, and composed to a great extent of followers of each, probably regretted that their man did not have the stage to himself. However, the excitement of the event may have led them to reflect,

9. See Chapter 12, on fundamentalism, for further discussion of this theme.

perhaps with humour, that they all belong to the same church, and that the true Christian challenge is not necessarily to share theological convictions, but to get along together in spite of their differences.

8

Scripture, Tradition and Interpretation

'All Christians share the conviction that Scripture is normative, therefore the biblical witness provides an irreplaceable source for acquiring greater agreement about the Church.' [1] Scripture therefore plays an indispensable part in the ecumenical movement and in any movement towards reform. All Christians see it as the principal source for learning about God's communication with human beings. This does not mean that the process of reading the Bible is simple and straightforward. For centuries there has been a conviction in Catholic theology that God is revealed in both Scripture and Tradition. In short, not all of God's revelation is to be found in Scripture alone.

Consequently there arose a major difficulty at and after the Reformation. There could be agreement about Scripture; but Tradition was another matter altogether.[2] Tradition, when interpreted as a separate source of God's word, and located principally in the papacy, was totally unacceptable to Protestants and later to liberal Catholics. The Second Vatican Council was to make a major contribution to the resolution of this difficulty. In its Dogmatic Constitution, *Dei Verbum*, it states:

> Sacred Tradition and sacred Scripture make up a single sacred deposit of the Word of God, which is entrusted to the Church. (art. 10)

It may be reasonably claimed that the most theologically seminal of all the reforms carried out by Vatican II was in a sense tacit: it simply abandoned the two-source theory of revelation which had dominated Catholic theology since the sixteenth century. This theory proclaimed that divine revelation is to be found 'partly in Scripture and partly in Tradition'. The

---

1. World Council of Churches, *The Church: Towards a Common Vision*, art. 11, p. 9.
2. When Cardinal Filipo Guidi, a liberal, opposed the definition of papal infallibility, Pope Pius IX shouted at him: *'Tradizione ... La Tradizione son' io'* ('Tradition ... I am Tradition'). Pius was only expressing in histrionic tones the self-understanding of many other popes.

Council of Trent did not actually employ the words 'partly ... partly', but this soon became the common interpretation of the Tridentine text, and it divided Catholic and Protestant theologians sharply. To say that revelation was contained partly in Scripture and partly in Tradition gave official Catholic theology the stimulus to disconnect developed Christianity from its biblical origins and therefore from the inspiration and restraints of its original setting.

This had two results: firstly, it discouraged the reading of the Bible by ordinary Catholics, lest they 'misinterpret' it, *i.e.*, interpret it in a sense not prescribed by the magisterium. Secondly, it elevated Tradition above Scripture and more or less identified it with papal teaching, which became the 'proximate norm' for orthodox Catholic belief and practice. Scripture remained significant in Catholic theology, not because it served as a protection against institutional development in a direction that is incompatible with the Gospel. It remained important largely because it was believed to be the word of God, and it could be raided for proof texts for theses that were not biblically originated, but rather were prefabricated under institutional prompting and supervision. Catholic authority made it very clear that Scripture was to be interpreted exclusively by the magisterium. This effectively robbed the New Testament of the control it should have had over such teaching agents as the magisterium. To attempt to interpret Scripture 'privately' (i.e. without having recourse to the magisterium) was roundly forbidden. One left that sort of thing to Protestants.

Here, then, were two major areas crying out for reform. Vatican II would provide it. Nonchalant Catholics today, who make little of the significance of the council, need to study not simply its texts, but its history: what preceded it and what followed from it. We can begin with a glance at the Reformation.

In 1521 at the Diet of Worms, in the presence of the Holy Roman Emperor Charles V, Martin Luther, a German Augustinian friar, was instructed to disown his writings. He asked for time to think things over. The following day on the floor of the Diet, with great courage, he declared:

> Unless I am convinced by the testimony of the Scriptures or by clear reason (for I do not trust either in the pope or in councils alone, since it is well known that they have often erred and contradicted themselves),

I am bound by the Scriptures I have quoted and my conscience is captive to the Word of God. I cannot and will not recant anything, since it is neither safe nor right to go against conscience. May God help me. Amen.

Luther had previously appealed from the pope to a council. Here, having rejected the authority of both popes and councils, on the grounds that they have often erred, he makes the radical assertion that Scripture and reason alone are his final court of appeal. It was a sensational defiance of both church and state, and, in consequence, he was declared a heretic by the church and an outlaw by the state.

Luther's appeal from both papal and conciliar authority is to the Word of God. He did not set up a dichotomy between Scripture and Tradition. Protestant commentators, however, quickly turned his protest into an appeal to Scripture alone (*'sola Scriptura'*). The Catholic response was in effect to make Tradition the primary instrument of divine revelation and to identify it with church teaching, *i.e.*, the teaching of those who are in power at any given moment. Thus Protestants became 'people of the Book', while Catholics became 'people of the church' – 'church' in practice meaning the papacy and its court.

It was a lamentable situation, and it lasted until the Second Vatican Council recognized the need for change and defined the church as 'the people of God'. There can be no question today of a formal return to those preconciliar days – the texts and history of the council stand in the path of such a return.

At the end of the sixteenth century Robert Bellarmine spelt out the classical Catholic position on the relationship between Scripture and Tradition, when he argued that if we find that the church has embraced as a dogma of the faith, or observes some practice, which only God could prescribe, but is nowhere to be found in Scripture, we must say that it is a tradition from Christ and his apostles. Thomas Cranmer had already pointed out the fallacy of this argument in some memorably blunt words:

If we be bound to believe certain things delivered from the apostles by word of mouth only, without writing, as they would make us believe … it should hereof follow that we are bound to believe we wot not what.

Cranmer's argument is still valid, even where the circumstances are different. Rome has no business making an *a priori* declaration based on existing conditions that may be in need of reform in the light of Scripture.

The World Council of Churches (WCC), meeting in Montreal in 1963, pointed out that the role of the Bible in church life is to diagnose corruptions that occur over the years within church tradition. This was a problem that Vatican II had circled nervously around, but never explicitly admitted. Official Roman Catholicism has never liked to acknowledge the presence of structural corruption in church life. (Moral corruption provides no serious problem and can be condemned without embarrassment to the institution: Pope Alexander VI's numerous fornications do not pose a problem for Church authority, which is content to condemn them while maintaining the validity of his office.)

At Montreal the WCC meeting noted that we all read Scripture in the light of our own traditions, which means that we cannot simply appeal to the Bible in disputed questions without accepting that interpretation is implied in what we are doing. All sorts of theological and philosophical questions arise from this simple observation.

At this point we need to note the significance and relevance of hermeneutics, that is, the philosophy of interpretation. Hermeneutics has the great value of clarifying some of the problems that arise from consideration of both Scripture and Tradition. It brings into the open what happens when we really attend to a text. Although hermeneutics goes back to the ancient Greeks, modern consideration of what happens when we attend closely to the meaning of a text – any text, but in the case of modern hermeneutics, the text of the Bible – is what lies at the heart of the matter. The philosophy of interpretation is a large and complicated subject that has been treated in depth, notably by German philosophers and theologians. Here I wish simply to draw attention to some basic principles that are relevant to the questions raised in this book.

To take a practical example: hermeneutics is immensely important in dealing with fundamentalist attitudes to the Bible, and with all topics that involve texts. Its most basic principle is that there is no uninterpreted human experience, when it is appealed to in support of an argument. This means that when Christians affirm that 'the Bible says', or 'the church teaches', they need to be challenged on what they think they are contributing to a debate. Their reasoning needs to be subjected to an examination of what is happening when they appeal to a text in support of a disputed position. To them it may seem to be a very simple business to read an obvious meaning off a text. It is important that they be shown the complexity of what happens when we read a text, any text, whether it be a telephone directory or the Bible.

There are three elements in the process of interpreting a text: (1) the author of the text; (2) the text itself; and (3) the reader of the text. It is commonplace in everyday life to distinguish between what is subjective and what is objective; but we need to understand that distinguishing between objective and subjective meaning raises some significant philosophical questions that have to be answered. To describe something as a 'fact', for example, implies a subjective judgment that has to be allowed for in any 'objective' treatment of 'facts'. Courts have to reckon with different factual or legal interpretations of an event, and judges and juries have to take into careful consideration the differences, before deciding which account to believe. There is no guarantee that they will always get it right: hence the existence of courts of appeal.

Historians can aim at 'objectivity' in their treatment of past events. In practice this means recognizing our biases and appreciating their influence on our judgements. The nearest one can get to 'objective' treatment is to recognize that there are many possible interpretations of 'what really happened'. There is no purely objective assessment of a situation or reading of a text. The reader brings an unavoidable *pre-understanding* to the enterprise. It is wise to remain alert to the phenomenon of pre-understanding and to recognize its presence in any judgment we make about texts or events. Pre-understanding is not the same as bias, which carries the mild implication of moral defect, whereas pre-understanding is a neutral description of a natural psychological process.

Interpreters can emphasize one or other of the three facets of interpreting a text. Thus romantic hermeneutics aimed at rethinking the original author's thoughts in its attempt to understand a text. Structuralists concentrate on 'the semantic autonomy of the text', holding that the text speaks for itself independently of the intention of its author or the contribution made by the reader. Reader-response theorists emphasize the role of the reader in setting up meaning. In this view, we read *into* as well as out of a text. Feminist theologians make considerable use of reader-response theory in their attempt to make women 'visible' in male-dominated documents like the Bible. They believe that women have to be 'read back' into texts which simply, if unconsciously, ignored them.

If we choose to emphasise one of these three elements in interpretation, as is our right, we need to know what we are doing and allow for it in our treatment of texts. The importance of hermeneutics for Christian theology is clear. The historical religions all have written texts, and this raises the question of assigning value and authority to these texts, and deciding how they should be used, for example in liturgy or in theological understanding. Thus Paul of Tarsus writes a letter to some Christian converts in Corinth in the first century C.E. That letter is read as Scripture in churches today. Since the conditions that obtained in Paul's apostolate no longer exist today, why should we bother to read what he wrote to the Corinthian Christians of that time?

What does it mean to regard some texts as 'canonical', giving them a special value above other texts? Most Christian churches believe that God has in some way 'inspired' these texts. What does this mean? To the fundamentalist it means that the text comes directly from God, and the mind of God can be read off it immediately. The human element does not matter to the fundamentalist, who regards attention to the process of interpretation as a trivial pursuit. Thoughtful Christians today recognise that the Bible, though inspired by God, has to be interpreted in the same way as any other text. The word of God is expressed in human words, and those human words have to be interpreted, if we wish to understand what God may be saying. The process is complex but unavoidable. We have to examine the text first in the light of the circumstances that produced it. Then we have to inquire into its application to our own circumstances. There may be differences in interpretation and application of the text. Some canonical texts have had an interpretative history that has played a crucial role in Christian experience. It is therefore important to examine that role.

A prime example would be the far-reaching influence of the prologue of St John's Gospel, where it speaks of Jesus as the Word of God. The phrase 'Word of God' proved to be immensely significant to philosophically minded Gentile Christians. It bore its doctrinal fruit at the Council of Nicaea (325), when the Christian Church finally broke with its Jewish origins and made a defined truth of a philosophical concept. It is not without significance that the first ecumenical council of the church put forward a doctrine that was not based on Scripture, even allowing for the prologue of John's Gospel, which was open to different interpretations, some of which would not have made much sense to the apostles.

Another instance of a biblical text that went on to have a distinguished history occurs in St Paul's Letter to the Romans in which he writes that it is faith that makes one righteous before God (Romans 1:17). It is one thing to understand what Paul means here. It is quite another to realize that the text has had a new and dramatic significance read into it since the sixteenth century, when it made a momentous impression on Martin Luther. In a flash it lifted a heavy burden from his shoulders by showing him that nothing he could do, such as penances, fasts and self-denial, would make the slightest difference to his standing with God. It is faith, not works, which makes one righteous before God. This insight was significant not merely for Luther himself; it also became a corner-stone of the Reformation, for all Protestants, but specifically for Lutherans. Luther's reading of Paul's Letter to the Romans is a clear example of reader-response to a text. What Paul intended the text to mean is arguably of less historical significance than the meaning that Luther read into it. The Lutheran doctrine of justification by grace through faith has made a significant contribution to Christian history and theology. In our own time, for example, it has influenced the Lutheran attitude to Liberation theology, which can seem to some Lutherans to be relying on good works for divine approval.

If one takes a literal view of divine inspiration of the Bible, Christians are faced with the problem of what to do with Old Testament texts that cannot be squared, for instance, with New Testament teaching on love of enemies. The very phrase 'Old Testament' is a relativising of the re-lationship between Christians and Jews. This is one of the many, usually unrecognised, problems that face fundamentalists.

Some years ago the American feminist theologian, Sandra Schneiders, trying to interpret biblical texts that are excessively male-centred, claimed that we do not need to disregard such texts on the grounds that they offend many modern women; on the other hand, we do not need to regard them as being directly and immediately the inspired word of God. The Bible, she says, is a witness to the *human* experience of divine revelation. In other words, it is a limited human testimony to a human experience of God's self-gift. The limitation is not God's; it is a natural property of all human experience and includes even historical mistakes and morally indefensible acts, which plainly cannot come directly from God. She makes the impressive point that Paul's teaching that the Mosaic law need not be imposed on Gentile converts will never be surpassed in radicalism. Ordaining women would be far less innovative, she writes.[3] Christian theological understanding can therefore change, and indeed has changed in the early church with Paul's teaching on the irrelevance of the Mosaic law to Gentile converts, to which can be added the arcane philosophical language of the Council of Nicaea, so different from the language of the New Testament.

In view of all that has happened to Christian interpretation of the Bible through the ages, we are impelled to ask whether there is an essence of Christianity, *i.e.*, some agreed truths that transcend their different historically conditioned expressions, and can be regarded as immune from the vagaries of historical and social influences. If such an essence existed, it would of course provide an interpretative key to the Bible.

One of the foremost nineteenth century theologians, Adolf von Harnack, held that there is such an essence of Christianity. It consists of three elements: (1) the Kingdom of God and its coming; (2) God the Father and the infinite value of the human soul; and (3) the commandment to love. Harnack was a liberal Protestant who dismissed as unimportant to Christian faith the philosophical structure of trinitarian and christological documents forged in the fourth and fifth centuries. In fact he believed that one of the greatest corruptions of the simple essence of original Christianity was its Hellenization in the post-Nicene church.

Official Roman Catholic theology rejected Harnack's views as being both liberal and Protestant. Moderate Catholic theologians, however, while fully accepting the existence of the phenomenon of Hellenization, would probably not agree that it amounted to corruption. Nevertheless, it remains a feature that must be reckoned with by historical theologians.

3. S. Schneiders, *Beyond Patching: Faith and Feminism in the Catholic Church* (New Jersey, 2004), chapter 2.

Hellenization certainly presents Christian orthodoxy with a problem that calls for careful consideration; but one need not see it, with Harnack, as a corruption. It may be seen as an inevitable consequence of thoughtful Christianity's engagement with the culture of the age.

In a famous lecture given in 2006 by Pope Benedict at the University of Regensburg, where he had taught theology from 1969 to 1977, he spoke about the appropriateness of theology's having a rightful place in the university.[4] In this context he took issue with Harnack's condemnation of Hellenisation as a corruption of Christianity. He went further by commending Greek philosophy as having a 'profound harmony' with 'the biblical understanding of faith in God'.[5] Many Scripture scholars might question this claim, which, as we might expect, lays heavy emphasis on the word *logos* in the preface to John's Gospel. Historical theologians might point out that defending the link between faith and reason does not commit one to the view that Hellenisation has been a sustained benefit to Christian and Catholic church life and thought, although such a view is altogether in keeping with Benedict's attack on 'modern reason'.

Roman Catholic officially-sanctioned nineteenth century theology was at least as problematic as Harnack's. Catholic orthodoxy in the nineteenth and twentieth centuries favoured the view of revelation known as 'integralism', which connoted the system of doctrines comprising neo-scholastic orthodoxy. It was a system that promoted the view that no one point could be detached from the others without endangering the whole. It distrusted any search for an essence of Christianity on the grounds that revelation must be seen as a package extrinsically guaranteed *as a whole*. Its propositions were graded, not in order of intrinsic importance, but according to the degree of authority bestowed on each proposition by theologians submissive to the magisterium.

Integralism is intrinsically authoritarian. It combines all the different components of Christian belief, large and small, into the one package, which it then guarantees as the one indivisible truth. It does not allow the serried truths to speak for themselves, and it makes no concession

4. This lecture is examined in Paul McPartlin, 'Theology in the University for Pope Benedict XVI and the International Theological Commission', *Milltown Studies*, No 72, Winter 2013.

5. Ibid. p. 3.

to the fact that these truths, some belonging to the creeds and others added later in the church's history, are not of equal importance. It fails to appreciate that decisions made in response to certain challenges may be adequate to the situation at the time but should not be permitted to accrue to the treasury of the church's unchangeable teaching. It relies on authority to impose certain beliefs on the entire church rather than allowing legitimate differences to emerge from discussion and debate. In short, it devalues conscience and shuns the idea of diversity as a healthy feature of church life.

The authoritarian mindset of integralist theologians discourages questions about the essence of Christianity, lest the non-essential be disregarded and, worse, lest authority itself be threatened. Vatican II undermined integralism by its doctrine of 'the hierarchy of truths'. In its Decree on Christian Unity it has this to say:

> When comparing doctrines with one another, they [theologians] should remember that in Catholic doctrine there exists a 'hierarchy' of truths, since they vary in their relation to the fundamental Christian faith (*Unitatis Redintegratio*, art. 11).

Integralism is still to be found in hard-line traditionalist attitudes, for example at the recent Synod on Marriage and the Family in Rome. A division of opinion between some curial cardinals and Cardinal Walter Kasper led to some questions that were put to Kasper by the media, one of which produced an interesting answer.

Q. Why do you think there is so much fear of a development in the church's discipline?
A. I think they fear a domino effect, if you change one point all would collapse. That's their fear. This is all linked to ideology, an ideological understanding of the Gospel that the Gospel is like a penal code.[6]

Kasper, an eminent theologian much admired by Pope Francis, here identifies integralism as 'an ideology' that interprets the Gospel as 'a penal code'. It allows traditionalists to lump together relatively peripheral matters with the central truths of Christianity – another kind of creeping

6. *National Catholic Reporter,* October 10-23, 2014, p. 2

infallibility, expanding the teaching of the church to include matters that should not be subject to the magisterial party whip. Such neo-integralism, backed up by legalism and punitive action, obscures the doctrine that there are priorities in Christian faith and practice. It also ignores the rights of local authorities, the existence of legitimate local differences and the doctrine of subsidiarity.[7]

In Christian teaching, love of enemies is vastly more important than, say, clerical celibacy. That Rome has made the prohibition of female ordina-tion and contraception settled positions of the Catholic Church suggests that it still views the magisterium with an integralist mindset that does not grade its teaching in terms of priorities, as the Second Vatican Council taught. In this way of looking at things, fidelity and loyalty to the magis-terium have to be practised with no distinction between what is central and what is relatively peripheral; consequently it places an unwarranted value on institutional obedience..

One illustration of the practical effect of integralism is Rome's control over liturgy throughout the Church. It was recently able to inflict upon the English-speaking areas of the Church a liturgical text that is linguisti-cally incompetent and theologically questionable. When will local church authorities have the courage to refuse to comply with instructions that are so clearly an unwelcome and gratuitous imposition upon churches whose clergy have had to teach uncomprehending congregations a new text without any explanation of why it has been ordered? Perhaps the most objectionable aspect of the imposition of the Latinized liturgy is that it attempts to achieve by command what it is unable to achieve by discussion and argument.

In refusing to accept the newly imposed liturgical text of the Mass, the German church has proved to be more courageous than the English-speaking ones. Moreover, German bishops are not afraid to disagree with one another, as they have done over the admission of divorced and remarried people to the Eucharist.

Reform will not be brought about by local considerations alone. The centralizing way in which the Catholic Church is being run at the moment is at the heart of many of the problems facing local church communi-

7. The notion that senior levels of authority should not do what a lower level is capable of doing.

ties. The fear engendered by the authoritarianism existing at all levels of Catholic life is a crucial obstacle to the sort of reform that many in the church are calling for. The nineteenth century distinction between the Jesus of history and the Christ of faith placed justification by faith alongside a critical approach to the Bible. This enabled Protestant biblical scholars to adopt one of the leading principles of form criticism, namely, that the needs of the early church controlled the choice and use of sources about Jesus in the New Testament.

The Catholic systematic theologian quickly becomes aware of how German Lutheran scholarship, consciously or unconsciously, has assumed justification by faith alone as the interpretative key to understanding the entire New Testament. It is everywhere. Often it is invoked to make a virtue of necessity: for example, when the original quest for the Jesus of history is shown to be an impossible pursuit, the concomitant statement is made that one must never appeal to history in support of one's faith. That would be to intrude a work into what should be pure faith. Hence the most destructive historical criticism can be carried out with a glow of virtue. *Pecca fortiter*: the more destruction you wreak in the critical area, the more room you leave for existential faith. This was why Rudolf Bultmann, a deeply radical interpreter of the Bible, came across as an evangelical preacher, in spite of the destructive character of his historical criticism of the New Testament.

As the Catholic Modernist, Lucien Laberthonnière, humorously remarked more than a century ago: With the Liberal Protestants you have faith without beliefs, while with the Catholic neo-scholastics you have beliefs without faith! No wonder that Catholic theologians, new to modern biblical criticism, have felt that to escape from the excesses of an intolerant magisterium into the hands of radical biblical critics is to go from the frying pan into the fire.

When Edward Schillebeeckx wrote two large volumes, one on Jesus, the other on Christ, he was commendably attempting to bridge the gap between biblical criticism and systematic theology, only to find that the biblical critics were telling him that his efforts were old hat. It seems that you can't win; for when systematic theologians try to be responsibly biblical in their work, they may well find that the biblical critics have moved the goal posts! It all seems part of the divine purpose not to be found too easily or too cheaply.

I must refer briefly to the question of the canon of Scripture, namely the decision by the church to accept certain texts as authentically the word of God, while rejecting others as inauthentic. It is a very large question which I cannot consider at length here. In the context of this book I want briefly to enquire why the question of the canon is important for the Christian church in every age, from its earliest period down to our own time. There are some theologians who have suggested abandoning the notion of a canon altogether, on the grounds that it is too bound up with the 'house of authority', which they feel has been gratuitous and controversial. Many modern Catholic theologians would regard this suggestion as too radical a departure from Tradition. The Protestant appeal to Scripture alone made the canon an important alternative to the Roman Catholic magisterium.

Just as reform-minded Catholics are impelled to criticize the tyranny of Roman integralism, Protestants have to face the question of who decides what is to be included in, and what is to be excluded from, the canon. Who makes the decision about whether this or that document should be admitted? Historically, it would seem that local churches made their choices pragmatically, occasionally comparing notes with each other and enquiring into the practice of their neighbours. The final settling of the canon took some time and was not the product of one official decision for Catholics until the Council of Trent in the sixteenth century declared the number of the canonical books in the Bible.

The canon of the four gospels was finally decided by the end of the second century. There is scholarly debate about the date of *The Gospel of Thomas*, which was probably written, if not at the same time as the canonical gospels, then shortly afterwards. It was excluded from the canon, mainly, it would seem, because of its Gnosticism. The inclusion of Paul's letters in the canon was probably influenced by the prominence given to him by Luke in Acts of the Apostles. The formation of the canon is historically complex, but its importance transcends history and must also be seen as theologically as well as historically significant.

The theological consequences are interesting: Luther's appeal to Scripture over against church authority had far-reaching implications. Protestant theologians continued to appeal to Scripture over against a

church magisterium; but, after the Enlightenment, they were also committed to the discomfiting task of biblical criticism. This exposed them
to questions about the canon, especially about who decided which documents were and which were not authentic. The distinguished Yale biblical
scholar, Brevard Childs, put the problem with commendable bluntness:

> The skandalon of the canon is that the witness of Jesus Christ has been
> given its normative shape through an interpretive process of the post-
> apostolic age.[8]

Something of a blow to the *sola scriptura* principle!

Study of the canon has demonstrated the interplay between Scripture
and church Tradition. The Bible can be thought of as written tradition,
which gives the church an indispensible role in the production and canonization of Scripture. We need to note, however, that in the early church
it was not a process dictated by a centralised magisterium. It was pragmatic
and communitarian, in the sense that different local communities decided
on what they wished to include as authentically biblical. Realization of the
significance of what happened helps to show that Tradition, properly understood, is wider by far than any Roman magisterium. Taking it seriously
is a challenge to both Catholics and Protestants, each in their own way.

8. B. Childs, *The New Testament as Canon: An Introduction*, 1985, p. 28.

9

The Reception of Vatican II

Glendower: I can call spirits from the vasty deep.
Hotspur: Why, so can I, and so can any man;
But will they come when you do call for them?[1]

Hotspur's question prompts the reflection that it is one thing for a general council to meet, deliberate and issue documents; it is quite another for its deliberations to have an immediate or lasting effect on the church at large. However, response to a council's teaching may take some time to produce an effect, and there may be a reaction against it. The process whereby such an effect occurs is technically described as 'reception'. Sometimes the reception of a council can be long and contentious, as, for example, was the case after the Council of Nicaea (325, C.E), which condemned Arianism, namely the doctrine that the Son is inferior to God the Father.

The questions therefore arise: How well has the Second Vatican Council been 'received'? What difference has it made to the Catholic Church? Is its reception to be even more drawn-out than that of Nicaea? These are particularly apposite questions to ask today, when only an ageing generation remembers the stir the second Vatican Council caused in the 1960s. Was it simply an occasion that happened then, and now belongs to past history, and can in practice be safely disregarded as having no relevance to contemporary Catholic life? Or was it an occasion that produced important changes in the Church which, *if they were fully and consistently implemented*, would bring about a significantly different mentality from what had existed beforehand, and exists again today?

Vatican II differed from previous councils, especially from its immediate predecessors, Vatican I and Trent, by issuing no statements claiming to be infallible doctrinal definitions of faith. Sadly there are reactionary Catholics today who argue that this means that Vatican II can be safely disregarded. As we shall see, some of the younger generation of priests in the

---

1. Shakespeare, *Henry IV*, Part 1

church may regard concern with the council as a preoccupation of their elders, and one, moreover, that is tiresome and tiresomely controversial.

Traditionally the young have always reacted against their elders; and it is normally an honourable tradition that allows fresh ideas to enter society. What seems to be happening among young priests today, however, does not follow the usual sequence of events, where the younger generation is more liberal than their elders. Today there seems to be a curious reversal of roles.

Not long ago some young priests were interviewed in two national Irish newspapers. What they told their interviewers is disturbing. They could not see the significance of Vatican II or the Association of Catholic Priests, and they thought that those priests who did were out of touch with everyday ordinary reality. It gives me no pleasure to comment adversely on the self-satisfaction of fellow priests; but I do so only to show how necessary a body like the Association of Catholic Priests is in Ireland. Other countries have their own similar associations. Vatican bureaucrats dislike all of them. One can only hope that the Association will be listened to, so that people may know that there is more to pastoral life than the short-sighted sacramental managerialism that seems to have been adopted by some young priests, one of whom spoke of the silencing of fellow priests by the CDF as 'something I only read about in the paper. I still have to get into school for the confirmation of children, I still have to talk to the family about the funeral tomorrow.'[2]

Another interviewer gave a description of another young priest:

> He is representative of a new breed of cleric who is proud to be seen in his collar, has no hang-ups with the Vatican, and believes the future of the Catholic Church in Ireland is rosy. Nor has he any desire to see Rome change its stance on clerical celibacy.[3]

In other words, he is placidly incurious about the reality of his surroundings and blind to the need to widen his conception of his pastoral mission. He is quoted as saying: 'There is a certain vintage of priest who seems a little disgruntled, perhaps, with the church and discipline. That is not the same attitude the younger generation have.' As one of the 'dis-

2. *The Irish Times,* June 4, 2012, p. 6.
3. *The Irish Independent*, Saturday, July 7, 2012

gruntled vintage', I am happy to wish him every success in his ministry, and I hope that he will not be discouraged when he is ejected from his Garden of Eden and has to encounter the real world in a few years' time. He may then discover that the future of the Church is rather less rosy than he expected. Although these young men say that their attitude is to be found generally among their contemporaries, I cannot believe that all their contemporaries think this way. These worrying examples, however, raise the question of how well the council was received, when we find some clerically educated priests displaying such a passive acceptance of how things are in our church, and who appear supine in their acceptance of the status quo.

We would do well to recognize that there are many other priests who are very different from these young men. The Association of Catholic Priests is an example, in Ireland, of pastorally engaged priests who appreciate the problems that face us all, and who give encouragement to those of us who are struggling with life in the contemporary church. With the ACP, I am attempting to criticize from the inside the Roman authorities of the church that we care about. Such criticism is often more deeply resented by authority, because it is closer to the bone than anything external critics can say. Rome may preach evangelical engagement with the world, but it must be on *its* terms, which it gratuitously describes as 'the teaching of the Church', and which leaves no room for alternative and perhaps fresher voices.

We shall see in the next chapter how the Holy Office hounded the French Dominican theologian, Yves Congar, who was to have such an important influence on Vatican II. Although, to the best of my knowledge, he never received an apology, he was given a Red Hat shortly before his death. Honours, such as being appointed a cardinal, help the church to forget what he went through, when he was a defenceless friar and scholar in the years before the council authenticated his scholarly insights into Tradition.

Mention of Congar brings me to ponder some of the major theological issues that arose during the council. They are at the root of what is happening in the church today. The most relevant and basic theological issue is the meaning of revelation, that is, of how God communicates with us through historical events, especially through the life and death of Jesus of Nazareth. Before Vatican II, it was commonplace in Roman Catholic theology to regard revelation as a series of divine statements that had to be accepted by an act of faith interpreted as intellectual assent to the propositions of revelation. It was a view that facilitated coercion and control, and it suited curial purposes ideally. Vatican II abandoned this view of revelation, not of set purpose, but indirectly by using a different kind of language than that used at previous councils. The abstract language of scholasticism had buttressed the whole doctrinal system favoured by those who were resisting the reforming views of the conciliar majority. In fact, one of the major achievements of the council was to have tacitly reformed this view of revelation and faith. That it has done so makes nonsense of the fundamentalist claim that church teaching has been consistently the same in every age.

Some traditionalist members of the church continue to read the documents of Vatican II through the eyes of those who framed the documents of Vatican I, thus missing the point of Pope John XXIII's address to the members of Vatican II at its opening, that they should avoid definitions, condemnations and anathemas. Debates in the council chamber clearly manifested the radical division of attitudes in the Catholic Church.

There are two conflicting mindsets in the church, which can be loosely described as conservative and liberal; and there is no possibility of consensus between them. To pretend that there can be substantive intellectual accord between them could involve mental dishonesty and lack of transparency. Every Christian is bound to seek peace and loving care; but that peace must not offend against truth and logic. To seek agreement between two opposing mindsets may seem a laudable venture; but it must be an agreement to accept the differences rather than pretend that there is intellectual compatibility between them. Consensus on mutually contradictory intellectual and moral convictions is not possible without self-deception. The truly Christian task is to enable the two to live charitably together while disagreeing with each other's convictions. There can be a consensus only on accepting diversity and living together without violence, personal or institutional. One can only hope and pray for greater tolerance of views which are perceived by one mindset as wrong, yet which cannot be proved to be at odds with Christian orthodoxy.

In order to analyse further the impossibility of bringing about consensus between two opposing and contradictory positions, we can take an analogy from Irish history: there is no possibility of political consensus between Nationalists and Unionists: the two political ideologies contradict each other. The peace process is based not on ideological, political or religious agreement; it is based on agreement to live in peace with each other without having to give up their conflicting political and religious convictions. The Peace Process leaves each free to argue for their own position while forswearing all resort to violence or terrorism.

There is something analogous in the case of divided Catholics. They should feel free to hold their own ecclesial convictions while leaving others free to hold theirs. Each should be open to the truth in the other's position and should be ready, if convinced by argument, to make concessions to it in the name of truth. However, if we are to make progress towards the ideal of a truly united church, those with authority and power must refrain from using punitive measures against fellow Catholics whom they like to describe as dissenters, or worse, as heretics.

There was a serious move at the council to reform the curia, especially the Holy Office; but the attempt finally failed, because the council closed after four years, and the bishops were once again dispersed throughout the world, with consequent practical loss of their collegial authority. Since then they have had little opportunity or inclination to press for continuing reform of the Vatican's internal administration. A Church that emphasises monarchical centralization, and consequently depreciates the very Catholic notion of subsidiarity, overlooks a principle which was revered by Pope Pius XI:

> Just as it is gravely wrong to take from individuals what they can accomplish by their own initiative and industry and give it to the community, so also it is an injustice and at the same time a grave evil and disturbance of right order to assign to a greater and higher association what lesser and subordinate organizations can do.[4]

It would appear that the teaching of Vatican II on collegiality, so energetically fought for at the council, has not been received in practice by the Vatican curial authorities. The theory is on the books, as it were, but the

---

4. *Quadragesimo Anno* (art. 79)

practice is one of non-collegiality, though Pope Francis is showing clear signs of recognising and promoting its importance. The bishops on their *ad limina* visits to Rome continue to report to the pope as subordinates rather than equals. No one is left in any doubt about who is reporting to whom. We have, it would appear, returned to the practice of unrestrained papal primacy, with consequent disregard for one of the foremost reforms of the council. The pope – but especially the curia that acts in his name – remains free to act as he pleases, with no check on his actions by his fellow bishops. The minority at Vatican II would indeed have rejoiced, had they known that with the passage of time this would happen.

Whereas the First Vatican Council practically criminalized its dissenting minority, the Second Vatican Council treated its dissenting minority with consideration and sympathy. Even where the whole thrust of a minority position was in an opposite direction to the views of the majority, the minority's views have been awkwardly incorporated into the text, often with damage to its coherence. The peaceable method, adopted by the council in an effort to pacify the defeated minority, was to juxtapose in its documents two conflicting mentalities with the result that the primary intention of the majority is obscured and indeed may seem to lack overall coherence. This has been a heavy price to pay for a gesture of toleration that was neither appreciated nor reciprocated by its recipients.

For instance, in the Constitution on Revelation, *Dei Verbum*, the unity of revelation is set alongside the Tridentine position on the relationship between Scripture and tradition, which was originally meant to be a deliberately divisive measure, condemning the Reformers, and is now obsolete. The majority at Vatican II had agreed to lay aside such divisive thinking. In the Constitution on the Church, *Lumen Gentium*, the doctrine of collegiality is juxtaposed with a renewed yet unqualified statement of papal primacy. In the Decree on Ecumenism, *Unitatis Redintegratio*, recognition of the ecclesial truth in other churches is awkwardly aligned with the doctrine of 'the one true Church', which in practice means that ecumenically minded members of other churches are graciously invited to measure their beliefs against a narrow and partial interpretation of Roman Catholic dogma. The overall effect of this juxtapositioning, though intended as an eirenic gesture, seriously weakens the thrust of the main argument.

It was a response of sorts to the bluster of the conservative minority at the council; but it amounted to capitulation rather than being simply a dialectical tactic, and it negated the reforming effect of the significant changes achieved at the council. Fundamentalist Catholics today can appeal to these conciliatory statements, taken out of context, without any acknowledgement that they obscure the intended thrust of the text, and are included merely to accommodate a minority opinion. It is a seriously misguided act to try to establish a consensus between two mutually exclusive mentalities, especially if one side is concerned with power and control, not exchange of ideas. It diverts attention from the true path of reconciliation: to agree to live together in peace in spite of contradictory convictions. This is not an easy task, but it is enjoined on Christians by the message of the Gospel.

There are circles in the church where the Second Vatican Council has been rejected out of hand. Institutional schism was diagnosed and condemned by Rome, but it was at least an open and honest rejection of the achievements of the council, and it resulted in excommunication. Archbishop Marcel Lefebvre's unambiguously negative assessment of the council is a clear instance of straight opposition to almost everything it stood for. Lefebvre outlandishly blamed Vatican II for introducing into the Catholic Church the principles of the French Revolution: collegiality corresponding to *égalité*, religious freedom to *liberté*, and ecumenism to *fraternité*. The more one considers all that Lefebvre stood for, the greater one's perplexity over the extraordinary efforts that have been made by Rome to appease and reconcile his followers.

Rome makes it all too clear that church members who think about the Gospel for themselves, in a manner that strives to be relevant to contemporary men and women, are a danger to orthodoxy, while ultra-conservatives, some of whom adopt a fascist attitude (a Lefebvrite bishop has denied the existence of the Holocaust), have been offered a 'personal prelature', on condition of accepting the authority of Vatican II together with some other prescriptions. For anyone who is looking for real reform in the church it is a slap in the face, and a throwback to the attitude fostered by Pius IX and the First Vatican Council. In a word, right-wing extremists are treated with concessions that suggest that Rome regards them more or less as having their hearts in the right place and merely sinning by excess of zeal. Meanwhile those who have attempted to make their church more relevant to the modern world have been condemned out of hand.

Pope Benedict XVI disliked the word 'reform', and regarded those who criticize the institution that he headed before he became pope as diverting attention from the church, understood as a mystical reality. It is surely impossible rationally to defend the notion that the state of the institution is irrelevant to Christian life, thus evacuating the meaning of the hallowed slogan, *Ecclesia semper reformanda*. It is still more indefensible to hold or imply that the institution always acts with divine approval of its political purposes and managerial tactics. Even a glance at the history of the papacy should disabuse us of that delusion; yet some Catholics continue to act as if the pope is the proper subject of personal adulation, and has a right to regard any criticism of his institutional defects as a kind of moral failure and religious infidelity. Concentration on the papacy, at the expense of giving bishops, priests and laity adequate consideration, produces an imbalance in one's attitude, and takes attention away from other more important matters. Those who like to trumpet the cliché, 'the church is not a democracy', should be brought to concede that neither is it a dictatorship.

A word on that other tiresome cliché: '*à la carte* Catholicism'. Some of those who want all members of the Church, and all commentators, to conform to their narrow conception of orthodoxy, like to employ the clichéd phrase, '*à la carte*'. Let's continue the metaphor: If one has a '*table d'hôte*' view of church discipline, then, by definition, those who are described as '*à la carte*' must logically be seen to be challenging, or perhaps simply ignoring, the 'correct' doctrines. It all depends who is writing the menu. It is an ingenious, though superficial and discreditable, tactic for getting certain ideas accepted in advance of all further discussion, and it would not be employed by anyone who believes in fairness, objectivity and pursuit of the truth.

Since the CDF is authoritarian to the core, it takes little notice of modern canons of human rights and civilised legal practice, perhaps its members might listen to the words of a solemn prescription of an important General Council of the Church, in 1215:

He who is the object of an enquiry should be present at the process, and, unless absent through contumacy, should have the various headings of the enquiry explained to him, so as to allow him the possibility of defending himself; as well, he is to be informed not only of what the various witnesses have accused him of but also of the names of those witnesses.[5]

The Congregation for the Doctrine of the Faith routinely contravenes that prescription of the Fourth Lateran Council in every respect. It seems to have actually regressed to pre-thirteenth century canons of legal behaviour, yet it is a conciliar prescription of an ecumenical council called by the most powerful pope of the middle ages! What has become of a clear and authentic teaching of a pope and council, that is routinely ignored by present-day bureaucratic members of the CDF who accuse fellow members of the Catholic Church of non-correspondence with 'the teaching of the church' without according them the forensic procedures laid down 900 years ago?

The international jurist, Paul Sieghart, in his Cardinal Heenan Memorial Lecture, reiterated a complaint he had made many times before.

The complaint is simple but also stark: within its internal structures, my own Church – that is, the Church of Rome – has not yet even begun to practise what it has so forcefully preached for twenty-five years and more in the matter of human rights.[6]

The fathers of Vatican II unaccountably allowed the pope to reserve to himself the very matters that Rome has, since then, made a test of obedience to the magisterium. It would appear that the Pope and the ultra-conservative minority knew what was likely to happen if the topics of contraception, homosexuality, female ordination and clerical celibacy had been left to free debate on the floor of the council. The papacy, unchecked by the council, was later able to impose its will on the church, with no attempt to consult the faithful on matters that concerned them most closely. It seems reasonable to conclude that the council has been by no means fully received by some of the highest authorities in the church,

5. I have taken this quotation from Bernard Treacy in *Doctrine and Life*, November, 1998, p. 451, where he writes an editorial introduction to Ladislas Örsy's stimulating article 'Are Church Investigation Procedures Really Just?'

6. Paul Sieghart, 'Christianity and Human Rights' in *Law and Justice*, no. 100/101, 1989, p. 16.

though allowance must be made for what the new pope may try do to change this.

A tacit revolution occurred at Vatican II: the church no longer insisted that scholastic philosophy and theology were essential for Catholic orthodoxy.[7] No great fuss was made over this radical change brought about by the council; yet it was a major achievement made tacitly rather than expressly in response to Pope John XXIII's vision of *aggiornamento*. John had made it plain that he wanted a change in language and style from the language and style of previous councils. It was a momentous change, because Vatican II showed that style and language were not a collateral effect of substantial change; they were a vital element in it.

John O'Malley, the American Jesuit historian, makes this point with clarity and vigour:

> Vatican II, however, largely eschewed Scholastic language. It thus moved from the dialectic of winning an argument to the dialogue of finding common ground. It moved from abstract metaphysics to interpersonal "how to be." It moved from grand conceptual schemes or *summae* with hundreds of logically interconnected parts to the humble acceptance of mystery. In so doing it largely abandoned the Scholastic framework that had dominated Catholic theology since the thirteenth century.[8]

This change of style was no mere aesthetic flourish. It was a substantive move that favoured a different sort of theology. It went hand in hand with the major changes of attitude brought about by the council in the fields of ecumenism, religious liberty and the task of relating the church to the modern world. Scholasticism had favoured the expression of abstract doctrines and the notorious anathemas which often accompanied conciliar statements. This new style facilitated greater openness to other churches, to other faiths and to a non-condemnatory view of the secular world. It also facilitated a break with the view of revelation as statement and faith as mental assent which, in turn, advanced the move from essentialism and integralism.[9]

7. See Chapter 12, on Fundamentalism, for fuller treatment of this highly significant topic.
8. John W. O'Malley, *What Happened at Vatican II?* (Cambridge, Massachusetts, (2008), p. 46.
9. On essentialism see *infra* Chapter 14, Essence and Existence; on integralism see Chapters 1, 5 ,8, and 12.

In 1864 Pius IX had published a *Syllabus of Errors* which in many respects reflected the Catholic Church's response to the spirit of the age. Its last article is notorious for its condemnation of the view 'That the Roman Pontiff can and should reconcile himself and make peace with progress, with Liberalism, and with modern culture.' It must be said that Pope Leo XIII would have broadly agreed with this condemnation, though he normally expressed himself in a less intemperate way than did his predecessor. Leo's appeal was to medieval thought and this was in harmony with nineteenth century romanticism, and, more significantly, it led to a flourishing of historical and especially philosophical studies of the Middle Ages. He saw his action as a much-needed reform.

Pius X extended the same principle of reform to music in the liturgy, giving the instruction that plainsong and classical polyphony should replace the theatrical music which was redolent of the 'profane' world and ill-fitted the sacred words of the liturgy. His native Italy, the home of opera, was notoriously guilty of the operatic treatment of sacred texts sung in the liturgy. Pius's Instruction on Sacred Music, *Tra le Sollecitudini*, of 1903, made plainsong, together with classical polyphony, the model for all liturgical music. This was a reform that liberals might favour aesthetically, as long as it did not promote segregation of church from world. There is a case to be made for music that may help to draw young people to liturgy, though it may be aesthetically repugnant to others. Pius' reform was motivated by a desire to segregate the church from the world; and as such it may be seen as an attempt to withdraw to an island of holiness in a sea of worldliness. He clearly believed that the age called for withdrawal from a sinful world. One can regret his judgemental attitude, while looking for music that suits the occasion and one's own aesthetic tastes.

Pope John Paul II was concerned to show how faith and reason complement each other and how faith is a rational procedure in no way at odds with revelation. His encyclical, *Fides et Ratio*, is at pains to show that not merely is there no conflict between faith and reason, there is a kind of knowledge that is distinctive of faith:

On the basis of mistaken and very widespread assertions, the rationalist critique of the time attacked faith and denied the possibility of any knowledge which was not the fruit of reason's natural capacities.

This obliged the Council to reaffirm emphatically that there exists a knowledge which is peculiar to faith, surpassing the knowledge proper to human reason, which nevertheless by its nature can discover the Creator. (*Fides et Ratio*, Art. 8)

John Paul wishes to defend both the autonomy of philosophy and its dependence on the epistemological effect that Christ has on it. This is a daring thesis that makes Christ a guarantor of the potential that philosophy has for truth and ultimate meaning.

Nonetheless, in the light of faith which finds in Jesus Christ this ultimate meaning, I cannot but encourage philosophers – be they Christian or not – to trust in the power of human reason and not to set themselves goals that are too modest in their philosophizing. (Art. 56)

John Paul sees faith as a force that extends the boundaries of reason and enlarges its scope. In this impressive encyclical he puts forward a highly integrated synthesis between the two, which unifies the natural and the supernatural. During the neo-scholastic period a chasm was dug between nature and supernature. In *Fides et Ratio* the believer sees science and religious faith as two sides of the one coin. In an age of scepticism about the ability of reason to find meaning in the world, John Paul encourages philosophers to trust their discipline and use it to its fullest extent. Without apology he portrays Christ in epistemological terms and not merely as the bringer of salvation.

The coming of Christ was the saving event which redeemed reason from its weakness, setting it free from the shackles in which it had imprisoned itself. (Art. 22)

This is a challenging assertion of the mysterious harmony that exists between creation and redemption. *Fides et Ratio* does not set out to argue the case for Christian faith in an adversarial way; it tells unbelieving philosophers to have confidence in their ability to pursue transcendent meaning in a secular setting, and it will bring them to find Christ as the human face of God. It is a notably unscholastic method of apologetics and is a triumph for Pascal's *faite intérieure*. Pascal has a nicely balanced view of faith and reason, when he says that in faith there is enough light for those who want to believe and enough shadow to blind those who don't. John Paul comes near to this in his encyclical:

> Of itself, philosophy is able to recognize the human being's ceaselessly self-transcendent orientation towards the truth; and, with the assistance of faith, it is capable of accepting the "foolishness" of the Cross as the authentic critique of those who delude themselves that they possess the truth, when in fact they run it aground on the shoals of a system of their own devising. The preaching of Christ crucified and risen is the reef upon which the link between faith and philosophy can break up, but it is also the reef beyond which the two can set forth upon the boundless ocean of truth. Here we see not only the border between reason and faith, but also the space where the two may meet. (Art. 23)

Those words would have gladdened the hearts of Maurice Blondel, Lucien Laberthonnière and George Tyrrell. We see here the 'method of immanence' in action. A combative scholastic like Louis Billot, a Jesuit theologian, whom Leo XIII had called to Rome in 1888 to lecture at the Gregorian University, was contemptuous of any appeal to experience or the 'heart'. One scarcely dares to imagine what Billot would have made of *Fides et Ratio*! Compare John Paul's encyclical with something that Laberthonnière, a dedicated proponent of the method of immanence and a sworn enemy of Billot's 'extrinsicism', wrote in 1904. He later recalled it as the core of his philosophical and religious position, which one of his biographers has described as 'critical mysticism':

> We do not set out from knowledge so that faith may follow. We believe as we know and we know as we believe. The outcome is a complete transformation of the soul.[10]

Lucien Laberthonnière, a Modernist reformer, censored by the Holy Office, makes an unlikely predecessor of an authoritarian pope! Nonetheless, he and Pope John Paul II share an intriguingly similar view of the relationship between faith and reason. Laberthonnière was treated with disgraceful prejudice and forbidden to publish; John Paul was a pope of undoubted authority and conservative orthodoxy. Neither of them

---

10. See Gabriel Daly, *Transcendence and Immanence: A Study in Catholic Modernism and Integralism* (Oxford, Clarendon Press, 1980), p. 106.

takes any notice of the general thrust of Pius X's encyclical *Pascendi,* and in effect they bring about the end of the anti-modernist crusade and an acceptance of the need for reform in a pilgrim church.

Blaise Pascal, the seventeenth century mathematician and mystic, profoundly influenced Laberthonnière by his famous distinction between the *esprit de géométrie* and the *esprit de finesse.* As a mathematician of genius he was a fervent advocate of the scientific method for examining nature. (For example, the Aristotelian philosophers had decided *a priori* that 'nature abhors a vacuum'; Pascal proved *a posteriori* by scientific experiment that vacuums do in fact exist in nature.) However, in spite of his high regard for science, the scientific spirit was, in his view, incompetent to demonstrate the truth of religious matters. They required what he called the *esprit de finesse,* by which he meant what Laberthonnière would later call 'the method of immanence', an awareness of the inner dimension in an approach to religion. Pascal spoke of the heart's having its own reasons which saw deeper into transcendent reality than scientific observation could do.

This approach to creation and redemption goes back to St Augustine's unquiet heart in search of eternity and preceding all purely rational thought. Neo-scholastics like Louis Billot ridiculed what they saw as subjectivity expressing itself as unsatisfied desire, which they chose to depict as irrational sentimentality. It has been pointed out that the French authors of *Gaudium et Spes,* Vatican II's Constitution on the Church in the Modern World, were heavily influenced by Pascal's concern with the *'faite intérieure',* the interior, subjective aspect of faith which relies less on evidence and more on the logic of a yearning heart.

John Paul II was a man of contradictory convictions. He may have tried to claim that his negative attitude to the ordination of women was infallible, thus showing that he followed Paul VI's attitude to the teaching of his papal predecessors; but he also showed, in his encyclical on faith and reason, that, unlike his predecessors, he adopted the alternative paradigm of belief and reason that goes back through John Henry Newman, Lucien Laberthonnière and Blaise Pascal to the restless heart cherished by Augustine. It can be argued that John Paul retained a basically, if unrecognised, Thomist perspective, but if his words are taken at face value, he does not see neo-scholasticism to be necessary for Catholic orthodoxy. His position signalized a partial reform of the church's attitude to theology, in spite of his autocratic attitude to church governance. His abandoning of neo-scholasticism, however, may have robbed him of a coherent foundation for his authoritarianism.

In Chapter 14, I will try to show that the cause of many of today's theological and moral problems in the Catholic Church is a continuing devotion to an essentialist perspective on its doctrine and moral thinking. Essentialism, conscious or unconscious, may arrogate to itself the right to judge moral actions like contraception from an exclusively *a priori* theoretical viewpoint which brooks no dissent, and refuses to listen to moral arguments based on experience. The assembly of 150 bishops called to advise the Pope on marriage and the family will be of mostly elderly male celibates with no existential experience of marriage and probably imbued with an essentialist view of what marriage *should* be like, rather than what it *is* actually like.

Pastoral care itself may well depend on the willingness of these men not merely to listen attentively to the experience of married laity, but also to be prepared to consider the matter from a very different perspective than that of the probable essentialism of their early theological training. If they prove ready to do this, they will be receiving not alone the teaching of the Second Vatican Council but, more importantly, of the Spirit who inspired it.

10

Faith, Theology, Doctrine and Freedom

Doctrines in the Christian church are shaped by serious efforts to understand all the implications of what we find in Scripture, in the creeds, in the personal and social experience of the believer and, ideally, in the signs of the times. The process is as much an effort of imagination as of mind, which is why symbols and images matter and should never be lightly regarded. Anselm of Canterbury classically described theology as faith seeking understanding, but that understanding may be tacit, nonverbal, and dependent on images. Francis of Assisi is reputed to have made the point with perceptive wit: 'Preach the Gospel at all times, and when necessary, use words.'

The freedom of faith demands the freedom of the theologies derived from it. There must be no external restraints, however prelatical, if religious faith is to be authentic. Because cultures change, the theologies attendant on faith must be open to re-expression in language that is understandable to people of any age and place, while preserving the essence of what was originally proposed to belief. This is why the philosophy of interpretation (hermeneutics) is so important in the reading of sacred texts. Insisting on the literal reiteration of formulas without any effort to make them intelligible and relevant in a later age can actually betray the original experience that was expressed in the language of a different age. Sophisticated philosophers may not be the best interpreters of Galilean peasants – which is possibly part of what Jesus meant when he said that children would enter into the kingdom before the learned. 'He called a little child to him, and placed the child among them. And he said: "Truly I tell you, unless you change and become like little children, you will never enter the kingdom of heaven."' (Matthew 18:2-3)

Doctrine is an attempt to make an intellectually coherent statement of what one believes. Of its nature it is second order activity at a remove from the original experiences. We have no access to the experience that made some fishermen give up their normal lives to follow a wandering craftsman and become the founders of a following numbered in billions. Doctrine is made up of ideas, images and language that are borrowed from a specific culture; and with the development and change of cultures the original experience becomes ever more complex and dependent on second-order reflections. Revelation does not employ a heavenly language which survives unchanged through subsequent different cultures: it takes place through the medium of obsolescent cultures and in dependence on the possibilities and limitations of different and developing languages. Revelation is given through an inherently unstable medium and is always dependent on the process of interpretation. That thought ought to give pause to authoritarian fundamentalists. The Bible is the word of God, not literally, but filtered through the experience and linguistic limitations of a Middle Eastern people, more than 2,000 years ago.

A markedly essentialist attitude to culturally controlled statements will tend to absolutise what is relative and treat it as an eternally valid truth instead of as a linguistically limited expression of the transcendent. The term *homousios*, for example, translated into literalised English as 'consubstantial', is taken from a culture that has long gone, but is still recognised as an integral part of a conciliar definition and, as such, binding on the church permanently.

The first requirement in teaching and writing theology is honesty in saying what one really thinks, as distinct from what one is supposed to think. Concern for authenticity applies as much to teachers as to professional theologians. It severely damages the credibility of an author or preacher who is seen to be repeating 'orthodox' ideas out of a misguided sense of loyalty. Bishops, for example, may damage their own credibility in their efforts to be obedient to bureaucratic departments in the Vatican, over which they are, in point of fact, superior, but on which, in a power-based structure, they depend for security of their standing and possibly of their careers. To refuse, for example, to ponder in depth and transparency the implications of the shortage of priests today, in the Northern hemisphere, because Roman bureaucrats might not like some obvious remedies for it, is regrettable, and may actually amount to a failure in pastoral responsibility.

Great Christian theologians, like Augustine, Aquinas, Luther and Tillich, wrote what they did in an effort to understand the Christian Gospel and apply it to their own circumstances, thus seeking to give cultural relevance to the biblical account of the Good News. Until Pope John XXIII made public his celebrated distinction between the substance of faith and the manner of its formulation, the guardians of orthodoxy in the Catholic Church usually operated under the assumption that their statements about faith remained eternally valid and timelessly relevant, and that any attempt to depart from them would amount to unlawful dissent and even heresy. However, theology needs to change in order that faith may remain constant through every change of culture, yet do so with complete fidelity to the original message in the New Testament. To illustrate this crucially important point, I shall consider two modern theologians, Yves Congar, a French Dominican, and Elizabeth Johnson, an American Sister of St Joseph of Brentwood, one writing before, and at, the Second Vatican Council, the other writing in its aftermath. Both incurred the hostility of the Vatican.

Congar's case is particularly relevant to the topic of reform, in that he suffered greatly from the hostile attentions of the Holy Office, now known as the Congregation for the Doctrine of the Faith (CDF). The opposition was to his books, *Divided Christendom* and *True and False Reform,* and to his support for the worker-priest movement. However, he went on to be recognised as perhaps the most influential theologian at Vatican II. A year before he died, Rome made him a cardinal, without any sense of irony or shame! During Vatican II, Congar, who was a *peritus* at the council, wrote a journal which became a very large book that is an eye-witness account of a reforming council in action.[1] The journal is a record of that council; and the life of its author is testimony to a scholar who was pursued as a theologian by the Holy Office but survived to become one of the foremost influences at the council. Yves Congar's story illustrates how genuine reform can turn a persecuted theologian into a conciliar celebrity.

The Holy Office, which had pursued him relentlessly in the years before the council, was still trying to discredit him without success, even while the council was sitting. His *Journal* is taken up with the contest between

1. Yves Congar, *My Journal of the Council* (Dublin / Adelaide / Collegeville; Dominican Publications /ATF Press / The Liturgical Press, 2012). The original French edition was published in 2002.

what the media at that time accurately described as the 'conservative' minority and the 'progressive' majority. He makes it very clear that if the conservatives had managed to control the council, it would have meant the end of reform in the church. Fortunately that did not happen, and from the outset of the council, Congar became one of the main contributors to the cause of reform. He never wavered in its pursuit, and in spite of conservative bluster he made it clear that there had to be a change in theological thinking if there were to be real reform. First and foremost he believed in *ressourcement, i.e.* a return to the sources, namely, to study of the Bible and of the early ages of the Church.

Congar recognized that it would have been dishonest of him, having committed himself to the modernisation of Catholic theology, not to take sides in a contest that would shape the character of the whole church. He sets a very high standard for those who are aware of serious deficiencies in the government of the church in any age, and are trying to do something about the situation, in spite of the hardship such action may draw down on them. Though Congar made no secret of his critical convictions, he believed in and practised fairness and the avoidance of sectarianism – no mean achievement, in view of the disreputable tactics resorted to by the conciliar minority. He told Hans Küng that they must avoid conveying the impression that they were a 'para-council of theologians'. Küng wanted a meeting of theologians of similar mindset. Congar replied that unless theologians of a conservative cast of mind were present, he would not attend.[2] He appreciated the need for the free expression of beliefs and convictions, and he deplored the use of coercion in the pursuit of a narrowly defined conception of orthodoxy.

He had to face curialists like Cardinal Alfredo Ottaviani, Prefect of the Holy Office, who often interfered, in a partisan manner, with conciliar documents, and was shamelessly biased in his choice of speakers at meetings where he was chairman. He was unscrupulous in the tactics he employed against people like Congar, who was a reformer prepared to defend his convictions vigorously, but in an open and non-partisan way. Return to the sources would in Congar's view, and in the view of other, mainly French, reformers, be an implicit critique of the kind of papal centralisa-

2. *Journal,* p. 82.

tion which had grown up in the church over the centuries, especially since the Council of Trent in the sixteenth century. New Testament and early church practice, if examined historically, were, to Congar, a standing witness to what the church had been before the conversion of the Emperor Constantine had drawn it into the maelstrom of political life, prompting it to emphasize its hierarchical structures and develop princely attitudes.

Return to Scripture and early Tradition would, the reformers hoped, lead inevitably to a much-needed reform of church governmental structures. In his opening address to the council, Pope John XXIII had called for *aggiornamento*, a bringing up to date. It was also a reforming concept, having aims similar to those of *ressourcement*. The two schools of thought blended during the council in opposition to the tight grip that the curia had exercised over church government and the oppressive appeal to doctrine as an instrument of coercion.

Before the council, Congar had lectured and written on topics that were highly suspect in Rome, and he paid a heavy price for it. In his own words, 'since 1938, I have been UNCEASINGLY under suspicion, pursued, reprimanded, limited, crushed'.[3] In 1954, the Master General of the Order responded to Roman hostility to French theology by banning Congar and other French Dominicans from teaching. Exiled to Cambridge until the end of 1956, he was later assigned to the priory in Strasbourg where he found that the bishop of the diocese, Jean-Joseph Weber, was favourably disposed towards him. Weber brought him to the council as his *peritus*. He remained forbidden to teach, but he was able to do research and to write.

In one of the early entries in his *Journal* Congar wrote:

> The announcement of the Council aroused great interest and great hope. It seemed that, after the stifling regime of Pius XII, the windows were at last being opened; one could breathe. The Church was being given its chance. One was becoming open to dialogue.[4]

This last remark is a reminder that he had made a distinguished and courageous contribution to ecumenical relations with other Christian churches. This, it need hardly be said, was regarded unfavourably in Rome at that time.

3. *Journal*, p. 370.
4. Ibid, p. 5.

One highly significant feature of Congar's work during the council was his educational contribution to it. In theory, bishops take the lead in promoting the practice and theory of the faith. In reality, however, many of them are out of touch with important theological developments and need to be informed about them, if they are to fulfil their episcopal duties and not be imprisoned in the formulas of their past. Congar remarked that many of the assembled bishops had lost the habit of study and of deciding matters for themselves, and had consequently acquired the habit of allowing Rome 'to do all their thinking for them'.[5] That thinking was shaped by late nineteenth century attitudes to theology and the magisterium's role in it. It should be remembered that it was theologians from the Roman clerical universities who wrote the initial draft texts submitted to, and rejected by, the Second Vatican Council. Congar had little time for them.

These Rome-based theologians have no respect for the Tradition. All they can see are papal utterances. That is where the great battle will continue to be waged. The truth will prevail.[6]

He recognised that Pope John XXIII, although he was unaggressively traditional in his piety and theology, nevertheless saw the need for change. Congar depicts him as a 'cordial, very simple, Christian'.[7] He quotes the Pope's remark to Cardinal Leger that 'they have not understood what I wanted in summoning this Council [to bring the Church "up to date"]'.[8] To a new French ambassador to the Quirinal Pope John said, 'I want to shake off the imperial dust that has accumulated on the throne of St Peter since the time of Constantine'.[9]

Congar's views on Pope Paul VI are more complex. He recognised that Paul made some admirable ecumenical gestures, but he also felt that he lacked the ecclesiology to support them. Paul was well disposed towards ecumenism but he was careful not to cross swords with the hard-line traditionalists. Those who were urging Paul to defend the papal monarchy were speaking to his deepest convictions and fears. He usually hesitates but ends up in favour of the conservative direction. He saw himself as

5. *Journal*, p. 8
6. Ibid, p. 58.
7. Ibid, p. 93.
8. Ibid, p.208.
9. Ibid, p. 282.

being above the church rather than within it; this belief was, of course, at the roots of curial action which was dedicated to 'doing EVERYTHING to prevent the episcopate from recovering the rights which have been stolen from it'.[10] He believed in collegiality, but he saw no way to combine it with papal primacy.

Congar's mind constantly returns to his trials before the council, and while he appreciated the benefits of belonging to a religious order, he reflects ruefully on the usual collusion of his religious superiors with the CDF: 'since 1938 I have been UNCEASINGLY under suspicion, pursued, reprimanded , limited, crushed'.[11]

Joseph Ratzinger and Karol Wojtyła would later proclaim, in the CDF Instruction, *Donum Veritatis* (1990), that freedom of conscience does not extend to doctrinal pronouncements. (art. 38) For them, the single most important authority in matters of faith is the magisterium, which takes precedence over conscience, conviction and scholarly research.

In May 1990, the Congregation for the Doctrine of the Faith, presided over by its Prefect, Joseph Ratzinger (later to become Pope Benedict XVI), published a document, *Donum Veritatis*, at the command of Pope John Paul II. It was a statement on the ecclesial vocation of the theologian issued by two notable and powerful conservatives.

A careful reading of it shows that it was conceived within a markedly essentialist and authoritarian mindset, and it was clearly intended to act as an *a priori* justification of the activities of the Vatican magisterium, which it saw as being willed by Christ and having precedence over all other interpretations of the Christian message.

> God graciously arranged that the things he had once revealed for the salvation of all peoples should remain in their entirety, throughout the ages, and be transmitted to all generations.[12] He bestowed upon His Church, through the gift of the Holy Spirit, a participation in His own infallibility.[13] Thanks to the 'supernatural sense of Faith', the People of God enjoys this privilege under the guidance of the Church's liv-

10. Ibid, p. 425
11. Ibid, p. 370.
12. *Dei Verbum*, art. 7.
13. Cf. Congregation for the Doctrine of the Faith, Declaration *Mysterium Ecclesiae.* n. 2:AAS 65 (1973) 398 f.

ing Magisterium, which is the sole authentic interpreter of the Word of God, written or handed down, by virtue of the authority which it exercises in the name of Christ.[14]

This quotation from *Donum Veritatis,* obsessed as it is with revelation-as-statement, makes artful use of the Vatican II Constitution, *Dei Verbum,* on revelation by intertwining a conciliar document with a declaration from the CDF, as if equating a conciliar with a curial document. This integralist view of church authority manages to imply that Jesus, in committing his Good News to his followers, would actually have approved of how today's CDF thinks of itself and behaves towards others.[15] It is one thing to say, with *Dei Verbum,* that the task of interpreting the word of God has been given by Christ exclusively to the living teaching office of the church; it is quite another to claim that: 'the Magisterium is, in its service to the Word of God, an institution positively willed by Christ as a constitutive element of His Church' (*DonumVeritatis,* art. 14). Any dissent from its judgements is a grave matter that invites an 'intervention' (shameless euphemism) by the CDF. The human element in all this is conveniently ignored and the dice are loaded against any theologian who dares to take issue with the magisterium. Any faithful Catholic looking for reform is up against a powerful *a priori* systemic defence of the very institutions most in need of reform. Argument has no significance here.

Today the matters that concern the magisterium are moral, behavioural and disciplinary, but in calling them the teaching of the church, Rome is raising them to equality with the central message entrusted by Christ to his followers – an injudicious and reckless move. The Instruction is careful to assert that revelation also contains moral teachings that can be infallibly taught by the magisterium. (art. 16) This preoccupation with infallibility suggests a lack of confidence in the ability of the message to speak for itself, and it signals a return to late nineteenth century anxieties. It goes on to claim that magisterial teachings must be received with 'the religious submission of will and intellect'. (art. 23)

The second section of the *Instruction* is headed, 'The Problem of Dissent'; and it is notable that the Instruction regards diversity of theological

14. Cf. *Dei Verbum,* art. 10.
15. It is the CDF, not *Dei Verbum,* which mentions infallibility.

views as a 'problem' rather than as a normal healthy feature of human intellectual commerce; but it makes plain how the magisterium continues to see itself as a primary source of Catholic theology, and declares that

> Dissent has different aspects. In its most radical form, it aims at changing the Church following a model of protest which takes its inspiration from political society. (art. 33)

This implicit denial of the political aspects of institutional church activities, especially of its 'interventions', is disingenuous. In the eyes of the creators of *Donum Veritatis*, dissenters who regard statements of the magisterium as the expression of one school of thought among several are setting up a 'parallel magisterium'. [art. 34] Why do these magisterial bureaucrats always have to think in terms of authority rather than of the essential elements in the Good News? There is nothing here about truth speaking for itself; everything is about authority and the imposition of its own views as 'the teaching of the church' – an attitude that is not only outmoded but, in addition, cold and ultimately unevangelical. It fails to grasp all the implications of the abandonment of the notion of revelation as divine statement and faith as intellectual assent to it.

The Instruction, in its supernaturalist conviction that 'Magisterial teaching, by virtue of divine assistance, has a validity beyond its argumentation' [art. 34], proclaims magisterial teaching to be immune from legitimate intellectual criticism, and it tries to make itself intellectually impregnable. Since God is on its side, it claims, it has no need of argument or involvement in the free market place of ideas. That God is on its side is essential to its validity, but the fact is that it is an unproven assumption. One is compelled to consider all this as the manifestation of a special kind of fundamentalism buttressed by some powerful theocratic assumptions. It ill befits a body that sees itself as the source of all Catholic theology, since it discourages all serious theological thinking.

When the magisterium withdraws 'the canonical mission or the teaching mandate from a dissenting theologian', it is seeking 'to be faithful to its mission of defending the right of the People of God to receive the message of the Church in its purity and integrity and not be disturbed by a particular dangerous opinion'. (*Donum Veritatis*, art. 37) The hand of Joseph Ratzinger, who liked to speak of 'the right of the faithful to be nourished by true doctrine', is all too evident here. It reveals an attitude that resists reasonable argument; it is fundamentalist in the sense that intellect is overpowered by will; in short, the document is true because 'we', in our privileged way, say it is true.

Human rights are irrelevant to this sort of authoritarian traditionalism, for which 'thinking with the church' means accepting the point of view of the ruling party in the church, because their point of view belongs to a higher order of existence that owes nothing to politics, ideology or academic rigour. (art. 37) The magisterium has no obligations towards such earthly matters as human rights, hence it can safely remain in its doctrinal enclave, ordering the lives of others. It simply proclaims the theological impropriety of appealing to conscience in matters of doctrine.

> Finally, argumentation appealing to the obligation to follow one's own conscience cannot legitimate dissent. This is true, first of all, because conscience illumines the practical judgment about a decision to make, while here we are concerned with the truth of a doctrinal pronouncement. This is furthermore the case because while the theologian, like every believer, must follow his [or her] conscience, he [or she] is also obliged to form it. Conscience is not an independent and infallible faculty. It is an act of moral judgement regarding a responsible choice. A right conscience is one duly illumined by faith and by the objective moral law and it presupposes, as well, the uprightness of the will in the pursuit of the true good. (art. 38)

Because the authors of the Instruction feel no need to put forward a reasonable argument in its defence, this autocratic voluntarism is logically necessary: their withdrawal to a sacred environment, to which others have no access, dispenses with the need to justify their beliefs or behaviour rationally. With this kind of theocratic fideism there is no need for convincing argumentation - only magisterial affirmation is needed.

I am aware that in looking closely at a document of the CDF, I run the risk of boring the reader, but I am convinced that I should present the case against theological freedom as far as possible in the words of the magisterium. It helps to ward off the charge of misrepresentation and to explain the nature of the persistent attack on Yves Congar by the Holy Office, and, as we shall see, of the American Bishops' attack on the

Fordham University theologian, Elizabeth Johnson.

One question remains insistent: How is it that the Roman Curia never seem to learn from their mistakes? Time and again they persecute people who do not share their ultra-conservative beliefs. Their victims undergo humiliating condemnations and censorship, and are left with no recourse to a higher tribunal. Sadly, it would appear that the CDF sometimes relies on the probability that its action will cause anguish not alone to their victim but also to his or her family and relatives. Congar wrote to his mother explaining why he had been silenced by church authorities: 'What put me wrong [in their eyes] is not having said false things, but having said things they do not like to have said.''[16]

That any Christian should have to undergo this sort of harassment by fellow Christians deeply offends one's sense of justice and one's awareness of the Gospel. It is outrageous that Yves Congar should have had to endure this treatment from people who quite possibly lacked the ability or the will to appreciate what he was saying, but who nevertheless had the power to make his life a misery.

The Committee on Doctrine of the United States Conference of Catholic Bishops have attacked Elizabeth Johnson's stimulating book, *Quest for The Living God.*[17] The Committee's claims reflects the case laid out by the CDF in *Donum Veritatis* and it deprecates all efforts to think in a fresh way about old beliefs, which is what Johnson does so impressively in her books. Later in the document the Congregation encourages the practice of theology but asserts that it is a 'risky' business. The advice is to engage in theology, but be very wary. It is difficult to see how this behaviour has anything to do with Jesus and his preaching of the Good News.

Donum Veritatis gives guarded advice to theologians:

> It is the theologian's task in this perspective to draw from the surrounding culture those elements which will allow him [or her] better to illumine one or other aspect of the mysteries of faith. This is certainly an arduous task that has its risks, but it is legitimate in itself and should be encouraged. (art. 10)

16. Yves Congar, 'Silenced for Saying Things Rome Didn't Like to Have Said,' *National Catholic Reporter,* (June 2, 2000), p. 3.
17. Elizabeth Johnson, *Quest for the Living God: Mapping Frontiers in the Theology of God* (Bloomsbury, London, 2007).

Elizabeth Johnson unquestionably draws on the surrounding culture to illumine aspects of the mysteries of faith. She takes into consideration such areas as politics, feminism, evolution, ecology, liberation and other contemporary cultural concerns, all of them capable of illuminating her theological interests. Central to her spiritual and theological experience has been her awareness of the way in which male experience has dominated Christian theological images of God over the centuries. Hence her book, *She Who Is* (1991), shows very clearly how female images and models for God have enlarged the ways we think about, and approach, the divine. She shows that Feminist theology is not merely a matter of gender politics: it plays a sizeable part in extending our ideas and images of God and of God's graceful and loving action in the world. The persistence of predominantly male images of God since the early days of Christianity is conspicuously in need of the correction that is being supplied by female theologians who are taking the lead, especially in the US. Their work appears to be problematic for the American bishops.

In the impressive first chapter of her book, *Quest for the Living God*, Johnson draws some rich implications from her feminism which illustrate how language about God works. Making perceptive use of Sallie McFague's *Metaphorical Theology: Models of God in Religious Language* (1985), Johnson, in remarkably few words, examines the significance of the nature of metaphor, and emphasises its bipolar character: if for literary reasons we say that something is something else, we know that this cannot be literally true. If, for instance, we say that Richard has a lion's heart, we are not describing his anatomy. All language about God expresses what is true within its limitations, followed immediately by a recognition that in a literal sense it is not true: From the human experience of wise men and women we derive a concept of wisdom, which we can apply to God, though only with the rider that God is wise in an infinite and utterly transcendent way. All language about God necessarily limps, and it is a wise person who accepts this fact and does not try to act as if he or she were sprinting effortlessly towards an open goal.

In every instance the permanent tension between the "is and is not" dynamic of metaphor has to be maintained in order for its intellectual and affective power to work. Religious tradition with its habitual repetition in ritual and teaching is liable to forget this pivotal point.[18]

The Commission makes great play with Johnson's alleged failure to differentiate between metaphor, symbol and analogy. She has no need to do so, since her point is to counter the bland use of literal statement about God. Her episcopal critics seem to think that one cannot make true statements about God that are metaphorical or symbolic. Their literalism is what Johnson rightly criticises. Many misunderstandings arise from thinking that one can make literally true statements about God. In Johnson's phrase, 'As history shows, dead metaphors make good idols'.[19] We have no approach to God except through our image of God; but we need always to remember that our image is not God; it is a distorted depiction that easily becomes an idol, if taken for literal accuracy. (See 1 Corinthians 13:12-13) It is remarkable how some defenders of orthodoxy overlook Aquinas' warning that what we do not know about God vastly exceeds what we do know. We need a profusion and variety of images to think of, and approach, God. As Johnson puts it: 'Since no one term alone is absolute, a positive revelry of symbols pours forth to express divine being.'[20]

Nor does the mystery of the incarnation change the differentness of God, which defies univocal predication. 'Christians believe that God has drawn near in Jesus Christ, but even there the living God remains unutterable mystery and cannot be encompassed.'[21] A lively spiritual relationship with Jesus does not shatter the otherness of God and may indeed trivialise the impact of the transcendence of God by a sentimental union with an historical being who emptied himself so that God could be seen in his Galilean ministry some 2,000 years ago. There is a danger that we can mar the mystery of God by domesticating our eschatological relationship with Jesus, forgetting that *kenosis*, self-emptying, is at the centre of the mystery of the incarnation. (Philippians 2:7)

Throughout her book, Johnson displays a mental inclusiveness which enables her to visit diverse cultures and draw from each of them further enlightenment on how God deals, not exclusively with Christians, but with all human beings, offering them love and salvation. This prompts

18. *Quest*, p. 20.
19. Ibid.
20. Ibid, p. 21
21. Ibid, p. 17

the bishops to return to the alleged exclusivity of Christianity and affirm that Johnson 'denies the uniqueness of Jesus as the Incarnate God'. In all this, the Second Vatican Council seems somehow to have escaped the attention of the Bishops' Committee.

It need hardly be said that she has a chapter on the importance of women's experience for a properly balanced theology.

In the middle of a chapter that reflects on the South American experience of liberation, she has four pages on popular religion which I found personally illuminating and instructive.[22] Reading these pages has thrown new light for me on popular religious practices with many of which I have usually felt uncomfortable and which I have too easily written off as superstition. Popular religion, often an embarrassment to more sophisticated Christians, enables ordinary people to find the presence of God in the events of everyday life. They, especially in South America, take part in colourful ceremonies that give expression to their experience of God. These ceremonies are not clerically inspired (though clerics are often co-opted into them); they are not filtered through hierarchical regulations; they come from the imaginations and passions of the people, and are more Dionysian than Apollonian.[23] They appeal to people for whom the prescribed niceties of liturgical regulation mean nothing. (For obvious reasons, ecclesiastical authorities are usually uneasy with the Dionysian, since they can't control it.)

Belief in apparitions is a way of finding the presence of God in everyday life. As a result of reading Elizabeth Johnson, I am acquiring more sympathy with apparition-seekers than I used to have. God can reach people

22. *Quest*, pp. 136-139.

23. The distinction between the Apollonian and the Dionysian goes back to Greek mythology and is given modern reference by Friedrich Nietzsche in his book *The Birth of Tragedy* (1872). The Apollonian element is rational, ordered, restrained, while the Dionysian is spontaneous, wild, untamed, undisciplined. Human life, including its religious aspect, is often characterised by a struggle between the two, one seeking control, the other demanding unhindered expression. An ordered and regulated liturgy may be fairly described as Apollonian, while the religious element in a South American *fiesta* is clearly Dionysian in its spontaneity and emotional outpouring. Certain kinds of religion deal mainly with the Apollonian. The Dionysian, if present, is at best a side effect; other kinds are mainly Dionysian in their inspiration. What is needed is something like a balance between them and a recognition that temperament and tastes can differ. For instance, not all Christians can be charismatic, and they are none the worse for that, provided they do nothing to interfere with that kind of worship which may do for others what more restrained kinds of worship fail to do for them.

through what some of us may thoughtlessly call superstition. Church authorities are not usually disturbed by alleged apparitions, which are normally controllable by a judgement of the magisterium that leaves the magisterium in charge, which is their principal concern. People who have jurisdiction in the church can usually control the impact of apparitions by ruling on whether they are authentic or not.

Unfortunately they can also use liturgical worship as a field for the exercise of their authority, as we have seen with the imposition of a new and unnecessary Latinised text for the Mass, to say nothing of instructing the celebrant at Mass not to leave his place at the altar to go to greet his fellow worshippers!

Elizabeth Johnson's book, *Quest for the Living God*, has been a striking success in the USA, to the extent of seriously worrying the traditionalist establishment. Johnson is doing something that pastorally-minded theologians do who write not merely for other professional theologians, but also for thinking Christians – a class often neglected by official pastors who sometimes offer them uninspiring restatements of old formulas in an atmosphere of authority, infallibility, power and control, all of which are guaranteed to repel many practising Catholics and would-be believers.

It is important to understand what Johnson means by the term 'modern theology'. She points out that the Enlightenment in the seventeenth and eighteenth centuries tried to introduce a purely rational scheme for understanding the world. This put Christians on the defensive, and they mirrored the stance of their enemies by adopting a heavily Apollonian and rationalist approach to defending their faith.[24] She shows how this meant allowing the enemy to choose the weapons for both sides.

> Now, however, to counter the Enlightenment's criticisms, they [religious people] switched to the same playing field as their opponent. Leaving behind Christian sources and adopting philosophical methods of thinking that sought objective knowledge about the universe on a rational basis, they set out to shape "clear and distinctive ideas" about the divine.[25]

24. In Chapter 1 I described how I began my theological life in a Roman clerical university that practised this approach. Vatican II helped me to see its weaknesses.
25. *Quest*, p. 15.

This immensely significant development, adopted by René Descartes and utilised gratefully by many defenders of the faith in more recent times, led to the church's emphasis on a purely intellectual concept of revelation and faith, concomitantly emphasising the importance of control through magisterial teaching – the very feature that most alienates people today. The doctrine of infallibility was greatly facilitated by the prominence given to statement as the keystone to an 'orthodox' idea of revelation and faith. It also gave overpowering significance to the magisterium as the alleged source of all orthodox Catholic theology. Congar tried to oppose this idea by his appeal to *ressourcement*, a return to the real sources of Christian faith.

It may help us to understand the unhappy divide in the church today between liberals and conservatives, if we consider briefly the nature of the attack made by the North American bishops on Elizabeth Johnson's book. They make it quite clear that they were disturbed by the fact that the book is immensely popular in universities and theological colleges in the US, becoming virtually a textbook. Instead of asking why she is being listened to and they are not, they decide that her thinking does not conform to theirs, and therefore she must be condemned as unorthodox – a *non sequitur* of startling proportions.

The bishops have entered into an uneven 'discussion' with her that has never been face-to-face, and they have had the last word by replying to her observations on their original judgement, flatly denying her complaint that they have misunderstood and misinterpreted her. The fact that they attempted some sort of dialogue with her is an improvement on the normal procedures of the CDF. If the CDF would only restrict itself to making traditionalist statements without inflicting institutional penalties or demanding prior censorship of guest speakers at gatherings, as Gerhard Ludwig Müller has done with the US-based Leadership Conference of Religious Women, it would be a crucial step towards reform. We should then have something like a healthy diversity of theologies in the church, with ultra-conservatives having to contend with others by free discussion and argument – an alarming prospect for them.

It would be beyond the scope or purpose of this book to examine here all the charges made against *Quest for the Living God*. I shall consider some of the more pertinent ones to show that there could be no meeting of minds: they are operating out of mutually contradictory mindsets about the meaning of Catholic Christianity.

The bishops' charge against Johnson's book is that it 'does not take the faith of the church as its starting point.' What do the Committee mean by 'faith' here? If they mean the New Testament and the creeds, the accusation is palpably false, since Professor Johnson clearly takes these very seriously indeed. If they mean the developed theology of the church, one must concede that the whole purpose of her book is to try to present fresh theological thinking that seeks to escape from the formulaic restraints of traditional doctrinal statements that no longer speak to modern men and women.

As I have already said, it is quite inaccurate to claim that we are bound to use the precise words of a teaching council. We do not, for instance, have to use fourth century language in order to be faithful to the church's teaching on the Trinity. Instead, we have the more difficult task of translating fourth century language into something more intelligible to modern men and women – a task that Professor Johnson performs so well. In the world of today there are many different cultural streams that can enrich our understanding of what we believe as Christians. Elizabeth Johnson's presentation of the implications of the incarnation speaks forcibly to contemporary men and women, and it chimes with the ecological concerns of thinking people today. It proclaims that science and religious revelation come from the hands of the one Creator.

The protest of Christian feminists that our language about God has been heavily male is a perfectly legitimate, and much needed, critique. In the subsequent discussion between Elizabeth Johnson and her episcopal critics, she points out that she is not proposing to replace the excessively male language used in magisterial teaching about God, but rather to supplement it with newer, more culturally relevant, language that takes into account the concerns of many believers and would-be believers, especially women, today.

Johnson speaks a language that modern intelligent young people understand, and her accusers regard as deviant. She also speaks a language that many contemporary theologians speak, and her accusers do not. It seems that to enter into serious and open discussion with the 'liberals' would threaten the fortress of their institutional certainties. They postulate a situation that can be discussed only in terms that have the properties of a perennially valid language – and that is historically impossible, since language emerges from evanescent cultures.

Her treatment of the Trinity in the last chapter of her book is fresh and stimulating. The Episcopal Conference takes especial offence at it, because it makes a point of not repeating the abstract language of classical Trinitarian theology. Her accusers try to extend the scope of revelation to include speculation about what is called the 'immanent Trinity', *i.e.*, the Trinity as it exists in itself, as distinct from the 'economic Trinity', which is concerned with the triune God's relations with creation, notably through human beings. She quotes Karl Rahner's well known remark : 'the economic Trinity is the immanent Trinity and vice-versa'.[26] What God has done for human beings is the subject of revelation. How the 'persons' of the Trinity relate to one another is in no way a revealed matter. To be sure, it became accepted theological speculation – which, however, is not the same as revealed Christian truth. The Bishops' Committee seem unable or unwilling to see this. Instead, in their reply to Johnson's observations, they affirm that

> it is … impossible to understand who Jesus is as pre-existent Logos, as ontologically the eternal Son of the Father, and what the incarnation means without an understanding of the relations between the persons of the Trinity.

In other words, they make the astonishing claim that we cannot address ourselves to God's revelation in Jesus Christ without first adopting some purely speculative theological ideas from a later era. Projecting fourth century scholarly speculations back on to Scripture is anachronistic and both historically and theologically indefensible. In addition, the Bishops identify their own opinions as 'the teaching of the church', and in consequence they lay a gratuitous obligation on Elizabeth Johnson, and on all of us, to conform her thoughts to their judgement – a totally unreasonable demand, which would, incidentally, invite her to be unfaithful to her conscience and to her intelligence.

The Bishops demand that she employ all the abstract adjectives of the classical treatment of the doctrine of God, such as 'incorporeal, impas-

26. *Quest,* p. 210

sible, omnipotent, omniscient and omnipresent'. She quite rightly avoids them, since they arose as abstractions in a different culture and do not speak convincingly to our age about the redemptive love and mercy of God. Catholic theologians are not bound to use ancient language in order to remain orthodox. In fact the attempt to do so can actually betray the primary purpose of evangelisation: incomprehension and boredom are not mental states favourable to reception of the Gospel.

Johnson has just published a book with the intriguing title *Ask the Beasts: Darwin and the God of Love.*[27] It makes complete sense when we are reminded of Job and his reply to one of his 'comforters': 'Ask the beasts and they will teach you'. (Job 12:7) This impressive book shows Johnson at her best, making principled contact with the world of science and, in the process, bringing together the theology of creation and redemption by taking Darwin and his theory of natural selection with theological seriousness.[28]

Her treatment of incarnation is breathtaking in the way it portrays God drawing near, not merely to us humans but, through us, to all creation. The flesh of Jesus can be truthfully related to the Big Bang, the primeval beginning of our universe. 'The flesh assumed in Jesus Christ connects with all humanity, all biological life, all soil, the whole matrix of the material universe down to its very roots.'[29] She derives this reflection from a careful exegesis of the word '*sarx*', flesh, in the prologue of John's Gospel, which she invokes as a powerful refutation of Docetism, a second century heresy which taught that Jesus only appeared to be human. The retreat to a purely 'spiritual' perspective on Christianity remains a constant temptation for some Christians who like to oppose 'soul' to 'body' and the supernatural to the natural.

I have referred here to a contest between the conservative teaching body in the Catholic Church and two distinguished theologians, one of whom puts forward a view of creation that the American bishops seem unable to comprehend. She and they are speaking different languages

---

27. E, Johnson, *Ask the Beasts: Darwin and the God of Love* (Bloomsbury, London , 2014)
28. I am indebted to Professor Terence Tilley for drawing my attention to this fascinating book. I should add that Elizabeth Johnson devotes a large part of the early chapters of her book to a detailed explication of the science of evolution and natural selection which non-scientists may find hard going but which amply rewards careful study.
29. *Ask the Beasts*, p. 196.

about the one mystery. The truly Christian answer to this situation is for both sides to put forward their ideas in freedom, listening to each other, and not trying to prevail by the (unproven) assertion that their opinion is the (binding) teaching of the church. The church has indeed taught through abstractions, when that kind of thinking was favoured by scholars, and when it represented the highest kind of intellectual culture at the time. That culture retains its validity, but it is no longer dominant, or even intelligible, in an age that looks to science as the best way to understand the cosmos which Christians, Jews and Muslims identify as creation.

One has no right to identify one's own opinions as 'the teaching of the church', unless one can give convincing theological reasons for making the claim. The Catholic Church needs theologians like Yves Congar and Elizabeth Johnson, so that the Gospel may be heard anew in every age with liberating joy, and not in a disagreeable atmosphere of threat and grim insistence on the kind of unity that precludes the divinely willed gift of diversity.

11

Athens and Jerusalem

God was in Christ reconciling the world to himself. (2 Corinthians 5:19)

I believe in one Lord Jesus Christ, only-begotten Son of God, born of the Father before all time, God from God, light from light, true God from true God, begotten not made, consubstantial with the Father, by whom all things were made. (Council of Nicaea, 325 CE)

Something of considerable significance has happened between these two professions of faith, separated by little more than two centuries. The first is a beautifully simple statement, 'God was in Christ', which uses language in a direct and uncomplicated way while professing the central truth of Christian faith. The second is a complicated formula that uses a highly technical term, 'consubstantial', in line with Hellenistic philosophy. Geza Vermes puts the situation crisply:

> The way of thinking of the Church Fathers was very different from that of Jesus. The principal task of the prophet from Nazareth set in front of his Galilean followers was the pursuit of the Kingdom of God in the immediacy of the here and now. By the early fourth century the practical, charismatic Judaism preached by Jesus was transformed into an intellectual religion defined and regulated by dogma.[1]

The reign of the Emperor Constantine is signally important for the history of Christianity. Early in the fourth century, persecution of the Christian church ceased by imperial decree, and the church proved ready to assume all the trappings of power. Constantine is in many ways an ambiguous figure who took a strong political interest in the church. There is some debate about his actual Christian faith. He was baptized on his deathbed; but that was not uncommon at the time. He was a politician to his fingertips and as such he took a particular interest in church unity.

---

1. Geza Vermes, *Christian Beginnings from Nazareth to Nicaea (AD 30-325)*, (London, 2012), p. xvi.

He felt that religious divisions were a threat to the unity and peace of his empire. Released from the persecutions inflicted by pagan Rome, the church witnessed a proliferation of Christian intellectuals schooled in the disciplines of Greek philosophy, who conducted their debates in public.

Attention had fallen on the question of precisely how Jesus Christ was related to God. All were agreed that polytheism was not an option; hence they had to face the task of relating Jesus the Messiah to the God whom Jesus had called his Father. The fourth century saw the definitive break of the Church with its Jewish origins. By and large, when the New Testament showed people answering the question of who Jesus was, they generally used the terms 'prophet' or 'Messiah', and left it at that. Later erudite Christians were unable to leave matters there.

The Hellenists, under the influence of Greek culture, wanted to take the matter into greater philosophical depth, and the result was the introduction of technical terms in keeping with Greek philosophy. Thus Constantine's search for theological as well as political peace and unity coincided with the increasing Hellenization of Christian thought. The adoption of philosophical terms played a large part in fomenting divisions between different schools and even between bishops, each of whom declared himself to be orthodox and his opponents to be heretical.

The notion of orthodoxy seems to have formally originated in the fourth century, and it became important for more than theological reasons. It also put more emphasis on technically correct terminology, sometimes at the expense of fidelity to the Gospel. The Emperor left it to the church to decide which theological opinions were orthodox, but he made it very clear that any divagation from the declared orthodoxy was politically unacceptable. This led to the unhappy precedent of the persecution of dissenters, which, in changed historical circumstances, continued through the centuries. Hellenization had the effect of making philosophical reflection on the nature(s) of Christ more important than the simple vision of the meaning of the reign of God and Jesus' role in it. In effect, at Nicaea Athens went some way towards complicating the message of Jerusalem. Although the Catholic Church of today is no longer actively concerned with philosophical problems about Jesus Christ, the trinitarian and christological formulas approved at Nicea remain its formal teaching on God and Jesus. Today, sound preaching and catechesis is thankfully more concerned with Jerusalem than with Athens; nevertheless, theologians have to keep a weather eye on the fourth and fifth century councils, because, although the formulas of these councils were framed in what is to us today a culturally remote age, they constitute the defined teaching of the church. To be christologically orthodox in the twenty-first century, faithful Catholic theologians are forced to return to the culture of the fourth century to find a definition of what they are bound to believe. This illustrates the problems that arise from a rigid conception of orthodox church teaching that disregards the theological significance of changing cultures and issues definitions that are deemed to be timelessly valid.[2]

One can only regret the alleged gap between doctrinal orthodoxy and the real daily concerns of Christians today. The magisterium of the Catholic Church seems to regard obedience to its teaching, in any age, to be the touchstone of faithful membership of the Church. It gives the impression that the fact of its teaching seems to be more important than its content. At least in the fourth century the debates, although conducted in recondite language, were about the central issues of God and Christ.

The Emperor Theodosius the Great (347-395) completed Constantine's vision of a united church-state by outlawing paganism and making Christianity the exclusive imperial religion. The establishment of Christianity as a state religion set a truly unfortunate precedent for centuries to come, when secular rulers imposed their own religious opinions on their subjects. What happened in the fourth century played a major part in creating the sort of church structures we have today, even though most states have ceased to see church institutions as relevant to national politics.

Definitive reform of the church may well depend on a radical break with the precedent of establishment and the consequent persecution of non-conformists. Establishment can be formal, as in the Church of England, or informal as in the Irish Catholic Church since the foundation of the State in 1922. In England the incorporation of the Anglican Church into social and political life is not retained today by the State for religious reasons, but rather for constitutional convenience. Disestablishment would have intricate constitutional consequences. There are members of the Church of England who support establishment largely because it keeps

2. For an example of this cultural / theological problem, see the account, in Chapter 10, of how Elizabeth Johnson's tackles it.

some vestige of religion in the public arena, such as prayers in parliament or the presence of bishops in the House of Lords. Others, however, would like to see disestablishment as creating a truly free Church. The Church of Ireland was disestablished in 1869, and some of those who had earlier opposed disestablishment made a virtue of necessity by accepting the State's politically inspired decision, and proclaiming that 'today the Church goes free'.

In Ireland the current influence of the Catholic Church has been greatly diminished, because secularism and a more relaxed view of religion have become increasingly prevalent in society, and because there is resentment of the authoritarian way in which the church has behaved in the recent past, and especially of its creation of fear throughout Irish society.

Leaving aside the matter of establishment, the influence of Nicaea can still be seen in the employment in the Creed of the highly technical term *homousios*, translated in the latest version imposed on the English-speaking Catholic Churches as 'consubstantial', though previously more sensibly and intelligibly rendered as 'of one Being with' the Father. The recent imposition of a new translation has reverted to 'consubstantial', perhaps because it sounds more 'orthodox'.

Many Fathers of the first ecumenical council were unhappy that a solemn teaching of the church was employing a non-biblical term. The main reason why this had happened was that a presbyter named Arius had used the term to deny the eternal Son's equality with the Father. The bishops of the council felt obliged to rule out the teaching of Arius in as firm and decisive a manner as possible; and they clearly felt that the best way to do this was by a formal rejection of Arius's denial that the Son is 'one in substance with the Father'. They used the term *homousios* affirmatively by denying Arius' denial, and thus the church was left with an unavoidable non-biblical term in the first of its solemn professions of faith.

The fact that the liturgy of the Mass today again employs the term 'consubstantial' in the creed, and that few people in the congregation can be expected to understand what it means, makes its use hard to justify. What is being achieved by doing so? It would be interesting to know why the re-introduction of the technical term 'consubstantial', was considered necessary by liturgists responsible to the guardians of orthodoxy. Why has the church continued to employ a non-biblical term in a solemn profession of faith, when a plain biblical one would be more suited to the liturgy? The reason would seem to be that the verbal interpretation of doctrine, conservatively understood, remains in force, in spite of Pope John XXIII's distinction between the substance of faith and the manner of its formulation. Arianism is not a live issue in the church today; so the original reason for using the term 'consubstantial' is no longer relevant, unless one asks questions about the nature(s) of Christ in the philosophical language current in the fourth century. Are we still embedded in a verbal understanding of how God communicates with human beings?

This verbal understanding of technical terms can be found elsewhere in church usage. Transubstantiation, for example, is a highly technical term which ought never to have been brought into everyday usage. It should have remained in the studies of theologians where it was first conjured up. Today it is bandied about as if its meaning is self-evident – which it most certainly is not. One cannot 'believe in' transubstantiation, which is a philosophical term at one time conveniently expressing, for theologians, the real presence of Christ in the Eucharist. The church has said that it is not competent to impose any philosophical system in the name of faith, though it can say that a particular philosophy fittingly expresses a doctrine, as the Council of Trent did with the notion of transubstantiation:

> [T]hrough consecration of the bread and wine there comes about a conversion of the whole substance of the bread into the substance of the body of Christ our Lord, and of the whole substance of the wine into the substance of his blood. And this conversion is by the Holy Catholic Church conveniently and properly called transubstantiation.[3]

As long as Catholics are speaking the same philosophical language as the Fathers of Trent, they may fittingly use the technical term 'transubstantiation' as a description of what happens to the elements in the Eucharist. Trent does not say that Catholics have to use the term, only that its use was 'fitting and apt' in the sixteenth century. After all, the church got on without the term for a thousand years; therefore it follows logically that it cannot be an indispensable part of Christian teaching.

3. Session XIII, October 1551. Englans translation, Henry Bettenson and Chris Maunder (editors), *Documents of the Christian Church*, fourth edition (Oxford: Oxford University Press, 2011), p. 267.

Rather, it is a theological development that is valid only in its own highly specialized culture.

I realise that many people are bored with theological niceties; but if they use complex theological terms like transubstantiation, they cannot reasonably avoid attending to the theology involved. If they misuse the term, they may cause needless confusion. People who are self-appointed guardians of orthodoxy too often misuse the term transubstantiation.

Catholics sometimes employ the term as a synonym for 'real presence' – which it is not. Real presence is an essential element in Christian doctrine, though it may not be the best way of conveying the truth and relevance of the Eucharist. In any celebration of the Eucharist, Christ is really present not only in the elements of bread and wine, but also in the entire liturgical assembly. That the Eucharist is a meal is of primary importance to its meaning. Perhaps one of the most disturbing features about the use of the term transubstantiation as an ordinary word is that, detached from its proper theological context, it is sometimes taken to mean physical change, which would be not alone heretical but plainly and empirically untrue.

Transubstantiation is a metaphysical term, and, in an age that is heavily influenced by science, and especially by scientism, people rarely think metaphysically or ontologically. If the term transubstantiation is removed from its metaphysical context and used empirically, it loses its proper meaning and easily acquires a meaning that is false.

I would wish to argue that this is what has happened today. It is quite incorrect to claim that Catholics have to 'believe' in transubstantiation; yet this is what one hears time and again, because it has become a mindless and needless slogan to distinguish Catholics from Protestants. One cannot 'believe' in a metaphysical term: one either accepts it, modifies it or rejects it. One can be a perfectly orthodox Catholic and never use the term transubstantiation. If one does use it correctly, then one must believe that in the Eucharist the 'substance' changes while the 'accidents' remain. The fact is that people today do not think metaphysically, in terms of 'substance' and 'accidents', and so the word transubstantiation means little or nothing to them. They use it as a slogan: 'Catholics believe in transubstantiation' (with the implication that Protestants don't).

To those who were present at the Last Supper it was the occasion that mattered, and without being scholars they were able to think poetically and with imagination about the meal that Jesus left them as a memorial of his passion, death and resurrection. They were accustomed to Jesus speaking symbolically and parabolically. He used this kind of language to make people think, and, in the case of his disciples, he explained his meaning later in discussion with them (Matthew 13:34). Mark puts the matter particularly directly: 'He did not speak to them except in parables, but he explained everything in private to his disciples.' (Mark 4:34)

'How can this man give us his flesh to eat?' (John 6:52) Even in biblical times there were people who had literal minds! Chapter 6 of John's Gospel makes it clear that Jesus employs the symbol of eating his flesh and drinking his blood to refer to the total attitude of believers towards him as Son of the Father. The Eucharist is a tacit liturgical expression of a comprehensive act of faith in Jesus Christ, and not simply of his presence in the elements of bread and wine. Chapter 6 of John's Gospel provides a theologically rich background to the last meal that Jesus ate with his disciples on the eve of his crucifixion.

In the course of the meal, he took a loaf, broke off pieces of it and distributed them to the disciples, saying, 'This is my body'. Then he took a cup of wine and gave it to them to drink, saying, 'This is my blood'. (Mark 14:22-25). Both offerings were a clear symbolic gesture of his union with them. One cannot think that any of them wondered what had happened to the bread and wine that he had just given them. They were focused upon the meaning of the entire occasion, including his washing of their feet, which theoretically could have become an officially sanctioned sacrament and is an important part of the liturgy of Holy Thursday.

St Paul, reflecting on the significance of the last supper, adds that Jesus exhorted his disciples: 'Do this … in remembrance of me. For as often as you eat this bread and drink the cup, you proclaim the Lord's death until he comes'. Thus Paul links the supper with the sacrifice of Jesus' life that was to occur on the next day. (1 Corinthians 11:25-26) It was a daring thought, and it opened up a valuable direction for eucharistic theology; but it was also one that was later to prove needlessly contentious, because there were Protestants who believed that Catholic doctrine proclaimed that every celebration of the Eucharist was a new sacrifice; and Catholics did little enough to disabuse them of this belief.

Speculation about the meaning of sacrifice would follow in the later church; and it would become another cause of utterly needless division between Catholics and Protestants. The eucharistic liturgy is not a separate, new act of sacrifice each time it is celebrated. It is a liturgical and sacramental re-presentation of Christ's once-for-all sacrifice of himself on Calvary.

The early church practised the discipline of the secret (*Disciplina Arcani*) as concealment from pagans of certain doctrines and practices in a time of persecution, and from catechumens, possibly to heighten their expectation of learning about the mysteries of their faith in and after their Baptism. It could be interesting to ask whether a similar kind of reticence might be fruitfully practised today. Certainly it is of no benefit to Christian faith to allow a technical term like transubstantiation to be so freely bandied about and misinterpreted. Speaking in Dublin in 2012, Richard Dawkins, the well-known professional atheist, remarked in his familiar and magisterial fashion: 'If they don't believe in transubstantiation then they are not Roman Catholics'.[4] So there: now you know. The atheistic magisterium, which often has a poor grasp of reputable modern Christian theology, has spoken and defined how Catholics should think about the Eucharist! The fact that an intelligent man like Dawkins can make an *ex cathedra* pronouncement of this kind is a warning of how easily popular misconceptions can become dogmas in the minds of even intelligent people like Professor Dawkins, whose desire to attack religion sometimes overpowers his understanding of it.

In a non-metaphysical age like ours, the term transubstantiation, if not used correctly, can actually promote a misunderstanding of the Eucharist. This can happen if Athens is mindlessly allowed to replace Jerusalem instead of complementing it. Cultures change; and the culture which produced the term transubstantiation is gone. The term was always technical and should never have been used in ordinary parlance, least of all as a test of orthodoxy.

The journey from the simplicities of the Gospel to the complexities of subsequent Christian thought is engrossing, and sometimes disconcerting. Responses to it range from acceptance of it as an inevitable develop-

4. As reported in *The Irish Times*, Thursday, June 7, 2012, p. 13.

ment, on the one hand, to resounding disapproval, on the other. We can hardly deny that there is often a difficulty, at any given time, in relating the complexities of later ecclesiastical situations and statements to the simplicities of the Galilean spring, when the Good News of salvation was first proclaimed. Athens can sometimes overwhelm Jerusalem.

What needs to be preserved is not a literal reproduction of life in Galilee 2,000 years ago, even if that were possible, but interpretation of the spirit that inspired the Gospel in that age. The Good Samaritan could be flying in a space ship just as easily as walking along a road. It is true that some people take refuge from the materialism of the present age by living an artificially simple way of life. Most Christians, however, would see this way of life as anachronistic and possibly contrived. There are undeniable problems in applying evangelical attitudes, which occurred in a rural setting, to the complex situations we encounter in the northern hemisphere today, especially in cities. Trying literally to recreate today the conditions that obtained in Galilee 2,000 years ago is implausible, and any attempt to do so runs the risk of artificiality.

From early in the church's history attempts have been made to establish places dedicated to living the Christian life in as perfect a way as possible. Monastic life has been an attempt to express the simplicities of evangelical life in secluded locations. The Rule of St Benedict regulated monastic life in Europe from the sixth century, and it attempted to adopt a form of religious life that was a moderate reflection of the austere ideals of the more primitive Desert Fathers of an earlier age. Throughout the Middle Ages monasteries often grew rich and powerful, and were reformed by monks intent on recovering the relatively austere simplicities of the Rule of St Benedict. Reform in this context normally meant a return to a simpler and more ascetic way of life.

In the thirteenth century the expansion of towns called for a different and more active form of religious life, and the call was answered by the mendicant friars who chose to live in the towns rather than in segregated monasteries, so that they could minister to the spiritual needs of the people.

After the Reformation came the Jesuits and a host of other congregations dedicated to meeting the needs of the developing modern world. The new forms of religious life did not replace the old ones, which continued to exist in tandem with them and often to be influenced by them. In each case, religious orders responded to the spiritual needs of the age and reflected the religious values of society.

Today in many parts of the western world members of religious orders are experiencing a crisis of meaning, as well as having to face an unnerving diminution in members. As the distinguished English Dominican, Timothy Radcliffe, has put it: 'We are like blacksmiths in a world of cars, looking for a new role.' Quite possibly that role will call for a very different kind of life. At present in many religious houses the middle-aged are looking after a growing body of elderly brothers and sisters. The challenge will always be to try to express Gospel values in a contemporary setting and willingly to undergo the discomfort of responding to historical change.

For most thoughtful Christians today what needs to be done is to study the Gospel in its own original setting, and then to interpret it in ways that are appropriate to ours. In carrying out this task there is room for differences of interpretation; but that enriches rather than militates against the effort to remain faithful to the Gospel.

From the earliest age of the Church it became clear to some influential Christians that they had to engage with secular culture, if they were to fulfill Christ's mandate to teach all nations. (One early and notable convert to Christianity, Justin Martyr, who was a philosopher by profession, chose to become a Christian for explicitly philosophical reasons.) The problem was, and still is, how cultural accommodation of the New Testament to later ages could be achieved without loss of its original directness and simplicity.

The Christian Church has been contending with that problem for two millennia, and it is why we need constantly to keep in mind that we are members of a sinful but unceasingly forgiven church, not members of a triumphant society, free from all blemish and set up by God to be honoured as a theocratic and sinless establishment. (Pope Francis' obvious discomfort with his palatial surroundings points to the desirability of a simpler and less monarchical style of papal leadership.) Christians are forgiven sinners; and the societies to which they belong are flawed, though always capable of being 'justified' by God's grace. We are well used to the notion of individual and personal repentance; we may, however, be rather less inclined to think of the church as being in need of institutional repentance, in spite of the copious evidence provided by history.

Furthermore, it is appropriate to regard even our theology as being in need of repentance, since it tries presumptuously to explicate the unfathomable mystery of God. Christian theology comes about when the meaning of Christian faith is subjected to cultural, especially philosophical, examination. This process is always at risk of obscuring the message of the Gospel; but the risk has to be taken in the light of that same Gospel. The parable of the talents seems relevant here (Matthew 25:14-30). If it is to win a hearing for itself among thoughtful people, Christian faith has to encounter the prevailing culture of any age, and possibly to use the cultural and philosophical currency of the age for clearer contemporary understanding of Christian belief.

Whether this could be done without damage to the integrity of faith was, in the early ages of the Church, an urgent question for many thoughtful Christians, and opinions differed on it. In the first few centuries of its existence Christianity had to face the question of whether it should try to engage with the prevailing Hellenistic philosophy. In the pre-scientific era Greek philosophy was regarded as the highest exemplar of human intellectual life, and it might have amounted to a culpable lack of confidence in the robust truth of the Gospel to have failed to engage with it. There have, however, always been Christians who feel called upon to warn against the involvement of their faith with human wisdom and scholarly techniques. It has to be immediately admitted that they have some impressive biblical authority on their side. No less an authority than St Paul can be quoted pertinently. In a letter to his unruly and largely unlettered flock in the commercial seaport of Corinth, Paul wrote:

> Christ sent me ... to preach the gospel ... not with eloquent wisdom, lest the cross of Christ be emptied of its power. For the word of the cross is folly to those who are perishing, but to us who are being saved it is the power of God (1 Corinthians 1:17-18).

Inspired by texts as uncompromising as this, Christians have sometimes been ready to decry the dangers for the church of associating with the world of contemporary learning.

Tertullian, the fierce and puritanical North African scholar, sent a defiant question hurtling down the ages: 'What has Athens to do with Jerusalem?' (*'Quid Athenae Hierosolymis?'*)

What has the Academy to do with the Church...? Away with all attempts to produce a Stoic, Platonic and dialectical Christianity. We want no curious disputation after possessing Christ Jesus; we need no learned seminars after receiving the Gospel.[5]

Tertullian was a distinguished lawyer who engaged with many of the intellectual issues of his day and frequently broke with his own unfavourable view of the Academy; but if he had had his way, theoretically there would be no developed Christian theology. This may sometimes seem an attractive possibility; but consider what it would have meant: There would only be what church leaders of a later age have patronisingly called 'the simple faithful', by which they meant illiterate men and women ready to submit unthinkingly either to the authority of an administrative élite or to the authority of a book read for them in isolation from its historical context. With the advance of education in the developed world, the primitive concept of 'the simple faithful' has disappeared, and the Gospel has had to be presented in a more sophisticated way; and this holds out the challenge of doing so without loss of the simple directness of the original message. Today we have to reckon with the need for a 'second naiveté' that can look at the simplicities of the Gospel through educated spectacles. From earliest times Christian theology has witnessed to the church's theoretical rejection of an uncritical faith.

I say 'theoretical', because the sad truth is that the Christian Church has often failed to live up to the implications of its professed conviction that faith needs to be both intelligent and free, that it should never be imposed by decree, and that it must win a hearing for itself in conditions of exterior and interior liberty. Freedom of faith is inseparable from a freely practised theology – a sentiment that is at the heart of reform in the Catholic Church. Christian theology is no more than faith's inadequate attempt to understand itself and to give an account of itself to intelligent enquirers. It refuses Wittgenstein's famous (and later disowned) dictum: 'Whereof one cannot speak, thereof one must be silent'. The theologian may not indeed be able to speak with the assurance of, say, the economist or the sociologist, but he or she can at least stammer purposefully. If there is a place for wise silence (and many Christian mystics have dwelt on the

5. Tertullian, *De Praescriptione Haereticorum*, VII.

need for silence in its rightful place), there is also a place for humble stammering. We have to speak about God so that God may use our halting words to speak to us. The influential German theologian, Rudolf Bultmann, regarded theology as a sinful activity. He had, of course, the advantage of being a Lutheran and therefore he could add, 'Get on with it, *pecca fortiter*, be confident in spite of sin, since God forgives us even our theology'!

Theology is not faith; it is faith's conscience, guardian and sometimes hair shirt. Responsible theology helps to keep faith honest and tries to prevent it from turning into just another ideology, or from falling victim to fundamentalism.

St Augustine answered Tertullian, his fellow- African, effectively when he wrote:

> Far be it from us to suppose that God abhors in us that by virtue of which he has made us superior to other animals. Far be it from us, I say, that we should believe in order that we may reject reason, or cease to seek it; since we could not even believe unless we possessed rational souls. [6]

This was the reflection of the former professor from Carthage, who, while he bitterly regretted his extracurricular social activities, never regretted his pursuit of knowledge through passing in and out of different philosophical schools.

So long as intelligent men and women ask questions about the transcendent, about the realm beyond sense experience, in short, about God, so long will there be a discipline called theology. It may have to be an 'unknown god', as St Paul is reputed to have put it in Athens.[7] Theology no longer has the role, and the prestige, that it had in the Middle Ages, when it was regarded as the 'queen of the sciences', and the challenge of modernity lay still in the future. Adversity should have educated it in a becoming humility and inspired it with repentance for past and present arrogance. Today, Christian thinking has to win a place for itself in the currency of modern commercialism and the dominance of science and technology, so that it wins the right to criticize secular society when the

6. Augustine, *Ep.*120:3
7. Acts 17:23. Some scholars have questioned the historical accuracy of Paul's visit to Athens, as described in Acts.

occasion demands. It can only criticize the secular world with authenticity, however, if it is willing to criticize its own faults publicly.

The voice of Tertullian speaks again, though without his learning and sophistication, through fundamentalists who believe that theologians spend most of their time and energy watering down the pure wine of the Gospel. Atheist critics may find it easier to deal with fundamentalists than with critically minded believers. Professor Basil Mitchell has remarked that the non-believing academic critic prefers

> theology to be doctrinaire enough to be discounted with impunity. We are more comfortable with stereotypes. We are happy to know that our theologians are doctrinaire and irrelevant, just as we are happy to know that our dons are remote and ineffectual. [8]

The message of Christianity will always present a scandal, a stumbling-block, to worldly wisdom. But it is the task of theology to see to it that the Christian Church confronts both itself and the world with the right scandal, not with one of its own shortsighted and arrogant devising. Christians are commissioned to preach the truth of a man who was nailed to a tree, to proclaim to the world that God raised Jesus of Nazareth from the dead, and that Jesus gives all life its ultimate meaning. That message is startling enough, without obscuring it with outmoded orthodoxies, backed up by acts that are embarrassingly inconsistent with the Gospel that it preaches.

8. B. Mitchell, *Law, Morality and Religion in a Secular Society*, (Oxford University Press, 1967) p.115.

12

Fundamentalism

'Fundamentalism' can be a rather slippery word. However, there was a time when it was used confidently and without embarrassment as a self-definition. Its origins are to be found in early 20th century American Protestantism. When it is used theologically in reference to Roman Catholicism, it is by way of analogy.

The defining element in original Protestant fundamentalism, and in all later derivations of it, is a fierce opposition to academic liberalism, understood as any attempt to bring Christianity into a fruitful relationship with modern thought. There are many different types of fundamentalism, but anti-modernism (or anti-liberalism) is a constant element in all of them. Fundamentalism, strictly speaking, is always a response to a perceived and unacceptable liberalisation of thought. It is a major obstacle to reform; and it has to be carefully reckoned with by anyone who is serious about reform. Fundamentalists can think of themselves as reformers when they are dealing with liberals; one therefore has to be aware of the context of every instance of fundamentalism.

When in the 1900s the Southern Californian oil millionaire, Lyman Stewart, was looking for an editor for what he planned as a series of paperback books intended to be a *Testimonial to the Truth*, he chose A. C. Dixon, a well-known evangelist whom he had heard preaching against 'one of those infidel professors in [the University of] Chicago'. The result was a series of twelve tracts published between 1910 and 1915 under the general title of *The Fundamentals*. In 1920, a Baptist editor, Curtis Lee Laws, defined a fundamentalist as one who was 'ready to do battle royal for the Fundamentals of the faith.' (Pugnacity is a common feature of fundamentalism.)

From the start, the term was not merely reactive; it was unapologetically adversarial. Fundamentalism set out to oppose any academic theology that struck it as watering down the pure doctrine of Christian faith. Dixon's phrase 'infidel professor' is a clue to what conservative American Protestantism was worried about. The battle, then, was between Christians who wanted to 'make their faith intelligible to the increasingly secular mind of the nineteenth and twentieth centuries',[1] and Christians who believed that this would be achieved only at the unacceptable cost of the integrity of the essentials, the 'fundamentals, of the faith'.

A public crisis for early fundamentalism came in 1925 when a Tennessee biology teacher, John Scopes, was prosecuted for teaching Darwinism in a public school. The prosecution was led by a prominent fundamentalist, William Jennings Bryan, and the defence was led by a brilliant and urbane agnostic, Clarence Darrow, who destroyed Bryan in court, largely by ridicule. The 'Monkey Trial', as it was sometimes known, became a *cause célébre* around the world. As a result, the word 'fundamentalism' received a particular focus and reference, and with it, a name for bigotry and opposition to science. It came to be seen in the USA as synonymous with small-town obscurantism. 'Organized ignorance' was how one hostile critic described it. Fundamentalists were not necessarily anti-intellectual; they were anti-academic. They believed that universities were doing damage to faith.

The theory of evolution had become, and was to remain, a major symbolic issue between modernists and fundamentalists. In hard-line Protestant fundamentalism, the theory of evolution has been seen as utterly opposed to Christian faith. The early chapters of the Book of Genesis are taken as a literal account of what actually happened historically. Science has long since shown that the earth is billions of years old, and that *homo sapiens* evolved from more primitive animal species. Fundamentalism flees from the task of reflecting theologically on what science has revealed. Religious fundamentalism simply invites the scorn of scientifically educated people, and thereby does gratuitous and serious damage to the reputation of the Christian Church and its members; and it confirms atheists and agnostics in the correctness of their rejection of religious faith.

On the whole, the magisterium of the Roman Catholic Church has reacted less intemperately to the theory of evolution, which it never formally condemned, as long as certain doctrines were safeguarded. Papal statements have evolved since the time of Darwin down to our own

---

1. Langdon Gilkey, *Naming the Whirlwind: The Renewal of God-Language* (1976).

century, and today the Vatican does not regard the theory of evolution as dangerous to faith. However, as long as one accepts that souls do not evolve but are directly created by God, evolution of the body can be accepted, indeed welcomed, as a theory. Platonist dualism rides again in this view of things, but at least it avoids the crude anti-scientific attitude of biblical fundamentalists.

Apologists for 'creationism' sometimes claim that evolution is 'only a theory'. This observation indicates a serious misunderstanding of the scientific use of the word 'theory'. All scientific claims are theoretically open to being revised by further evidence or convincing argument. Thus, Newtonian physics is supplemented by Einstein's physics, which in turn has been questioned by quantum theorists.

Theological language operates quite differently; and it is saddening to see religious fundamentalists setting up a totally unnecessary conflict between science and religion. Just as theologians have no competence to oppose science in the name of religious beliefs, scientists have no competence to oppose rational religious beliefs in the name of science. Fundamentalists play into their hands by declaring unscientific views to be religious orthodoxy. Religious fundamentalism, if taken as an accurate manifestation of religion, does enormous harm to Christianity by setting up a false dichotomy between religion and science. Scientists have good reason to deride anti-evolutionism, and theologically educated believers have every reason to protest against the kind of scientism that insists upon setting up a confrontation between a scientific and a religious interpretation of creation. As believing Christians, we need both: the God of creation cannot be different from the God of revelation.

Allowing for differences of content and context, there seems to be no reason why we cannot speak of Catholic fundamentalism. (After all, the term is widely used in reference to Islam, which is further removed from American Protestantism than is Roman Catholicism.)

Dr John D'Arcy May, recently of the Irish School of Ecumenics, in his contribution to a volume on the CDF's Declaration, *Dominus Jesus* (August 6, 2000), writes:

John Baptist Metz once remarked that there is no reason, in principle, why the Roman Catholic Church, despite its enormous size and global presence, could not become a sect. Sectarianism is a matter of mentality, not size, and one of its presuppositions is the fundamentalist mindset.

He goes on to quote James Barr, one of the first theologians to take fundamentalism with academic seriousness, as saying that fundamentalism 'is not organisationally, but only intellectually a sect'.

> Fundamentalism is a particular form of reaction to modernity, de-fensive and hostile yet in a paradoxical way rationalistic, for the basic strategy is to declare certain doctrines and principles of interpretation valid *a priori* and therefore immune from literary contextualisation or historical criticism.[2]

This could be read as an accurate description of the strategy adopted by some, at least, of the Roman Curia, and it might suggest a reason for concluding that the curia sometimes behaves in a fundamentalist manner, especially when it protects itself from rational criticism by taking refuge in an *a priori* claim to immunity from criticism!

When we use the term 'Catholic fundamentalism' we need to remember that the condition it describes preceded Protestant fundamentalism by at least a century, and is generally known as integralism. Catholic fundamen-talism reacted against what had happened in general post-Enlightenment thought, philosophical as well as scientific, which it saw as inimical to Catholic doctrine. Rome was, as it were, getting its retaliation in first.

Hostile reaction to Vatican II is merely the intensification of an instinct that was already potentially present since the pontificate of Pius IX. If one of the defining characteristics of fundamentalism is an antagonistic response to the challenge of modernity, and another is a strong inclina-tion to distinguish sharply between the supernatural and the natural, then the nineteenth century papacy anticipated much of what the authors of *The Fundamentals* were later to diagnose and prescribe against. In the period between the two Vatican Councils, the Catholic Church shared with conservative Protestantism an opposition to much modern secular culture. Its focus differed from that of twentieth century Protestantism,

2. John D'Arcy May, 'Catholic Fundamentalism? Some Implications of *Dominus Jesus* for Dialogue and Peacemaking', in Michael J, Rainer (ed), *"Dominus Jesus", anstöBige Wahrheit oder anstöBihe Kirche? Dokumente, Hintergrunde, Standpunkte und Folgerungen,* (Munster, no date), p. 114.

since Roman Catholicism traditionally tends to concentrate on authority, most notably on that of the papacy and its court.

Rome's condemnation of Modernism in the early twentieth century was a discreditable victory, achieved, as it was, by brute force rather than by argument, over an abortive attempt to bring Catholicism into fruitful relationship with the modern world. Intransigent conservatives at Vatican II were still talking, with anachronistic implausibility, about the dangers of 'Modernism'.

The condemnation of Modernism in 1907-1910 ensured that, with some distinguished exceptions, Catholic theologians would remain in protective custody for the next half-century. Eventually, Vatican II would let them out to undergo the same 'cognitive misery' as enlightened Protestant theologians had been experiencing for over a century.

Facing modernity has been, and continues to be, an arduous and, for Catholics, a hazardous task. It is not made any easier by the Roman assault on progressive Catholics who are trying to make their faith intelligible to themselves and to contemporary men and women. As an exasperated Nicholas Lash exclaimed many years ago about the Vatican: 'When will they recognise who their friends are?' There are, of course, some matters to oppose in post-Enlightenment secular thought, but the opposition needs to be informed, measured, reasonable and ready to make wise concessions when they are seen to be necessary. The Gospel does not require a retreat from living in the world of our time.

An important difference between Catholic and Protestant modernists is that Protestants have received and absorbed their shocks in comparatively small doses and over an extended period; while Catholics got theirs in one high tension burst, as they absorbed vast quantities of cognitive radiation from both the Reformation and the Enlightenment at the same time. In less than a decade, Roman Catholicism underwent what was for most of its theologians an exciting transformation of previous attitudes and beliefs, but which also left some Catholics severely shaken and disorientated. The very source of their ecclesiastically based faith – a pope and a council – was, it seemed to them, trying to shepherd them in a direction that was away from much that they had been taught to believe and to treasure as distinctively Catholic. A few, such as the followers of Archbishop Lefebvre, simply set up a schismatic church, and, in the event, ordained their own bishops. Rome is still trying to entice them back.

Most have remained in the church and hoped for a return to the old ways. They have been faced with a distressing dilemma: how to remain with the old ways without publicly disagreeing with a pope and a council. The argument from conscience played little part in their way of faith and life. Some of them simply appealed to the old ways, contrasting Pope Pius X, whom they regarded as the foremost pope of the twentieth century, with the majority of members of the council that had so rudely disturbed their way of life and belief. They made it abundantly clear that they repudiated the council, and they sought to justify their stance by appealing to pre-conciliar pronouncements.

The Second Vatican Council put an end to Catholic hostility towards Anglicans and Protestants. The resulting situation was one of openness to Protestant attitudes and a willingness to look again at the reasons for the Reformation. The fundamentalist reactionaries took to blaming ecumenists for a capitulation to Protestantism. They often resort to using the term 'Protestant' as an automatic condemnation of reforming attitudes. Ecumenically disposed Catholics have realised that there is little hope of dialogue with these unreformed fellow Catholics.

Reaction to post-enlightenment modernity took a different course. When the church turned to face the challenge to Christian faith of modernity, modernity itself was in trouble. The experience of facing its challenge, though exhilarating, has been not unlike joining a ship in keen anticipation of an exciting voyage, only to discover that the ship has been quietly corroding below the water line, and that much of the voyage will have to be spent manning the pumps. Catholic theology had been saved from biblical fundamentalism by the fact that it had been taught to prioritise Tradition (understood as papal and conciliar authority) over Scripture, and that its late rediscovery of the Bible went hand in hand with modern critical biblical scholarship.

The last half-century has been a unique period in the history of the Catholic Church. Many bishops at Vatican II had to be informed about modern critical biblical scholarship, because for most of them it had had no place in their clerical education. These years have witnessed a radical break with the recent past. From the start it was probable that there would be a backlash against the consequences of Vatican II, if not indeed against the council itself. Clearly, Rome, in spite of its frequent alarm at some of the changes made possible by Vatican II, could hardly take a public stance against the council or even be seen to disapprove of it.

In spite of their defeat at the hands of the progressive majority at the council, however, some of the intransigently conservative minority fought on in support of their cause. Most of them have been able to avoid public condemnation of the council by keeping their opposition private and by putting the blame on the initiatives that were taken in its wake. These initiatives, not all of which, admittedly, were prudent, were an inevitable consequence of the freedom from the restrictions of the pre-conciliar church. Many neo-conservatives today ascribe failures in the contemporary church to the spirit of freedom released by the Second Vatican Council.

Pope Paul VI fretted about much that was happening in the church, but before his stand against contraception, he was not a fundamentalist and was too committed to the vision and authority of Vatican II to give his approval to a revolution against it. Nevertheless, he remained disconcertingly ambivalent about the role of his own office and its relationship with the rest of the church. The ambiguity of his papacy resulted from his attempts to reach a consensus between the conciliar reformers and the intransigent traditionalists – something that Pope Francis is still trying to do.

The real problem lies in the fact that the two mindsets are mutually contradictory and are not open to compromise. The most damaging instance was one far-reaching decision, when, in his encyclical, *Humanae Vitae* (1968), Paul chose to reject the counsel of the group he had set up to advise him on marriage, sexuality and the family, and opted instead for a reiteration of the ban on contraception, not because of a concern with sexual morality, but principally because of previous papal pronouncements on it. *Humanae Vitae* was a highly symbolic act, concerned more with church authority than with the substantive moral issues that were its ostensible concern. It was not that Paul was inflexible in matters of sexual morality; what really worried him was what he felt to be the onus on him to preserve the integrity of his predecessors' teaching. Pius XI's encyclical, *Casti Conubii* had set a formidable precedent, and would remain an insoluble problem for any pope or bishop who believes in the permanent validity of papal statements.

Humanae Vitae created an instant crisis in the church marked by protests, defiance, a considerable number of defections and a great deal of disillusionment. The encyclical quickly became a rallying point for Catholic fundamentalists and a cause of dismay to those who were trying to meet the reasonable advances of modernity. Even bishops not known for liberal thinking sought to soften the impact of the encyclical, while preserving the image of fidelity to the Vatican. Many priests in the confessional, usually by their silence, encouraged their penitents not to confess contraception as a sin. Gradually most penitents have ceased to do so.

The non-reception of *Humanae Vitae* by the great majority of Catholics became a well-recognized fact, though Rome still refuses to accept that fact and resolutely insists on the permanent validity of traditional papal teaching on it by the Catholic Church. One cannot help describing this attitude as fundamentalist. Rome continues to describe the non-reception of *Humanae Vitae* as reprehensible dissent; but that does nothing to change the actual situation. Eventually the papacy will have to face up to the fact that it needs to engage with substantive issues in their own right instead of being obsessed with its own authority. That obsession will have to be reformed before the Vatican ceases to promote a comprehensively outmoded attitude to birth control and other moral issues.

Unwarranted emphasis on the continuity of church teaching ignores the cultural changes attested to by history. After all, today's papacy no longer shares the attitude of medieval popes who, for example, believed in the efficacy and rightness of crusades; yet it refuses to admit that papal teaching can change in spite of the demonstrable fact that it has changed many times. Pope John Paul II formally retracted the condemnation of Galileo by Pope Urban VIII and the Inquisition. If the magisterium can change its enthusiastic sponsoring of crusades, and its condemnation of Galileo, why can it not change on contraception? Concern for the sacredness of life was notably absent when the crusaders plundered Palestine with papal approval. The most momentous change of all occurred when, in the wake of Vatican II, neo-scholasticism was abandoned as a bastion of Catholic orthodoxy.

With few exceptions, Catholics took the conciliar changes in their stride. It was different in curial circles, which were unhappy with the apparent diminution of their power after the council. The less talk about collegiality, they felt, the better for them. In the atmosphere of freedom that followed on the council, there were, as one might have expected, some rather fanciful initiatives, but nothing a wise local leadership could not handle without having recourse to punitive action. Bishops should have been able by rational discussion to deal with any over-enthusiastic experiments; but they sometimes seem to have abrogated their own responsibility in the matter and have uneasily shifted the responsibility onto Rome as the safest course. This is the kind of ecclesiastical 'prudence' deplored by Pope Francis.

In spite of many similarities, there is one momentous difference between present neo-conservative thinking and the thinking that prevailed before the council. To the best of my knowledge, no attempt is being made today to reassert neo-scholasticism as a necessary philosophical substratum to orthodox Catholicism. That day has finally gone, to the relief of many contemporary Catholic theologians, who are now free to study Thomas Aquinas, not as the expression of mandatory orthodoxy, but in his own right as a brilliant thirteenth century thinker. However, the abandonment of neo-scholasticism leaves the papacy without an ideology strong enough to support its reactionary programme, and it poses the problem of explaining how Paul VI's encyclical must be obeyed, while Pius XII's encyclical, *Humani Generis*, can be tacitly set aside.

Abandonment of mandatory scholasticism has forced the papacy to turn a handful of scattered moral and disciplinary concerns into touchstones of orthodoxy – a poor substitute for a philosophical structure, which, however unconvincing as a standard of orthodoxy, was at least intellectually coherent. Benedict XVI's claim that Vatican II was 'in strictest continuity' with Trent and Vatican I was a controlling feature of his thought, though it is historically implausible:

There is no 'pre-' or 'post-' conciliar Church: there is but one, unique Church that walks the path toward the Lord.... There are no leaps in this history, there are no fractures, and there is no break in continuity. In no wise did the Council [Vatican II] intend to introduce a temporal dichotomy in the Church.[3]

To put it as kindly as possible, this is very special pleading indeed. It

3. *The Ratzinger Report*, p. 35. I am indebted to Jim Corkery, S.J., for quoting this passage in 'Vatican II and Its Reception in Ireland', *Doctrine & Life*, vol. 63, no. 6, July-August, 2013, p. 37.

chooses to ignore what ordinary historical observation reveals, and it proclaims a mystical image of church intended to obfuscate its human element. The real challenge is how to combine the mystical with the bureaucratic.

Catholic authorities traditionally like to affirm improbable continuities, even where discontinuities are historically plain. Matters of strict Christian faith may be said to be permanent; the theologies and politics that are associated with them are always changeable, and have changed, since they develop under the influence of different historical circumstances and evince obvious discontinuities.

During the Middle Ages the papacy presented itself as a politically active monarchy, and it had temporal estates to support its claim. At that time, to do so seemed the most effective way of establishing itself politically as a power to be reckoned with, although its actions could often be contrasted with the simplicity and moral teaching of the Gospel. Even leaving Gospel morality out of it, and appealing only to human rights, repression by the papal bureaucracy has often been manifestly unjust. The supernatural-ism that underlay traditional Catholic views of authority has been all too evident once again in its institutional structures and in the conduct of its leaders. Since the arrival of Pope Francis, there is some prospect of change in this respect, though he seems unduly sensitive to traditionalist anxieties about any relaxation of former papal teaching considered to be 'the untouchable teaching of the Church'.

Lord Acton's celebrated remark, that 'power tends to corrupt', loses none of its point when its context is religious (as it originally was). The purely human aspects of church government are acceptable in their place, as long as we remember that these aspects can easily corrupt or be corrupted, and as such must be constantly open to reform. God wills the church; but that does not mean that the church can apply to itself exclusively godly epithets.

When at Mass we pray, 'Look not on our sins, but on the faith of your church', we are using the word 'church' in its mystical sense. We could just as truthfully pray, 'Look not on the church's sinfulness, but on its holiness.' The church is both sinful and holy; and it takes a baptised imagination to be able to combine the two into a coherent expression of a faith that is made possible only by the conviction of divine forgiveness and acceptance. I am far from decrying the need for mysticism in its rightful place - which, however, is not to be found in church structures and the activities of aggressive curialists. Christians need to combine mysticism with common sense and with due regard for the weakness of the church as a flawed human community, presided over by a flawed leadership.

In point of fact, fundamentalism is a threat to the genuinely mystical element of religion. It is a narrow and rigid way of doing one's thinking. It is impatient with qualification, with shading, with hinting. It prefers plain blunt literal statements that destroy the possibility of nuance and imaginative suggestion. It dislikes the sort of dialectical thinking in which every assertion needs to be balanced against a counter-assertion, and which is particularly applicable to every statement we make about God. 'Negative theology' sees every statement made about God as being in need of correction by its opposite; and this serves constantly to remind us of the limitations of all theology. Fundamentalists rely on bald literalism to prosecute their case. Neither irony nor humour has any place in their thinking. John May remarks: 'As a Lutheran friend once neatly expressed it, "fundamentalists are people who don't understand poetry".' [4]

By way of further analogy, fundamentalism is a frame of mind that can be found also in scientists, journalists and positivist philosophers. I have seen university scientists distinctly nonplussed to find that there are modern Christian theologians who are more than happy to work with the theory of evolution, which they affirm, not as a concession to science, but with the same conviction as scientists do. Some scientistic[5] fundamentalists are under the impression that orthodox Christian faith rests squarely on a literal, historicized understanding of the early chapters of the Book of Genesis, and that therefore Christian ideas about creation are patently at odds with scientific truth. Biblical fundamentalists rejoice at this interpretation of creation, and like to parade it as an alternative to science; but it embarrasses most critically minded Christian theologians.

I have heard, on a radio programme, a university teacher dismissing religion with the remark, 'I'm a historian – I deal with facts.' The chairman and the other members of the panel let him away with a remark that was

4. Rainer,'*Dominus Jesus*', p. 114.
5. Scientism is excessive belief in the universal validity of scientific knowledge and techniques to the exclusion of all other modes of thought.

not merely arrogant but philosophically naive. He needed to have been asked: What is a fact? Who selects it, and who decides on its interpretation or on its relative significance? Athens can come to the assistance of Jerusalem when attacks on religion are as egregious as this.

The distinguished German-American Lutheran theologian, Reinhold Niebuhr, records in his notebook for 1927 the experience of being present as a young minister at an open forum at which he was asked when he thought the Lord would return, while another person tried to get him to agree that all religion is fantasy. Niebuhr wrote: 'How can an age which is so devoid of poetic imagination as ours be truly religious?' Interestingly, a year earlier, the Catholic poet and dramatist, Paul Claudel, reflecting on the aesthetic situation in eighteenth and nineteenth century Catholicism had written: 'The crisis ... was not primarily an intellectual crisis ... I would prefer to say it was the tragedy of a starved imagination'.

Niebuhr went on to remark that fundamentalists have one characteristic in common with most scientists: neither can understand that poetry and religion have a way of arriving at truth by giving a clue to the total meaning of things without resorting to an analytical description of detailed facts.

In the end, I believe that we are concerned here with imagination and what, in the eighteenth century, was called 'sensibility'. Fundamentalists seek a clarity in excess of the facts. As the French Catholic philosopher, Maurice Blondel, said about his neo-scholastic opponents, 'They see too clearly to see properly'. They have neither the imagination, nor a philosophy of interpretation, that would allow them to appreciate the poetic, symbolic and metaphorical character of religious language. They fail to see the value of multi-layered meaning of the kind that does not force us to choose between one layer and the others.

Can we describe today's Catholic traditionalists as fundamentalist? In many respects I believe that we can. It is a very different kind of fundamentalism from that of the American Bible belt. Authoritarian curialists are educated men who take a position on the immutability of doctrine and papal statements that is analogous to that taken by biblical fundamentalists on the text of the Bible. They see themselves as defenders of an unchanging deposit that is threatened by theological innovations introduced by many modern theologians. Their position stands foursquare in the path of any move for reform. As a result of their devotion to the immutability of doctrine, their view of revelation is essentially propositional, as it had generally been between the first Vatican Council and the Second.

In a very real sense the Modernist controversy at the end of the nineteenth and the beginning of the twentieth century is a valid and valuable guide to the theological division that still exists today in the Catholic Church. At Vatican II there were voices to be heard warning against a recrudescence of Modernism. This was the most convenient term to describe the kind of thought being brought forward by theologians who were to have a far-reaching effect on the council. I have described the traditionalist invocation of the dangers of Modernism as an anachronism, because the historical Modernist movement was virtually liquidated by Pius X in 1907-10. However, there was a tendency to label any non-scholastic approach to Catholic theology as 'Modernist'. The term became obsolete when the Catholic Church at Vatican II departed from the hallowed idea that Catholic orthodoxy was to be defined by subscription to neo-scholastic philosophy and theology. I describe this sensational development as a tacit reform that took place without fuss during the council. To understand the significance of the reform, we must examine the history of what happened after Leo XIII prescribed Thomism as the cure for the prevailing philosophical eclecticism in the church of his time.

In his Encyclical, *Aeterni Patris*, (1879) Leo wrote:

> Let carefully selected teachers endeavour to implant the doctrine of Thomas Aquinas in the minds of students, and set forth clearly his solidity and excellence over others. (art. 31)

Leo's appeal to medieval thought was in convenient harmony with nineteenth century Gothic romanticism. As so easily happens in Catholic theological circles, Leo's prescription quickly hardened into church doctrine. By the time of Pope Pius X's pontificate, Leo's intentions had developed into a threatening admonition delivered in the stern tones of Pius' *Motu Proprio, Doctoris Angelici* (1914):

> If Catholic doctrine is once deprived of this strong bulwark, it is useless to seek the slightest assistance for its defence in a philosophy whose principles are either common to the errors of materialism, monism, pantheism, socialism and modernism, or certainly not opposed to

such systems....

We therefore desired that all teachers of philosophy and sacred theology should be warned that if they deviated so much as a step, in metaphysics especially, from Aquinas, they exposed themselves to grave risk....

This is Our Order, and nothing shall be suffered to gainsay it. (Par. 4)

A small group of Catholic intellectuals, soon to be labeled 'Modernists', had staged a reaction against the Leonine programme and had been ruthlessly condemned in Pius' encyclical, *Pascendi Dominici Gregis* (1907). Modernism became the *bête noir* in Catholic theology for the next half-century, until it was finally laid to rest during Vatican II.

Shortly after the publication of *Pascendi,* one of the principal Modernists, George Tyrrell, an Anglo-Irish Jesuit, in an act of courageous honesty that was also an act of ecclesiastical suicide, wrote an article in the London *Times* criticising *Pascendi.* It led to his excommunication and, on the order of the Pope, expulsion from the Society of Jesus. It contained a pithy sentence that indicates the main point at issue in the Modernist controversy:

Whereas, *Pascendi* tries to show the Modernist that he is no Catholic, it mostly succeeds only in showing him that he is no scholastic.[6]

After World War II, the theologians advising Pius XII were disturbed by the philosophical problems thrown up by Existentialism, which appealed to some Catholic theologians as a corrective to scholastic essentialism. Furthermore, some French theologians, mainly Dominicans, were approaching the question of Tradition from a historical perspective. Rome did not like what was happening. In 1950 Pius XII issued an encyclical, *Humani Generis,* possibly drafted by Reginald Garrigou-Lagrange, O.P., (1877-1964), professor of the Pontifical University of Saint Thomas Aquinas, the Angelicum, and an ardent neo-Thomist, who is said to have been a dominant influence on the content of the encyclical, reinforcing the Leonine position with disturbing clarity:

All these [modern] opinions and affirmations are openly contrary to the documents of Our Predecessors Leo XIII and Pius X, and cannot

6. M.D. Petre, *Autobiography and Life of George Tyrrell* (London 1912), vol. 2, p. 337.

be reconciled with the decrees of the [First] Vatican Council.[7]

Papal teaching from Leo XIII's *Aeterni Patris* down to Vatican II made it very clear that the Catholic Church was not merely recommending, but requiring fidelity to, neo-scholasticism, and especially to the philosophy of Thomas Aquinas, as obligatory Catholic orthodoxy.

So effective was the tacit reform brought about by Vatican II, that in 1998 Pope John Paul II was able to write unblushingly:

> The Church has no philosophy of her own nor does she canonize any one particular philosophy in preference to others. (*Fides et Ratio*, art. 49)

This can be fairly described as a sensational development which raises serious questions about the alleged continuity of 'church teaching'. John Paul, in no sense a liberal pope, implicitly accepted that Vatican II had made a crucial difference to the church's outlook on the relationship between faith and philosophy. The council did not abandon Thomistic thought, as has sometimes been claimed; it abandoned its imposition as indispensable for Catholic orthodoxy. John O'Malley, the American Jesuit historian, in his book, *What Happened at Vatican II?*, demonstrates this with clarity and vigour, when he points out that the council, by not employing scholastic language, moved from abstract metaphysics and grand conceptual schemes to the humble acceptance of mystery.[8]

The abandonment of mandatory scholasticism at Vatican II opened up the possibility of a return to an interiority that had been ruled out at the highest level in the church by the papal-led anti-Modernist campaign. After Vatican II, Augustine's 'restless heart' could make its re-entry to mainline Catholic theology, and with it Blaise Pascal's *fait intérieur*, the heart of non-scholastic French theology, cultivated by the Modernists, especially by Lucien Laberthonnière. All the Modernists reacted sharply against scholastic 'extrinsicism', none more so than George Tyrrell, who, inspired by his friend Friedrich von Hügel's interest in the human experience of contingency, was absorbed, towards the end of his life, in exploring the

---

7. Pius XII, *Humani Generis*, (art.34). In chapter 1, I described how I was taught according to the principles of orthodox neo-scholasticism; so, I unknowingly experienced sophisticated Catholic fundamentalism at first hand.

8. John W. O'Malley, *What Happened at Vatican II?* (Cambridge MA, Harvard University Press, 2008), p. 46.

experience of unsatisfied aspiration, an undoubtedly immanent phenomenon, as the only valid road to the transcendent. It was an approach to transcendence disparaged by one prominent neo-scholastic, Guido Mattiussi, S.J., as 'Kantian poison'.[9] Even as late as the 1940s, Immanuel Kant was still featuring as the leading antagonist of scholastic philosophy and theology. Mattiussi, strongly influenced by a fellow Jesuit and dedicated opponent of Modernism, Louis Billot, described Modernism as 'watered-down Kantianism', intended as an automatic condemnation.[10] The anti-Modernists considered Thomism to be the only antidote to Modernism.

According to the Modernists, the human relationship with God is mystical and necessarily mediated indirectly through human experiences which serve as signals of transcendence that are expressed largely through symbols usually in metaphorical language. Laberthonnière described the process as 'the method of immanence'. The transcendence of God cannot be approached directly through the human mind, as the scholastics taught; it needs to be mediated to men and women through their immanent experience of unsatisfied aspiration. Tyrrell, in one of his most poetical expressions described contingent man beautifully: 'A cage-born bird, he wonders what his wings are for.'[11]

Pascendi condemned this approach to God as 'immanentism' and described it dismissively as 'Modernism', 'the meeting-place of all the heresies'. Subsequent development of Catholic 'orthodoxy' displayed many of the features of fundamentalism, in that Modernism was treated as the enemy, and the imposition of neo-scholasticism was seen as a return to the fundamentals of Catholic theology, which Pius X prescribed as necessary for all church institutions of teaching. (Coincidentally, all this took place at the same time as A. C. Dixon was laying the foundations of Protestant fundamentalism in the US.)

What are the consequences of all this for what is happening today in a new pontificate? Pope Francis, for commendable though questionable reasons, is attempting to seek a consensus between two mutually opposed wings of the church – which is logically impossible because their convic-

---

9. G. Mattiussi, *Il veleno Kantiano: Nuova ed antica critica della ragione, immanenza, filosofia dell'azione*, (Monza, 1907), p. 208

10. Ibid., p. 183.

11. George Tyrrell, *Christianity at the Cross-Roads* (London, 1909), p. 125.

tions contradict one another. Traditionalists are saying that no pope can change 'the teaching of the Church'. What is this teaching? The Gospel and the creeds, certainly; but papal teaching in recent times? Let's look at the evidence, by direct quotations from two popes. (1) Pope Pius X: 'All teachers of philosophy and sacred theology should be warned that if they deviated so much as a step, in metaphysics especially, from Aquinas, they exposed themselves to grave risk.... This is Our Order, and nothing shall be suffered to gainsay it.' (2) Pope John Paul II: 'The Church has no philosophy of her own nor does she canonise any one particular philosophy in preference to others.' Take your pick! These two positions are mutually exclusive; yet both are papal teaching. Which, then, is 'church doctrine', as traditionalists would understand it?

On the matter of the Catholic Church's teaching about the necessity of Thomism, most contemporary theologians would agree with Pope John Paul that the church espouses no particular philosophy. Those who have a fundamentalist view of papal statements have a difficulty explaining the choice of one pope over the other. Neither statement involves fidelity to the Gospel or the creeds, so if one is not a doctrinal fundamentalist, there is no problem. Pius X, however, regarded his words as binding on the entire church, and would have been taken aback by his successor's remark. Let's take the matter further than the question of the philosophical underpinning of doctrine.

Why should Pope Francis feel himself to be bound by Pope Paul VI's encyclical, *Humanae Vitae*, considering that it too could be said not to have involved fidelity to the Gospel or the creeds? Why should he not be free to say that his predecessor's view on contraception did not bind the entire church? Is he, under traditionalist pressure, professing allegiance to a view of such matters as contraception, female ordination and clerical celibacy, because he does not wish to offend the traditionalist wing of the church? As Vatican II showed, the majority at the council was in favour of reform and they outvoted the conservatives handsomely. The same battle is being fought today. If the traditionalist bloc, which has a fundamentalist attitude towards past papal statements and a rule-driven view of church and even Gospel, continues to influence the Pope, the liberating effect that Francis is having on the church may not outlive his papacy. *Carpe diem* may be a reminder that practical politics may be appropriate in circumstances such as these; the curial mind has proved itself more than capable of subverting a reform that threatens its power.

Catholic fundamentalism is more than a matter of private conservative beliefs that concern only those who hold them. This is a conservatism that identifies its own ideas with church doctrine and relies, not on free discussion, but on the use of power, to achieve its aims. Since those aims include an intolerant and punitive attitude towards those who reject them, their victory would mean an end to the promise held out by Vatican II. In these circumstances, one has every right to fight for what one believes to be true and desirable for the church.

There is a strong conservative impulse to decry any attempt to speak of two distinct mindsets in the Catholic Church. Some traditionalists describe this understanding of what is happening as 'ideology', intending the word in a pejorative sense and failing to accept that their own viewpoint is as ideological as the one they oppose. It is far better, and more principled, to accept the fact that there is, in point of fact, a radical division of attitudes in the church. The Christian challenge is, not to try to strike a balance between them (a logical impossibility), but to consider how they can live together as brothers and sisters, listen to and care for each other, and perhaps manage to inject some humour into the situation. Both sides would need to desist from striving to enforce their views on the entire church, but feel free to argue for their ideas and to dispute ideas with which they disagree.

The ongoing Synod on Marriage and the Family has opened up conflicting attitudes in the Catholic Church, and they bear not only on marriage and the family, but also on a host of other matters. The contest between them is a fact of life, and it bears on the need to accept that opinions may legitimately vary within the parameters of Catholic faith. Sometimes fundamentalist opinions simply do not have to be endured in the interests of tolerance and submission to a specious demand for uniformity. We have every right to oppose, not the freedom to *hold* the opinions, but the power to *impose* them on the entire church.

13

Catholic Substance and Protestant Principle

Before the Second Vatican Council, Roman Catholics were taught that Protestantism was a heresy, and there was an end of the matter. History has forced even the most supernaturalistic Catholics to concede that there was need of moral reform. However, nothing was said by the magisterium about structural or doctrinal reform. In a more ecumenical age, we have been encouraged to heal the wounds of past unedifying sectarianism. We are slowly learning to appreciate the insights and convictions of those we have been schooled to recognize as 'separated brethren'.

The beginnings of serious institutional ecumenism took place in the first decade of the twentieth century, and it was brought about mainly by Protestant missionaries who had recognized the scandal which Christian division had given to those they were trying to evangelize. It was a Protestant initiative, and official Catholicism looked on with instinctive disapproval: for how could a church which saw itself as already possessing the whole truth, go into any sort of dialogue with those it saw as being in error, apart from trying to encourage them to return to the 'one true church'? Although some Catholics, at considerable risk to themselves, did engage in cautious ecumenical contact, and although there was in some Catholic circles an increasing desire to make a contribution to Christian unity, it was not until the Second Vatican Council that the church as a whole, to murmurs of 'indifferentism' by intransigent conservatives, committed itself to the ecumenical movement.

In official Catholic circles it sometimes seemed that ecumenism meant trying to negotiate, as amicably as possible of course, the terms under which the 'separated brethren' could return to the one true fold. Those who are engaged in genuine ecumenical dialogue know that their project is a search not only for unity but also for truth. That is why reform of the Church is a necessary ingredient in the search for authentic unity. Every real dialogue entails the risk of a journey to an unknown destination. Interchurch dialogue helps to keep theology honest, precisely because, properly understood, it is a search and not an exercise in bargaining. The movement for Christian unity can, and should, act as a spur to self-examination and reform.

If ecumenical dialogue is not an honest search for truth and for new insights, it becomes an exercise in what John Macquarrie, in a lethal phrase, called 'ecclesiastical joinery'. (Macquarrie has been described as 'unquestionably Anglicanism's most distinguished systematic theologian in the second half of the twentieth century.'[1]) Although he was a committed ecumenist, Macquarrie was quite prepared to speak of the 'many dangers in ecumenism', especially 'the danger of submerging legitimate differences, and thereby impoverishing the body which is enriched and strengthened by these differences'. 'The genuine diversity-in-unity of the body of Christ needs to be defended against uniformity just as much as against divisiveness'. [2] If Christian unity is fought for at the expense of legitimate diversity, the enterprise is not worth the effort.

One might interpret Professor Macquarrie's robust attitude to ecumenism as a warning against promoting unity at the expense of truth – being ecumenical with the truth, as it were. I like the phrase 'unity in reconciled diversity', though I realize that it has a controversial history, and that it is judged by some reputable ecumenists to fall short of the highest ideals of organic unity. It may be a matter of perspective and priorities, but it is particularly to the point when we are dealing with the Roman Catholic Church, which is so preoccupied with authority, and so unwilling to allow for diversity within unity. As a result of joining the ecumenical movement, many Roman Catholics have begun to take the Reformation seriously, and not merely as a regrettable occurrence that divided Western Christianity in the sixteenth century.

The World Council of Churches has an interesting comment to make on the ecumenical implications of legitimate diversity in the Christian Church.

1. Timothy Bradshaw, 'John Macquarrie', in: Alister E. McGrath (ed.) *The SPCK Handbook of Anglican Theologians* (London, SPCK, 1998), p. 168.
2. J. Macquarrie, *Principles of Christian Theology* (London, SCM Press, 1977), pp. 403-4.

Legitimate diversity is not accidental to the life of the Christian community but is rather an aspect of its catholicity, a quality that reflects the fact that it is part of the Father's design that salvation in Christ be incarnational and thus "take flesh" among the various peoples to whom the Gospel is proclaimed.[3]

Leaders in the Catholic Church tend not to appreciate that 'legitimate diversity … is an aspect of its catholicity'. Their behaviour has sometimes been sectarian rather than catholic, and its vision has been narrow rather than being genuinely catholic. The WCC has gently pointed out that to 'take flesh' in diverse cultures, there needs to be diversity of theological insights within the unity of faith.

Thus Catholics have usually conceded that the church needed reform in the sixteenth century; but they have understood reform in a sense that left structures and doctrines unexamined. Furthermore, even the most intransigent Catholic could see the moral defects of some of the Renaissance popes and their courts, but the proclamation of the need for reform was couched in personal rather than in structural terms. Sale of indulgences was fervently condemned as simony, but the very idea of indulgences remained (and remains) unreformed.

I turn now to the theology of Paul Tillich for inspiration on how both the Protestant and Catholic traditions have something indispensable to contribute to a united Church. This does not mean that I have become a disciple of Tillich. I am just as opposed to party whips in academic life as in church governance! I find in Tillich constant stimulation to think in fresh ways about ideas that often remain unexamined and taken for granted. I do of course recognize that to anyone who is unduly sensitive to theological fashion, Tillich belongs to an age that has passed. The same, however, could be said of Augustine, Thomas Aquinas and Martin Luther. Fashions make little sense to a theology which is firmly rooted in historical consciousness and which holds its faith as a precious deposit while engaging in unremitting search for the enduring truth within it.

One of Tillich's seminal ideas is that a united Christian Church should embody within itself what he called 'Protestant principle and Catholic substance'. What did he mean by this phrase? J. P. Newport, an authority

---

3. WCC, *The Church: Towards a Common Vision*, Art. 12, p. 10.

on Tillich, puts it very clearly and is worth quoting at length.

> Catholic substance sees the holy as primarily incarnate. It is a present reality, represented by holy persons, objects, and functions. This view sees the sacraments as ontologically related to their sacramental function. As such, they (water, fire, oil, bread, wine) have 'inherent' qualities which make them adequate and irreplaceable for their sacramental function.
>
> The sacraments, however, are in the ever-present danger that ritual actions, which represent the holy, will claim holiness for themselves. They tend to become identified with grace itself. To counteract this tendency towards the distortion of the sacramental principle, Catholic substance needs to be maintained in polar tension with the Protestant principle. [4]

When in the sixteenth century western Christians became divided from one another, it was not only mutual love and unity that were damaged. Truth and the integrity of faith were fractured too, because the self-righteous hostility resulting from division suppressed any inclination to examine the truth of the other's position. Each side in the divide between Protestants and Catholics proclaimed itself to be unquestionably right and the other to be in mortal error. One of the most unfortunate – we can properly call it sinful – results of historical developments following the Reformation and Counter-reformation was the institutionalizing of difference. Exclusion of the other became part of the self-understanding and self-definition of both sides. Each defined itself with self-conscious virtue in terms of what it rejected in the other. Loyalty was to one's own church rather than to the truth. (In recent times this attitude could be seen in the institutional church's instinct to put its good name before the safety of children.)

Reform thus became difficult in the Roman Catholic Church precisely because reform would appear to be introducing what was already institutionalized as the heresy of Protestantism – which by definition must be wrong. For similar reasons, sacramental practice became difficult for Protestant churches because it was vulnerable to the charge of catholiciza-

---

4. J. P. Newport, *Paul Tillich* (Word Books, Waco, Texas, 1984), pp. 132-3.

tion. Thus the institutionalizing of difference has tended to blind each to the truth in the other's position. It is standard practice, for example, for ultra-conservative Catholics to accuse their more liberal confrères of being Crypto-Protestants, while some evangelical Anglicans may stigmatize as 'Romish' having candles on the holy table. A sense of humour probably offers the best defence against this kind of thing.

It cannot be said too often that true ecumenical dialogue with members of other churches is not merely an exercise in fellowship and amity, important as these are. It is also, and far more importantly, a journey in search of truth, above all, the truth of what the Spirit is saying to the churches. Some of that truth will come from the 'strangeness' of the other. It will often be expressed in unfamiliar language that will need to be learnt, if there is to be benefit from our encounter with the other. It will be a truth, or, more accurately, a perspective on truth, which we may hitherto have lacked, because it did not seem relevant to our characteristic preoccupations.

Paul Tillich's understanding of the relationship between Catholic substance and Protestant principle can, I believe, help us to recover something, at least, of what we have lost by our historical divisions. Catholic substance is not to be sought only in Roman, Anglo-Catholic or Orthodox Churches; nor is Protestant principle to be sought only in the Protestant Churches. Indeed it is possible to argue, as Tillich did, that the Roman Catholic Church is insufficiently catholic, while Protestant Churches are insufficiently protestant.

It is not a matter of Roman Catholics imbibing some protestantism from the Protestant Churches and Protestants imbibing some catholicism from the Roman Catholic Church: *All* Christian Churches need the presence and action of both protestant principle and catholic substance – and this for the sake of truth and not merely for the sake of unity. Unity and truth go together and ought always to be mutually related, quite irrespective of the quest for unity. The relationship is dialectical in the sense that each acts as a corrective influence on the other and is a bulwark against sectarianism.

Some years ago, to my great delight, I came across a fascinating book by F. J. Leenhardt, Professor of New Testament in the University of Geneva. The book is entitled *Two Biblical Faiths: Protestant and Catholic*,[5] and it presents the reflections of an ecumenically-minded Protestant theologian on some characteristic differences between Catholicism and Protestantism, both terms being taken in a positive, inclusive and affirmative sense.

In his book, Leenhardt, with a nice play of imagination, describes Abraham as an archetypal Protestant, and Moses as an archetypal Catholic. Abraham affirms the liberty and sovereignty of God while expressing his own total incapacity. 'The God of Abraham is the God of absolute beginnings.' 'He is, only in the act of his speaking ... He is not present in what He has said, but in what He says.'[6] Leenhardt then goes on to draw the challenging conclusion that faith of the Abrahamic type tends to remove any confusion of the word of promise with anything human, earthly, factual, historical. It aims at pure interiority.[7]

On the other hand the revelation made to Moses is much more concrete and external. It 'brings into play a bush, a mountain, and a storm'. 'The God of Moses is revealed by means of instruments which are raised to the dignity of efficacious signs.' From this thought-provoking opening, Leenhardt goes on to comment" 'Abraham ... Moses ... Two figures, two aspects of Biblical revelation, But also two styles of piety, two universes, each with its own internal logic, its implications, its consequences'.[8] 'Each with its own internal logic' is a valuable reminder that divisions, alienations and misunderstandings can result from interpreting the language of the other according to one's own categories or perspectives, which may well be inappropriate. There are many possible illustrations of this.

A primary one would be to note that the Reformers and the Council of Trent employed different languages for discussing sin and justification. I am not suggesting that there were no substantive differences between them. There were, of course. Nevertheless, a significant part of their mutual disagreement arose out of their different approaches, assumptions and preoccupations. Some of the most significant advances in ecumenics today stem from a willingness to recognize the cultural and linguistic character of doctrinal statements. In this spirit we can ponder a thesis

5. London, 1964.
6. Ibid., pp. 64, 66.
7. Ibid., p. 66.
8. Ibid., p. 74.

that Leenhardt puts forward: 'Catholic spirituality assigns to the notion of presence the same part as protestant spirituality assigns to the notion of the word.'[9] Presence abides; word is of the moment.

There are possibilities and dangers in each spirituality. A theology and spirituality which are principally concerned with presence can lead to the sacralizing of persons, events and things in a way that seems to endow them with qualities that belong only to God. That was the situation in the late Middle Ages, when Martin Luther protested against the superstitions to be found in popular religion and even in ordinary church practices of the time. One has only to recall the cult of, and worse, the trading in, relics and indulgences to realize that a spirituality of presence was thriving out of control and was badly in need of correction by Protestant principle. Luther's protest against relics and indulgences has to be pondered in depth and without confessional prejudice, if its deeper meaning is to be appreciated. Unfortunately, institutional division came about partly by Pope Leo X's intransigence, and partly by the politicizing of religious division by the German princes.

Leenhardt's distinction between presence and word blends well with Tillich's thesis of Catholic substance and Protestant principle. In a theology and spirituality of presence there is a constant danger that sacraments can have holiness attributed to them for themselves and not as instruments of divine action; whereas a theology and spirituality principally concerned with word can obscure the fact that God may approach us through the medium of symbols, and if we reject their potential holiness merely on the grounds that they could promote idolatry, we may be blocking off an avenue of communication between the transcendent God and ourselves, who live in time and space. In short, God too takes risks – including the risk of our idolatry.

Tillich always liked to argue that God's approach to us, and our response to God are made within culture, and that they utilize culture as their means of expression. Thus the Bible is written in the languages, and reflects the cultures, of the ancient Near East. This illustrates vividly how God approaches us indirectly and at a remove, through words and signs that are undeniably natural or human, but which are at the same

9. Ibid., p. 96

time charged with the reflected glory of God, whenever God wants them to be. In the revelation to Moses, the bush, the mountain and the storm are natural signs in which Moses recognizes the presence of God. That presence can rightly be called sacramental. It is what Tillich designates as 'Catholic substance', and having stated it to be a necessary bridge between God and human beings, he then sounds the solemn warning that constitutes the heart of the Protestant principle: 'I am the Lord your God … You must have no other God besides me.' (Exodus 20:2-3) The fact that the Holy Spirit uses persons, places and things as means of making God present to human experience does not imply that these persons, places and things become divine. Mediation is not identification. Such identification is idolatrous; its practice can be properly called superstitious and therefore in need of reform.

To return to the theme of quest: there is much in human religious experience that suggests that God does not want to be found too easily or too cheaply, and that the search for God should be a constant and continuing feature in a life of faith. God is never finally possessed, resists domestication and escapes from any attempt on our part to make God a tame, if exalted, denizen of our daily experience. This emphasis on search can be rightly interpreted as a manifestation of the Protestant principle. It warns against the dangers of domesticating God within human religious experience. Our institutional tribulations in Western Christianity today, especially the decrease in church attendance and other symptoms of the breakdown of traditional church membership, may be the price that has to be paid for the former presumptions and arrogance of an historical Christendom that discerned the presence and action of God all too easily, and identified that presence and action all too quickly with church interests.

It is not that God is punishing us; rather, we had placed a barrier between ourselves and God by turning the church and its authorities into unrecognized idols. Too much domestication of the divine in churchly activities may produce a need for distance and a fresh search for the unknown God. So perhaps our institutional tribulations provide us with a valuable occasion for repentance, self-reform and newness of life. Gloomy reflections on the iniquities of the secular world contribute little to our response to God's call, and may result in the unhealthy segregation of the church from the world. The Church of Christ is not a supernatural enclave in a sinful world. It shares in the fallenness of all humanity and all human institutions, even those of divine origin. It has been given the powerful remedies of forgiveness and hope, but it needs the faith to recognize and accept them.

Perhaps our institutional setbacks could help us to re-engage in the search for God, by the reminder that God may use, but never depends on, churchly institutions in order to reach us. The challenge is to look for God in the world around us, and not merely to find God in a domestic round of churchly activities. If we believe that God is everywhere, it follows that God can be found in places and circumstances that we arrogantly believe to be untouched by grace. Wise missionaries (domestic as well as foreign) do not think of themselves as bringing divine revelation to people who lack God: they set out to find the God who is always ahead of both themselves and the people to whom they have been sent. Preaching Jesus Christ to people who have never heard of him, or to nominal Christians who have forgotten about him, ought not to give the impression that God's favour is to be found only in submission to ecclesiastical authority, however legitimate. The Spirit of God breathes where it wills. A good missionary looks for signs of God's presence in any society, before he or she attempts to preach salvation in Jesus Christ.

The mystery of the uniqueness of Jesus of Nazareth can be understood in either an exclusive or an inclusive sense. If it is understood in an exclusive sense, we could be taken to mean that salvation depends upon an accident of birth, of history or of geography, that is, that the Saviour happens to be born in a certain place and age that has had the serendipitous opportunity to hear him preached. In spite of the recent liturgical translation 'many' for 'all' in the newly imposed text of the Mass, we need to reiterate our faith-inspired conviction that Christ died for all humanity, and not merely for those who belong to the Christian Church. That he is the only source of human salvation is a formal teaching of the church: Christ died for all humankind, including those who have never heard of him. They do not need to have heard of him in order to be saved.

The term 'anonymous Christian' was devised by Karl Rahner to deal with this difficulty. Hans Küng attacked it on the grounds that it is presumptuous in appearing to endow people of other faiths, or none, with the favour of being Christians unbeknown to themselves. I cannot agree with Küng here. Rahner is not trying to impose formal Christian status on members of other faiths or of none. He does not ask us to leave aside our Christian convictions in our approach to other faiths. (I can only say that if a Buddhist were to regard me as an anonymous Buddhist, I would feel honoured, not imposed upon.) I cannot see how speaking of others as 'anonymous Christians', if understood inclusively, is presumptuous or imperialistic. Küng approaches theology historically; Rahner approaches it philosophically. There is a place for both approaches. It seems to me that Küng overlooks the fact that he and Rahner are using two different languages and two different methods of interpretation.

Unsatisfactory or not, the notion of 'anonymous Christianity' was at least an effort to meet the problem intrinsic to what has been called 'the scandal of particularity' presented by Christianity. This was, in fact, one of the first difficulties that early Christian thought had to face in the Hellenistic culture of its time. That culture was preoccupied with the universal rather than with the particular. Philosophers like Plato paid little attention to Greek religion. Instead they appealed to reason as their mentor on transcendence. Theirs was an intellectual culture that regarded transcendence as a condition that escapes the limitations of history, and has universal validity. That is why in a later age philosophers like Plato and Aristotle inspired Christian scholars. Their philosophy lent itself to a Christian interpretation, as Aquinas showed in the case of Aristotelianism.

The problem is still with us. People can find it hard to believe that God's complete and perfect word to humanity was expressed in the person of a young Jewish craftsman and itinerant preacher who lived and died 2,000 years ago in an obscure part of the Roman Empire. How could universal truth be expressed in so particular and seemingly adventitious a way? The church, which proclaims him as its founder, has, through the ages, approved the efforts of artists to embellish his image through their art, as if in a bid to raise him above his original lowliness, (one might call it artistic monophysitism). It is surprising what a halo and some rays of light can contribute to an otherwise unpromising scene. The mystery of the incarnation, however, finds its true expression in the presence of God's word in powerless human form.

This is the basic message of Christmas, underlying the nativity stories which may captivate the imagination at Christmas, but are, at the same time, open to questions about their historical authenticity. Believers can be shaken to find that the gospels of Matthew and Luke, the only gospels to provide the infancy narratives, may not be accurate by our modern standards of historical accuracy. There are, however, other valid perspectives on truth that are not dependent on historical accuracy.

It matters not at all whether the nativity stories are historically true according to our modern standards of historicity. What finally matters is that Jesus the Christ was born somewhere at a possibly unspecified time of year. It is the fact of his birth, not the circumstances retailed in the gospels of Matthew and Luke, that challenged the minds and imaginations of the early Fathers of the Church, who loved to dwell on it, precisely because it was a scandal to human values. We find Justin Martyr repeating, as if to convince himself: 'the Word cried like any other baby'.

Universal truth was born in particular circumstances, and those circumstances were anything but fittingly grand. Christian preaching has constantly dwelt on the fact that Jesus was not born in a palace, and that throughout his life he shunned the trappings of power. At Christmas, infinite majesty is expressed, not in the guise of human power, but in that of human weakness. This is the counterintuitive and glorious scandal that has to be proclaimed to the world. It is a scandal to a world that esteems wealth, status and power. What a pity that we so thoughtlessly obscure that scandal by replacing it with our own gratuitous scandals, such as the misuse of power and authority.

As I have already said, there is much in human religious experience that suggests that God does not wish to be found too easily, and that consequently the search for God should be a constant and continuing feature in a life of faith. In this world we never arrive at a condition of finally realized truth that dispenses us from the need for further search. This emphasis on search can be properly interpreted as a manifestation of Protestant principle. It warns against the domestication of God within the daily practice of faith. Our institutional tribulations may be taken as beneficial reminders that we have no control over God through our sacramental celebrations. Church interests are not to be identified with God's will.

Catholic substance is necessary because we live in the cultural webs we have woven for ourselves, and because God's presence and action are mediated through them. It is dangerous, because we are also natural idolaters. John Calvin in the *Institutes* claims that the human mind is 'a perpetual factory of idols'.[10] It is because of this that we are in need of the Protestant principle at every turn.

Now it is worth noting at this point that the language of idols and idolatry may sound strange to Catholic ears, when it is applied to church usage and order. Catholics may need to learn it from Protestant ecumenists. In propounding the need for Catholic substance and Protestant principle Tillich is critical of both Catholicism and Protestantism in their actual historical manifestations. He notes that 'the whole protest of the Reformation was in fundamental opposition to the sacramental system of Catholicism'.

He then advances an important thesis, when he says 'the problem of the sacraments is a decisive one if Protestantism is to come to its full realization'.[11] 'A complete disappearance of the sacramental element (not the same thing, be it noted, as the particular sacraments) would lead to the disappearance of the cultus [liturgical worship] and, finally to the dissolution of the visible church itself.' 'No church can survive without a sacramental element.'[12]

Tillich is careful, however, to protect himself against fellow Protestants who might accuse him of conceding too much to Roman Catholicism: 'Protestant thinking about sacraments must not revert to a magical sacramentalism, such as has been preserved down to our own time [i.e., the 1940s]. No relapses to a pre-prophetic or pre-Protestant attitude should occur on Protestant soil.'[13] A sacrament, he says, cannot be a thing, an object beside other objects, nor can it be identified with nature, which does not have any intrinsic power to create a sacrament. 'It can only become a bearer of sacramental power'. Nature has to be related to the history of salvation if it is to be 'liberated from its demonic elements and thus made eligible for a sacrament'.

The invocation of the 'demonic' is interesting, coming as it does from a liberal theologian like Tillich. Catholics can fruitfully pay attention to

10. *Institutes of the Christian Religion*, volume 1, *Library of Christian Classics* (Westminster John Knox Press, Louisville, 1960), p. 108.
11. P. Tillich, *The Protestant Era* (Abridged Edition, Chicago, 1957) p. 94.
12. Ibid., p. 109.
13. Ibid., p. 110.

what Tillich is saying here, precisely because he is using language that may seem strange to Catholic ears. He is espousing the instinctive attitude of the classical Lutheran mind towards nature. For Luther, nature is radically fallen, whereas for the Council of Trent, it is 'wounded'. Perhaps a good theology of creation could reconcile these two positions.

The ecological crisis today is inviting all Christian theologians, Catholic and Protestant, to give renewed consideration to the theology of creation. Protestants have tended to place salvation history above creation; while Catholic theologians have tended to make too sharp a distinction between nature and supernature. Luther himself, as Tillich has noted, did not reject sacramentalism, once it had been purged of superstition and of all suggestion of justification by works.

Tillich regarded the application of scientific method to study of the Bible as one of the major achievements of the Protestant principle. There are Protestants who, reacting to critical biblical scholarship, protest against the subjection of a sacred book to this kind of investigation. The Bible, as the word of God, should, in their view, exist serenely above all irreverent attempts to study it as a set of human texts. This protest struck Tillich as a failure to live up to the demands of the Protestant principle: it turns the Bible into an idol. The same could be said of the common Catholic view of authority, especially papal authority.

The Protestant principle should enable and empower Christians to relate their faith to the contemporary world with all its cultural variety and development, because it is not afraid to take risks in the name of faith. There is some irony in the thought that biblical fundamentalism offends against the spirit of Protestantism, which claims to recognize that the sovereignty of God cannot be restricted by external circumstances like the creation of a book. There is equal irony in the thought that the institutional fundamentalism of papal government can offend against the spirit of genuine Catholicism, which is not sectarian and aims at universal validity. In Protestantism, 'preoccupation with word as the exclusive medium of divine revelation and salvific action created a pastoral dynamic which favoured the educated over the illiterate masses'. Tillich notes this and observes that 'Protestantism is a highly intellectualized religion'.[14] It

14. Tillich, op. cit. p. 227.

replaces the priest with the preacher and ultimately with the professor.

> Protestant education in its reasonable and moralistic attitude, although it was capable of educating selected individuals, failed in the education of the masses. More and more individuals became unable to endure the tremendous responsibility of permanently having to decide in intellectual and moral issues.[15]

In the USA, psychoanalysis has proved 'more desirable for educated people than religion, especially Protestant religion'.[16]

Tillich goes on to say that for Roman Catholics 'confession has been able to overcome many tendencies towards personal disintegration'. He was writing in the period before Vatican II, when the stern Tridentine conditions for a 'good' confession controlled confessional practice. Although church teaching has always insisted that it is Christ who, through the ministry of the priest, absolves the penitent, the penitent was nonetheless expected to be precise and detailed in his or her enumeration and description of sins. The customary model for the confessor was that of 'judge'. Looked at from the standpoint of Catholic substance and Protestant principle, the Tridentine model of sacramental reconciliation seems to encourage the notion that confession is as much a work as an exercise of faith. Some Catholics have experienced it as a burden, and have found little of Christ in it, especially when the confessor was severely judgemental.

The sacrament of reconciliation today is in ostensible crisis, because it is in need of a reform that is radical and far-reaching. In practice, however, any actual attempt to reform it has met with disapproval from Rome. General absolution has been discouraged, seemingly because in it penitents do not have to undergo the discomfort of giving another human being the details of their failings, and perhaps, even more, because it appears to lessen institutional control over the process of forgiveness.

The outcome of all this is that many people have stopped going to confession, because they experience it as a burdensome duty rather than as a joyful occasion in which they can know themselves as totally accepted and cherished in a manner which the world so often refuses them. In

---

15. 'Protestantism in the Present World Situation', *American Journal of Sociloogy*, vol. 43, no. 2, Septembner 1937, pp. 242-3

16. Tillich, *The Protestant Era*, p. 228.

practice, however, services of communal penance may be made to meet the strict requirements of Rome by each penitent approaching the priest and confessing their sinfulness, though in general and brief terms. It is a welcome though casuistic compromise, technically meeting the requirements of law, while pastorally trying to meet the needs of people. The necessity for such casuistry can to some extent rob the occasion of its joy and its experience of divine generosity. Once again, the institution intervenes to put its own small-minded legalism ahead of God's bountiful offer of forgiveness.

One additional and very good reason why the church should make the liturgical and sacramental occasion of reconciliation one of joyful celebration is that forgiveness is not a prominent feature of secular culture, which is often preoccupied with blame, retribution and punishment. In our adversarial method of court procedure, counsel for the prosecution regards it as his or her duty to convict the accused; concern with forgiveness can be regarded as an unwelcome distraction from the work in hand.

However, forgiveness (or, as Pope Francis might put it, 'mercy') lies at the very heart of Christian faith; and it is the obligation and privilege of the church to proclaim it joyfully to the world, most especially when the world rejects it as weakness. It is integral to the scandal of Christianity to proclaim to the world that it is loved and forgiven, whether the world recognizes it or not. Bleak judgment and condemnation from the Christian church do little to celebrate God's presence and action in the world.

Ungenerous and legalistic attitudes to the sacrament of forgiveness present a man-made scandal that conceals the gladdening truth of God's forgiveness. Petty laws and mean-spirited restrictions at a sacramental level, together with a generally glum outlook on the world, give a counter-image to the church's true vocation. Police are necessary in the world in order to promote human rights and preserve public order. The Christian Church, however, has a different mission, which is not that of police or judges. It has been sent to proclaim joy and hope, where the world often refuses to recognize the dignity of its members and promotes a spirit of power, force and retribution.

An attentive reading of the accounts of Jesus' attitude towards, and behaviour with, sinners could point the way towards genuine reform of the church's institutional embodiment of forgiveness. Instead of complaining

215

gloomily about the fall-off in attendance at the sacrament of reconciliation, and treating it in a legalistic and forbidding way, why not attempt to make it a jubilant celebration of God's extravagant offer of forgiveness in a fragmented world which is more concerned with apportioning blame than with the enthusiastic acceptance and understanding of offenders? That is a task that is given as a privilege to both Catholics and Protestants to be proclaimed to the world.

14

Essence and Existence

The question of gay marriage has come as a challenge to both secular society and to the Christian Church. Opinion polls suggest that, in Ireland as in other countries, there is increasing support for it. The Irish case is remarkable: in this, as in other matters that concern the church, a revolution has taken place in a very short time. Only a few years ago homosexual acts were crimes; now they have been decriminalised. Only a few years ago gay men and women were careful not to publicise their sexual orientation; now they regularly 'out' themselves with no embarrassment, and their right to marry has been recognised in the constitutional law of Ireland (by amendment approved in a referendum) and of the United States (by decision of the Supreme Court).

The sheer speed of change has left the Irish Catholic Church unsure of how it should behave in the circumstances. On the one hand, the duty to care pastorally for gays and lesbians and try to defend them from prejudice and persecution is obvious in the light of the Christian Gospel. On the other hand, traditionalists in the church see themselves as bound by law and morality to defend the exclusive character of heterosexual marriage. It is all too plain that some senior churchmen find it difficult to combine these two attitudes harmoniously, especially when the matter is exposed in the circumstances of gay marriage.

It is likewise true that gay people may sometimes feel discriminated against and lacking equality in the community. This thought is for me the most urgent reason why why it is right that gay marriage be given full recognition in law. I do not underestimate the difficulty that this presents for traditionalists who have a prevailing sense of the importance of law in Christian life; but I am convinced that in the light of the Gospel, it is the course that we should accept in today's church.

I propose here to discuss the matter in terms of essence and existence, which, though applicable to many more questions than gay marriage, can, I hope, throw light on an issue that is exercising the Catholic Church in so manyplaces at the moment.

The relationship between essence and existence is dialectical: each acts as a corrective to the excesses of the other. We are dealing here, not with an either/or, but with a both/and. An historical faith like Christianity needs both. The foremost obstacle to a healthy relationship between essence and existence in the framing of moral standards is the aggressive intervention of any authority, whether of church, state or media, that short-cuts the processes of rational enquiry and freedom of discussion. In an historical situation an essence needs to be expressed in concrete existents in order to become a lived reality; but it must not be allowed to encroach on God-given freedoms and rights to historical and cultural development. Such encroachments may produce an idealised situation that bears little resemblance to what actually exists.

This point has been forcibly made in the present synodical discussion about marriage: Catholic teaching on marriage seems to be supremely idealistic and unrepresentative of many actual marriages. It holds out the image of the essentially perfect marriage, which is structurally conceived but has little to say to those who fail to achieve it, even when they observe all the laws. Its talk of 'wounded' people is restricted by considerations of structure and regulation; it seems to have little to say about the wounds that occur within a structurally sound marriage. Essentialism in action often seems to leave no place for failure, repentance, or forgiveness and compassion; you either observe the law, or you break it and have to face the consequences.

If, on the other hand, existence is considered to be the controlling factor in human reality, we have a totally relative situation in which men and women create their own meaning; and an objective evaluation of the created world becomes impossible. The implication of this for religious faith seems clear enough: divine grace and the action of the Holy Spirit are disregarded and revelation is reduced to self-knowledge and purely subjective insights. Thoughts about God are superfluous in such a situation. In these circumstances it quickly becomes clear that some pre-existent limitations on the demand for total freedom are necessary for any well-run rational society. In short, there is a legitimate place for an essential input, as long as it allows for the freedoms necessary for a beneficial human existence and takes failure into compassionate consideration.

I shall argue for the desirability of a mutually corrective blend of essence and existence, which could operate productively, but only if there were no intervention by authoritarian functionaries. Reform could allow such a blend to occur, but only if there is time for discussion, trial and error and freedom from bureaucratic interference. A reformed church would be one that profits from a dialectical relationship between conservatism and progressivism. I envisage a church with conservatives and liberals living together, sometimes disagreeing with one another, not out of enmity, but because each side sincerely believes in the truth and desirability of their own convictions.

A healthy church needs the insights of both, recognising that it is not designed only for strictly observant rule-keepers and doctrinal rigorists. Christians are human beings wounded by failure, false promises and disillusionment. They live in a world where they hurt and are hurt. For most people, life is a combination of happiness and sadness, light and shadow, a twilit world of religious uncertainty and moral ambivalence. Through grace and by faith in divine forgiveness, the journey remains attractive, as we pick ourselves up and return to the path of righteousness. In such a world the gathering of Christians that we call the church must first and foremost speak of a merciful God's readiness to forgive, rather than discouraging people by an emphasis on the consequences of their sins.

For this situation to come about, there must be no premature intervention from church officials who have institutional authority and power and sit in bureaucratic judgement on their fellows. Pope Francis is calling for clerics to speak their minds as distinct from saying what they think their institutional superiors would want them to say. Bishops need to meet and talk with a variety of theologians, so that they do not judge from criteria that are one-sided and hostile to newer insights. They themselves are commissioned to teach the faith, though to do so proficiently they should be ready and willing to draw help from different legitimate theologies, rather than being captive to a single theology that leads them to judge legitimate developments as suspect, or even heretical. Passive aggression by withdrawal from honest discussions is not a Christ-like way of dealing with differences in the church.

Traditionalists often seem to be unaware of the collateral damage done by setting oneself up as a defender of unchanging moral attitudes and values. Insistence on rules and regulations at the expense of understanding and compassion can be self-indulgent and arrogant. It is exceedingly difficult to reconcile the expression of hard-line moral conservatism with a truly Christian attitude towards people whom traditionalists find themselves logically compelled to regard as sinners. The collateral damage done by legalistic conservatives may never strike them as actually making membership of the Christian Church unattractive, if not positively re-pulsive – hardly a comfortable situation for a strictly observant Catholic.

The sad fact is that many traditionalist prelates and priests have still to learn how to accept homosexuality as a given rather than as an embarrassing aberration. As long as they continue to think in this way, they will find it impossible to reconcile their membership of the church with behaving in a truly Christian fashion. I freely admit the difficulty, which I experienced myself a long time ago, of sloughing off the effects of the old pre-conciliar moral theology textbooks; but unless we do so, we will continue to avoid taking the 'signs of the times' (an innovative Vatican II phrase) seriously. Priests who think of unreformed theology as 'the unchangeable teaching of the church' do serious harm to God's people and can be an embarrassment to their fellow priests.

In the secular world there are people who believe that the case for gay marriage is utterly indisputable. On the other hand, there are Christians who have no doubt that gay marriage is plainly wrong. Many fundamentalists, disregarding the established principles of hermeneutics (the philosophy of interpretation) and the findings of modern biblical studies, believe that the Bible condemns any kind of homosexuality in as clear *and timeless* a manner as possible.

The Anglican Church has to face the problem of containing a wide spectrum of members ranging from Anglo-Catholics to Evangelicals. Justin Welby, the present Archbishop of Canterbury, was courageous enough to be interviewed by Peter Tatchell, a well-known campaigner for gay rights, who quoted the Archbishop as saying: 'I am in favour of the state recognising same-sex relationships but not in favour of redefining marriage.'[1]

He also quoted him as denying that the church was 'discriminating' against gays and lesbians. 'The Archbishop told me: "Gay people are not intrinsically different from straight people, but there is an intrinsic difference in the nature of same-sex relationships", and this is a sufficient reason to deny gay couples the right to marry, even in civil ceremonies in register offices. When pressed to say why this "intrinsic difference" justified banning same-sex marriage, he merely replied: "they are just different".'

However, Tatchell added magnanimously that the Archbishop had struck him as 'a genuine, sincere, open-minded person, willing to listen and rethink his position'. 'I got the impression that he wants to support

1. This and subsequent quotations are all from the interview which appeared in *The Church Times*, 20 April, 2013.

gay equality, but feels bound by church tradition'.

Much the same problem faces the Roman Catholic Church, but its manner of dealing with it is very different. In many respects the Anglican Communion, abroad and at home, faces the unavoidable but distressing problem of how to preserve unity in spite of wide differences of doctrinal and moral conviction among its members. Admirably, it has refused to install structures attempting to enforce uniformity in the name of orthodoxy. It pays an edifyingly heavy price for its unwillingness to excommunicate members of the church who take a stand on some such matter as homosexuality, or women bishops, which opposes majority consensus. Anglican leaders are ready to risk the structural disintegration of their church for the sake of the principle of comprehensiveness. It takes faith and courage to endure the lack of enforced unanimity, but at least it leaves Anglicans free to search for the truth rather than imprisoning them in a plethora of 'certainties' achieved by coercion.

Roman Catholic Church authorities normally settle such matters by decree rather than by free discussion and argument; and they have condemned same-sex marriage out of hand. They refuse to acknowledge that they might learn anything by listening to opposing viewpoints, and they fail to take seriously Jesus' exhortation patiently and humbly to seek the truth rather than claim to possess it infallibly.

The appointment only of bishops who can be counted on to favour, or at least not to oppose publicly, the Roman view of things reinforces the effect of pronounced centralisation and failure to appreciate the religious benefits of freedom and diversity. The local election of bishops would seem to be the surest way of promoting a healthy diversity of opinion in the church. It is unhealthy for the church to have its bishops all of one mind on matters that are not essential to Catholic faith and practice.

The American theologian, Richard A. McCormick, reflected interestingly on an episcopate that suppresses its real feelings in the face of Vatican pressure:

> If bishops are not speaking their true sentiments, then clearly the pope is not able to draw on the wisdom and reflection of the bishops in the exercise of his ordinary magisterium.[2]

Pope Francis would be very susceptible to this wise insight, since he

2. Cited by Bernard Treacy in *Doctrine and Life*, November 1998, p. 451.

has already consulted the faithful at large on their real opinions on the church's doctrines and practices. In this respect, he is fulfilling John Henry Newman's ideal of such consultation. The problem is that the Pope has done nothing about the structures of command in the church, and the fruits of the consultation pass through the hands of intermediaries who have no compunction about altering the result by giving the process a conservative slant.

The Bishop of Antwerp, Johan Bonny, has called for the church to recognise the church gay relationships.

> Just as there are a variety of legal frameworks for partners in civil society, one must arrive at a diversity of forms in the church ... The intrinsic values are more important to me than the institutional question. The Christian ethic is based on lasting relationships where exclusivity, loyalty, and care are central to each other.[3]

This is a carefully worded statement that implies rather than states approval of gay marriage. *The National Catholic Reporter* article in which the statement appears carries an interesting comment by Professor Rik Torfs, canonist and Rector of the Catholic University of Leuven, who is aware of conservative attempts to play down the significance of Bishop Bonny's words:

> Do not underestimate the significance of this. Bonny advocates a change from principles long held as unshakable, something no bishop could have done under the dogmatic pontificates of Pope John Paul II and Benedict XVI.[4]

Before the Second Vatican Council, matters considered to be essential to Catholic faith were normally doctrinal or in some way connected with doctrine. Today they are moral and disciplinary and are topics on which there is clearly no general agreement. It prescribes mandatory uniformity in a manner that suppresses all dissent and frequently offends against human rights and dignity. This is strange behaviour for a church in an age of increasing unbelief.

It gives me no pleasure to be critical of the serious flaws in the governance of my own church; but Catholics who wish to take part in the debate

---

3. *National Catholic Reporter* (January 16-29, 2015) p. 11.
4. Ibid.

on gay marriage find themselves officially committed to a position that is already decided for them and is not institutionally open to being modified.

One of the main theological charges that can be brought against a church authority that is so peremptory in its judgements is that it fails to recognise that the Holy Spirit may be trying to speak through the free discussion of its members with each other and with the world at large. In spite of the fact that the Second Vatican Council spoke of the theological significance of 'the signs of the times', recent authorities in the Catholic Church have seemed unwilling to appreciate that the Holy Spirit can speak through the normal human expression of differing opinions. Furthermore, convictions arrived at by free discussion are likely to be more authentic than imposed doctrinal and moral instructions. The contemporary debate over gay marriage is an appropriate illustration of what might otherwise easily become a rather dry philosophical disquisition.

The question of gay marriage is better seen, even by the believer, not from a religious perspective, but as a philosophical question. This, in spite of its technical difficulties, helps to bring to the matter an undogmatic attitude, and it has the advantage of providing a common playing field on which religious and non-religious minds can meet in amicable discussion. I am in no way suggesting that we simply exclude all religious considerations, which have their rightful place in a proper context. Christians cannot be expected to divorce their moral convictions from their religious faith; but they have no business trying to impose their religiously inspired convictions on those who do not share them, and this is material to the dispute over gay marriage. Furthermore, they may, on reflection, find that, in addition to a genuine concern to protect the institution of marriage, there is an unavoidable moral and pastoral dimension to discussing same-sex marriage openly and calmly.

I find that the notion of gay marriage presents me with a dilemma which is disconcerting, and which is at once pastoral and philosophical. Let me examine each horn of the dilemma.

If gay men and lesbian women feel that the right to marriage is necessary for their human dignity, social equality and a sense of belonging, I as a Christian instinctively wish to favour it, because not to do so seems uncaring of people who belong to a much misunderstood section of society. The church has a poor record in this matter; hence, ordinary Catholics have to try to make up for our institutional defects. We need to oppose anything that might make homosexuals feel in any way excluded from an equal and respected place in society and in the church. This seems to me to be rather more important from a pastoral point of view than worrying about ecclesiastical structures and essentialist concerns bequeathed by the past and quietly disowned by Vatican II. It is plain that many homosexuals feel that they need the possibility of marriage in order to achieve true equality with heterosexuals. It is up to the church to respond to that sense of need with empathy and pastoral concern, even where we may not be in broad philosophical agreement with the arguments advanced in its support. Deeply rooted essentialism, of the sort in which many bishops have been theologically educated, may make it virtually impossible for them to accept that homosexuality is a condition that is congenital and not, as they have been taught, 'an intrinsic disorder'.

One of the most influential books in Catholic theology has been Heinrich Denzinger's *Enchiridion Symbolorum et Definitionum.* [5] It is a valuable source-book that has been re-edited and expanded many times. Denzinger compiled it to introduce an historical dimension into Catholic theology. Paradoxically, because of the way in which it came to be used, it lost much of its historical character and became a collection of texts designed to be channels of the view that Christian revelation is contained in magisterial statements intended to be received by faith as intellectual assent. Karl Rahner and Yves Congar spoke and wrote disapprovingly of 'Denzinger theology', meaning that an historically useful book had been reduced to being 'a Bible of Catholic Doctrine'. It remains a valuable source book, when it is read as a collection, not of doctrines, but of historical documents, some of which are doctrinal statements.

In the context of gay marriage, the notion of 'Denzinger theology' helps to explain something of the attitude of curialists and bishops theologically educated in an age of unrestrained essentialism. They have no answer to the problems posed by a condition they are prevented from understanding by their essentialist training.

Modern anthropology and psychology, not being limited by a metaphysical preoccupation with essences, accept the givenness of homosexuality without necessarily being able to agree scientifically about its origins or causes. In this respect at least, existential concern with what is the case takes precedence over what one might think ought to be the case.

Nevertheless, in spite of these personal and pastoral considerations,

5. First published in Würzburg, 1854, it has had many editors, the most important being Adolf Schönmetzer, S.J. The present editor is Peter Hünermann.

we must necessarily attend to the structural character of marriage and its role in society; and this brings me to the second horn of my dilemma, which is philosophical rather than pastoral. Before I consider the philosophical implications of gay marriage, and because my position could easily be misrepresented or simply misunderstood, I will summarise why I believe that Catholics may vote 'yes' with good conscience to the civil recognition of gay marriage.

In Ireland, first of all, this is a matter of constitutional law that governs every citizen of the State. One does not have to agree with its prescriptions to agree to be bound by them. This is an issue for the State, not for the Church. Marriage as a sacrament is the proper concern of the church, and it is difficult to understand why, in the light of Vatican II's teaching on religious liberty, conservative Catholics still feel that they have a right to impose their own religiously informed values on those who do not share them.

I understand and respect those who, in the referendum of May 2015, refrained from voting either for or against. This was once my position, but further reflection led me to change it in favour of voting 'yes'.

The question of gay marriage is open to philosophical analysis, which makes it clear that, in its classical definition, marriage involves two sexes. Why, then, do I believe that I could legitimately and morally vote in favour of gay marriage? Quite simply because I believe that concern for the dignity and self-worth of any human being trumps legal and metaphysical considerations.

Relating permanence to change can be seen as a function of the relationship between essence and existence. When I returned to full-time theology just after the Second Vatican Council had concluded in 1965, one question still affecting theology was the philosophical movement of Existentialism, which was widely seen as an inescapably atheistic philosophy. Pope Pius XII, in his encyclical, *Humani Generis* (1950), attacked several new trends in Catholic theology and philosophy (known by its enemies as '*la nouvelle théologie*').

The Pope wrote his encyclical in the knowledge of the impression that the writings of Pierre Teilhard de Chardin, the French Jesuit paleontologist and theologian, were having on many contemporary Catholic intellectuals. Pius did not take issue with the theory of evolution (provided that the direct creation of each human soul was affirmed) but he clearly regarded Darwin's theory of natural selection as unproven and dangerous. The

Pope did not like any suggestion of mutability or challenge to essentialist determinism. He was less concerned with the relationship between science and Christian doctrine than with the effect that the idea of evolution was having on the traditional essentialism of Catholic thought. In this he was echoing the thought of two Roman theologians, Sebastian Tromp, S.J., of the Gregorian University, and Reginald Garrigou-Lagrange, O.P., of the Angelicum University (either or both of whom were probably involved in the drafting of the encyclical). Placed in historical context, *Humani Generis* is a useful inverse guide to the achievements of the Second Vatican Council, which, only ten and a half years later, would set aside many of its teachings.

Near the beginning of his encyclical Pius stated very succinctly what was worrying curial Rome:

> Such fictitious tenets of evolution which repudiate all that is absolute, firm and immutable, have paved the way for the new erroneous philosophy which, rivaling idealism, immanentism and pragmatism, has assumed the name of existentialism, since it concerns itself only with existence of individual things and neglects all consideration of their immutable essences. (Art. 6)

The encyclical also shows that its author recognised the potential conflict between existentialism and the authority of the magisterium, which is an authority that has depended heavily on an essentialist view of society and is always a neuralgic topic for Roman authority.

> Unfortunately these advocates of novelty easily pass from despising scholastic theology to the neglect of and even contempt for the Teaching Authority of the Church itself, which gives such authoritative approval to scholastic theology. (Art. 18)

In the close link between neo-scholasticism and the magisterium, papal power was heavily reliant on a propositional understanding of revelation, which in turn lent itself to tight curial control.

> Hence Our Predecessor of immortal memory, Pius IX, teaching that the most noble office of theology is to show how a doctrine defined by the Church is contained in the sources of revelation, added these words, and with very good reason: 'in that sense in which it has been defined by the Church.' (Art. 21)

This is sometimes known without embarrassment or sense of irony as the 'regressive method'. In effect, it tells the theologian to begin with the contemporary teaching of the magisterium and show how it can be found in the sources of revelation, namely Scripture and Tradition. This placing of the cart before the horse, of course, rules out all possibility of theological reform. Happily, Vatican II would later abandon the two-source theory of revelation, and this would rule out Tradition as a separate source of revelation. *Humani Generis* re-affirms the necessity of scholastic philosophy for Catholic orthodoxy:

> How deplorable it is then that this philosophy, received and honored by the Church, is scorned by some, who shamelessly call it outmoded in form and rationalistic, as they say, in its method of thought. (Art. 32)

In 1998, Pope John Paul II issued an encyclical, *Fides et Ratio*, which contains the following startling words: 'The Church has no philosophy of her own nor does she canonize any one particular philosophy in preference to others.' (Art 49) It was a remark that would have astonished Popes Leo XIII, Pius X and Pius XII, and it came from a staunch authoritarian conservative!

Back in the period between *Humani Generis* and the meeting of Vatican II some important Catholic theologians believed that existentialism was not irreducibly atheistic, and that in moderation it could have a beneficial effect on Catholic thought, when seen as a corrective to the essentialism that had dominated Christian theology from its conciliar encounter with Hellenism in the fourth century.

To be sure that my argument is free of ambiguity, I should at this point offer a definition of both essentialism and existentialism:

(1) Essentialism is the belief that existents have a fixed essence composed of qualities which belong exclusively to them and which define them in advance of their actual historical existence.

(2) Existentialism is the belief that existence entails the freedom to become what one wants to be. Human beings are therefore defined only by what they make of themselves and of the world that is their habitat, not by pre-existing Forms that determine their essence or nature.

A slogan of Jean Paul Sartre – 'existence precedes essence' – became virtually a definition of existentialism, and it spoke to some theologians who were reacting against what they saw as the disproportionate essentialism of much traditional Catholic theological and moral teaching.

Sartre's lifelong companion, Simone de Beauvoir, gave a feminist twist to his dictum about essence and existence, remarking that one is not born a woman; one becomes a woman. She thus attacked the idea that one's life is comprehensively predetermined not merely by gender but by one's nature, or essence, which pre-exists, and is independent of, one's life in the world.

When the Second Vatican Council tacitly abandoned mandatory essentialism, it became possible for Catholic theologians to express themselves in philosophical languages other than Platonism and Aristotelianism. Existentialism was fashionable in the 1960s, and it offered theologians and spiritual writers the attractive possibilities of an emphasis on experience – a word that was highly suspect in Rome since the condemnation of Modernism at the beginning of the century. The council had taken the emphasis off revelation as statement and had placed it on experience and history, and had spoken of faith as decision and commitment. Thus it was preparing the way for a modified form of existential analysis, totally in keeping with authentic Christianity.

Christian existentialism is usually seen as having its beginnings in the writings of the Danish philosopher and theologian, Søren Kierkegaard (1813-1855) who deprecated the role that reason had achieved in Christian thought and in post-Enlightenment philosophy, especially that of René Decartes (1596-1650) and Georg W.F. Hegel (1770-1831). For Kierkegaard, faith is a leap from rationality into experience and trust. Catholic essentialists tended to regard this as rank fideism and they occasionally ridiculed it. The First Vatican Council had stated solemnly that God can be known by reason and God's existence can be proved by rational argument. Moderate Catholic existentialists did not deny that God's existence could be proved rationally; they merely observed that revelation is necessary for a true understanding of who God is.

After Vatican II a new Catholic interest in the Bible included critical scholarship, and it directed attention away from what many saw as the rationalism of 'natural theology'. Existentialism was a contemporary philosophy which provided a much-needed corrective of essentialism. A few theologians, like Karl Rahner, and Bernard Lonergan, tried to bring about a synthesis between scholasticism and existentialism (Transcendental Thomism). Rahner's work dealt explicitly and technically with the effect of European Existentialism on Christian, and especially Catholic, theology.

Most theologians, however, simply rejoiced in the new freedom made possible by the council, and Catholic theology took several new turns. One thinks of ecumenical theology, Liberation theology and Feminist theology, as examples. I call all these developments 'existential' insofar as they mark a break with essentialism. Plural theologies have proved to be a new and exciting experience for Catholic theologians, but curial Rome is obviously ill-at-ease with much of what has been happening since Vatican II, and an unreformed CDF has used its institutional power to attack decent men and women for opening out to the modern world.

I use the term 'existential(ist)' loosely to describe theologies that broke free of scholastic essentialism and, inspired by the teaching of the Second Vatican Council on such matters as revelation, Scripture and Tradition, experience, collegiality, personalism, ecumenism and religious freedom, allowed a new generation of theologians to find fresh ways of expressing themselves which would not have been possible before the council. The word 'existential' is convenient as an antonym for essentialist.

Unfortunately the Vatican magisterium remains captive to the essentialism on which its power has been based, and it continues to judge modern theologians by its own criteria, backed by its power and institutional authority. The term 'existentialism' can be loosely applied to any departure from essentialist determinism; hence there are many opportunities for hostile action by the Congregation for the Doctrine of the Faith and American and other bishops intent on preserving their pre-conciliar authority.

Plato's influence on conservative Christian thought has not always been sufficiently recognised, notably on matters to do with essence and existence. It is not difficult to appreciate why the women's movement finds it necessary to escape from the tradition of male supremacy and wishes to espouse a less deterministic understanding of human nature: Being is not a finished state of existence, and in this world it must always be open to becoming.

This topic is often discussed less philosophically in terms of nature and nurture, nature being seen as given in advance of human intervention, and nurture being seen as what human beings do to and with nature.

Today's growing concern for our natural environment calls for strict limitations on what we are doing to our planet. Some encroachment on exaggerated freedom to do what we like with our environment has become alarmingly necessary. The interaction of genes with environment is another component of the nature/nurture debate. However, it is my contention that the relationship between essence and existence, though the product of metaphysical analysis, is a particularly valuable way of approaching the issue. Care for the environment demands that we curb our freedom to develop the natural world as we please. Pope Francis' encyclical on care for our common home, *Laudato Si'*, makes enviromental concern a serious matter for Catholics, and seems to be offending those conservatives who are opposed to the environmental movement and deny the truth of global warming.

Pius XII, in his encyclical *Humani Generis*, saw Existentialism as a philosophy that concerns itself only with individual existents and dispenses with immutable essences.

This comprehensively essentialist attitude had no truck with any kind or degree of existentialism; and it was intended as a warning to Catholic theologians not to stray from it. Existentialism professed the view that human beings are free to shape themselves and their world in accordance with conscience or with cultures current at any given time. A generation later, Pope Benedict XVI preferred to treat the matter as unacceptable relativism, which he excoriated as one of the most serious defects of modern secular thought.

Without essentialism the authority of the papacy would need to be re-thought: Vatican II attempted to do this, but came up against entrenched papal traditionalism. It was, of course, the teaching of the Second Vatican Council that made possible Pope John Paul's departure from mandatory Thomism with his affirmation that the church espouses no particular philosophy as a standard of Catholic orthodoxy.

Understandably, Benedict interpreted radical relativism as an assault on Christian faith but, going further, he actually saw the church as a victim, while allowing the CDF to oppress Catholics who publicly took a position that differed from official conservative orthodoxy on unessential matters!

Some concessions have to be made to the essentialist position. An outright existential attitude to the institution of marriage would rob it of its enduring character as the exclusive union of a man and a woman. In view of the inflated essentialism of the traditional Catholic view of marriage, proponents of same-sex marriage have necessarily had to adopt an existential approach to the topic.

I contend that for healthy church governance we need a balance between existentialism and essentialism, not a capitulation of one to the other. Where, on the one hand, much modern secular thinking in the developed world dispenses with the natural restraints provided by essentialism, the Catholic Church, at the opposite extreme, has tended to ignore the rightful claims of the existential and of cultural changes that have taken place in doctrinal and moral attitudes, especially since the Enlightenment. In many respects essentialism is an enemy of science, since, by professing pre-emptive knowledge of the nature of this and that, it has already determined what science is engaged in exploring. Strict essentialism allows for no exceptions. One remembers Blaise Pascal's rejection of the essentialist dictum that nature abhors a vacuum by showing that evidence for vacuums does in fact exist in nature.

Essentialism has been given its clearest shape in Plato's doctrine of the world of Forms, in which all mundane objects have to be related to a superior world of immutable Forms, where the perfect, essential and archetypal Forms give intelligibility to everyday objects. For Plato, we make sense of our sublunary world by reference to the transcendent world of perfect Forms, in which our souls dwelt contemplatively before being exiled in the body. Christian thinkers, like St Augustine, while avoiding the notion of pre-existent souls, identified these Forms with the thoughts of God, thereby stamping much subsequent Christian theology with the seal of Platonic idealism.

Neo-Platonism sharpened the distinction between soul and body. It saw the soul as the higher element in a union with the body, the lower element. In this way of thinking, the union of soul with body constitutes the human person, who has fallen into a state of alienation from its origins. This fall was converted by St Augustine into the doctrine of original sin. Neo-Platonism saw the body as the material element of human existence, and the soul as the spiritual element, which is exiled into bodily existence and is repatriated by contemplation and a good life. This led to a dualism between the two that continues to affect Christian consciousness and, among other things, has promoted an exaggerated distinction between nature and supernature.

St Augustine, owing to his own experience of the effect that sex had on delaying his conversion to Christianity, identified sexual desire with sin, thus creating a western doctrine, original sin, that the Orthodox Church of the east has never fully understood. Furthermore, by identifying sexual desire with sin, Augustine has given sex a totally exaggerated role in moral theology.

The essentialist character of Catholic moral theology lent itself to populist distortion, which can help us to understand the harmful effect that unsophisticated essentialism has had on popular religious and cultural life. Ireland during the first half of the twentieth century was an ideal place for populist essentialism to flourish. It had a powerful, scholastically educated clergy, a highly biddable State and a society that was still largely intellectually untouched by the Enlightenment.

Neo-Platonist dualism, when popularised and distorted, also led to a bizarre denunciation of sex and sexuality which, before the meeting of Vatican II, had suffused much Catholic preaching and spirituality to a degree that amounted to an implicit, if unintended, denial of the goodness of creation. I am old enough to remember the atmosphere of religiously inspired phobia about sex that prevailed in the Irish Catholic Church, and in secular life, in the early and mid-twentieth century. All other moral considerations were dwarfed by a ridiculous obsession with sex, which today can make one wonder how it was able to gain such a firm hold on Catholic moral consciousness. That obsession had a remarkable influence on Irish life and led to a national phobia about sex that spawned a secular censorship of gargantuan proportions, prompting one commentator to claim that the list of books banned in Ireland was an index to some of the finest works of modern literature. Although the obsession has now largely gone, there are lessons to be learned from the fact that it ever occurred and has never been formally disowned or publicly regretted by the church.

Catholic moral theology fostered a grim distinction between mortal and venial sin, not hesitating, in its teaching manuals, to declare that sexual offences admitted of no lightness of matter ('*parvitas materiae*'), and were always mortal sins. Many of us who underwent this reign of moral terror may be forgiven for a continuing sense of resentment at an utterly misplaced and distorted essentialist moral theology. In those days it was not easy being a scrupulous adolescent, with proverbially raging hormones!

Will future generations regard as equally unacceptable what is happening today in respect of rigid church authority and belief in the permanent validity of papal and curial attitudes? Can current Roman preoccupation with the irreformability of church teaching in matters that do not belong to the substance of faith survive credibly into the future?

More serious, however, than Catholic guilt feelings about the whole area of sex and sexuality was the effect of essentialist thinking on the theology of marriage. Reproduction was seen as virtually the only reason for sex in marriage. Reproduction, as it were, redeemed the intrinsic sinfulness of sex. In Ireland, reproduction outside of marriage was viewed with particular disapproval, which had a catastrophic effect on the treatment of mothers of 'illegitimate' children and on the lives of the children themselves. Enforced adoption was the common fate of these children and their mothers. Draconian measures were taken to prevent the mother of an adopted child from ever discovering or meeting her child again.

The institutions to which these children were consigned were mostly run by religious congregations. Regarded as products of shameful relationships, these children were denied the treatment and esteem due to every human being, rich or poor. The nuns who ran the institutions are today blamed for the part they played in this wretched state of affairs; but it is unfair to load the whole burden of guilt for the activities of their predecessors on the shoulders of today's religious sisters. In a country, the population of which was predominantly Catholic, it was inevitable, at that time, that religious orders were given the task of running institutions that were properly the responsibility of the state. Members of other churches ran similar institutions. Most of them reflected the Victorian values that continued to influence society in Ireland well into the twentieth century.

Even if we look at the situation historically and non-judgementally, we are forced to ask why the Christian education of dedicated women and men did not inspire them to revolt, in the name of the Christian religion itself, against a system that treated some mothers and their babies as second-class citizens. It can be reasonably argued that we should not judge the past by the moral standards of today; but that is not the point that should concern us most.

The basic moral obligations of Christians were laid down 2,000 years ago and are at least a theoretical constant in Christian life ever since. History provides us with grim evidence that Christians have often failed to see their relevance to contemporary socio-political situations. The most pertinent question to be asked about the Christian institutions that took in single mothers and their babies is: what prevented Gospel values from bearing on that situation? How was it that societal pressures blinded them to the message of the Gospel and the human dignity of a single mother and her child? Today many would blame it on indoctrination, which took the place of appropriate and humble Christian instruction. It is a warning of what happens when the church places inordinate emphasis on rules and regulations at the expense of mercy and compassion.

The same question could be asked about institutions that looked after delinquent boys. How was it that the spiritual training of religious brothers and priests seemed to have had little bearing on the diverse tasks they undertook in these institutions? Were they so preoccupied with practising the supernatural virtues, that the natural virtues and elementary Gospel values somehow seem to have been submerged by the social pressures of the time?

Though sexuality was not the only area in Catholic thought to be affected by an unrestrained essentialism, it is particularly memorable because of the suffering it inflicted on the young and vulnerable.

In a less dramatic but no less important way, when essentialism dominated ecclesiology, the result was the stern proclamation of allegedly timeless and immutable papal statements from which the magisterium declared itself unable to depart. This remains with us today as a source of unnecessary and damaging division and as an obstacle to badly needed reform. Pope Francis' attitude seems to point away from this direction, but it remains to be seen whether he can break out of a system based on entrenched bureaucratic power and on a fear of the consequences that would follow if it were to be seriously reformed. One wonders whether he recognises that the curia have not been curbed, and that he himself is continuing to attempt an impossible consensus between old world traditionalists and those who have been inspired by the reforming impetus of the Second Vatican Council. Much may be going on behind the scene.

Although many professional moral theologians have moved on from an essentialist philosophical underpinning of Catholic moral theology, papal teaching on some moral questions has remained unchanged in its philosophical structure, notably in its teaching on marriage and sexuality. This, together with the principle of integralism, helps to explain its highly questionable linking of contraception with abortion, except where abortion is used as a method of birth control. Many moral theologians today, having broken away from a predominantly essentialist approach to morality, would treat contraception and abortion as two distinct questions which have little or no moral relationship to each other (with the possible exception of the 'morning after' pill). They no longer see contraception as offending against 'natural law', while continuing to regard abortion as radically wrong, always with due regard for the life of the mother.

Some might hold that the Vatican's condemnation of contraception actually weakens its stand on abortion. People who might listen to its teaching on abortion may be repelled by its facile attitude to contraception.

Popes regarding themselves as bound by *all* their predecessors' teaching exacerbate this problem. Pope Pius XI's encyclical, *Casti Connubii*, (1930) cast a dark shadow over Catholic moral standards on sex and presented a teaching on contraception that has governed the thinking of successive popes.

> ... [N]o reason, however grave, may be put forward by which anything intrinsically against nature may become conformable to nature and morally good. Since, therefore, the conjugal act is destined primarily by nature for the begetting of children, those who in exercising it deliberately frustrate its natural power and purpose sin against nature and commit a deed which is shameful and intrinsically vicious (Art. 54).

Those rigid and uncompromising words are unequivocally essentialist, and are apparently bereft of an appreciation of the role of sex in marriage other than its reproductive function. They set the papal scene for the rest of the twentieth century and the beginning of the twenty-first. If read with an essentialist mindset and a strong conviction of papal inerrancy, even in matters which do not belong to the essence of the faith, they present an insuperable obstacle to a beneficial change of moral teaching. The notion of 'intrinsic evil' – a deeply essentialist phrase – coupled to a view of nature as immutable, has set papal teaching on marriage and sexuality in stone, taking no account of advances in modern psychology and anthropology. Needed reform may well depend on the ability to recognise that this philosophical standpoint can be changed without any infidelity to the substance of revealed truth. The present situation suggests that a cohort of celibates, with an idealised view of marriage and no regard for scientific advances, is deciding how the great majority of their fellow men and women should behave sexually and reproductively.

Nevertheless, by the 1960s, owing chiefly to the meeting of the Second Vatican Council, Catholic hopes were high that a change in papal attitude to contraception would occur. Possibly influenced by the hard-line traditionalists around him, and offending against the letter and spirit of the council's doctrine of collegiality, Pope Paul removed matters of marriage and sexual morality from the floor of the council, reserving them exclusively to himself. When he subsequently set up a group of experts to advise him on marriage, sexuality and the family, Catholic hopes for a change of papal attitude to contraception were high. It is known that most of the group of advisors were in favour of change. Those hopes, however, were dashed by Paul's encyclical, *Humanae Vitae* (1968), which caused, and continues to cause, major dissent in the church. Though it was a somewhat warmer document than *Casti Connubii*, and it allowed for 'natural' methods of birth control, it nevertheless basically re-affirmed Pius XI's condemnation. Paul recognised that the traditional teaching was no longer being widely received in the European and American churches, but, so great was his regard for the binding power of previous papal teaching, he chose to disregard this awkward fact.

Opposition to his encyclical was not confined to world-renowned theologians like Karl Rahner, Hans Küng and Charles Curran. Bishops like Christopher Butler, and, notably, Cardinal Leo Joseph Suenens, were unafraid to voice their misgivings. Suenens made the point that moral theology was not taking sufficient note of scientific progress that could help to determine what is according to nature (taken more perhaps in a physical than a metaphysical sense). In a strikingly courageous remark he expressed fear that the encyclical would be 'another Galileo affair. One is enough for the Church'. [6]

Suenens saw the ecclesiological implications of what the Pope had done, and he pointed out that *Humanae Vitae* offended against the collegiality that had been proclaimed by the recent council.[7] This was a crucial contribution to the debate, by a cardinal no less, though the Vatican has subsequently managed to ignore it with impunity. When Pope Paul VI chose to reject the advice of the group he had set up to counsel him on marriage, sexuality and the family, and opted instead for a reiteration of the ban on contraception, he did so less because of substantive moral thinking about contraception than because of previous papal pronouncements on it. Thus, in Paul's thinking, the immutability of papal pronouncements prevailed over all other moral and doctrinal considerations. There are Catholic bishops today who have put forward the ban on contraception as a touchstone of orthodoxy and an essential component of 'church teaching'.

Pope Francis' attitude to *Humanae Vitae* is difficult to understand, but it suggests an unfortunate halt to progress on this front, until, if ever, Francis comes to accept that Pope Paul's encyclical does not bind him to a similar view. An editorial in the *National Catholic Reporter* expressed the heartfelt feelings of many Catholics on the matter: 'If Francis wants the church to be a credible witness, if he wants to be the pastor we think

6. Peter Hebblethwaite, *Paul VI* (New York, 1993), p. 394.
7. Op. cit. p. 533.

he can be, he needs to take us beyond the *Humanae Vitae* impasse.'[8] One wonders why, in view of his concern for compassion, the Pope cannot see the effect that this is having on the whole church, as it is forced to accept the negative rule-driven attitude of its remaining essentialists.

As long as popes continue to see themselves as bound by previous papal teaching on topics not belonging to the substance of Christian faith, there is little prospect of amelioration of current theoretical papal attitudes to sex and reproduction. Rome needs to appreciate that, far from showing commendable firmness to the world by its intransigence on sex and re-production, it may actually be giving scandal to people who are looking on in some amazement at the behaviour of one of the last absolute mon-archies in the West, together with its backward-looking curial bureaucrats. Surely the time has come to look afresh at the institutional church in the light of the Gospel and to see how far it has strayed from the attitude and teaching of Jesus? At the moment, there is a sizeable gap between official church teaching and the attitude of most ordinary Catholics to contracep-tion. That the Vatican refuses to acknowledge the existence of this gap is a regrettable consequence of its essentialist and integralist principles. *Humanae Vitae* has not been 'received' by the church at large, yet Rome has never conceded this and stubbornly persists in making it a changeless feature of Catholic orthodoxy and in punishing some of those Catholics who take public issue with it – something that Paul VI never did.

This attitude employs theory that does not accord with what many Catholics conscientiously believe and practise. The clear implication is the conviction that whenever there is disagreement between them, even on a matter that is not an essential element of Catholic faith, Rome is always right and the rest of the church is wrong. This attitude is no longer credible and has to change if we are to save institutional Catholicism from itself. It might have been in some way credible in the days when Christian revelation was considered to be propositional, and a sharp distinction was made between the teaching church and the learning church; but this crude distinction is today disowned as totally unacceptable by most ecclesiologists.

John Henry Newman wrote a famous essay about consulting the faith-ful in matters of doctrine. In the pontificate of Pius IX this was a danger-ous thing to do, and Newman had to defend himself against widespread

8. *National Catholic Reporter*, January 30 – February 12, 2015, p. 28.

conservative criticism. Leo XIII, however, gave him a Red Hat, which protected him from posthumous attack during the Modernist crisis. And he almost certainly would have been attacked, for he was no scholastic, and that made him a prime target during the Modernist crisis.[9]

It is illuminating to compare Newman's theology with Roman theology of that age. He went to Rome shortly after his conversion, a 45- year-old man, sitting among youngsters and being instructed in scholastic theology. No wonder he slept during some of his lectures! His teachers, theologians like Giovanni Perrone (1794-1876), did not know what to make of him. Perrone is credited with the judgement that Newman 'mixes and confuses everything'. This is how a neo-scholastic would react to someone whose thought-patterns were less abstract and tightly defined than his own. To rigid traditionalists, with no conception of different legitimate views in the church, all opposition to their way of thinking is 'confusing'; it is a popular word with ultra-conservatives who are worried by the diversity of modern Catholic theology. Newman was showing how one could be a believing Catholic without being a scholastic essentialist. He came from a tradition profoundly influenced by a romantic reaction against the rationalism of the Enlightenment, combined with an emphasis on the imagination.

In England, rationalism had taken the shape of reliance on evidence for such basic issues as the existence of God. William Paley (1743-1805) was the foremost English natural theologian of his age. He became Bishop of Carlisle, though he was not greatly interested in clerical administration. He preferred the life of an academician. He wrote a book entitled *Natural Theology: or, Evidences of the Existence and Attributes of the Deity; Collected from the Appearances of Nature.* [10] It was a celebrated book that set out to prove the existence of God from rational 'evidences' in nature. It appealed to rationalists of the eighteenth century, though most scientists and many philosophers found the analogy between nature and God to be too remote to be logically valid. Charles Darwin, early in his life, was influenced by Paley, but he later pointed out that the principle of natural selection completely invalidated Paley's arguments.

By the time Paley died in 1805, the romantic era had begun and was being led in England by Samuel Taylor Coleridge, the poet and philosopher, who deplored the rationalism of the post-Enlightenment age. His thought, almost certainly, influenced Newman who liked to speak of

9. See *John Henry Newman and Modernism*, A.H. Jenkins (ed.), Sigmaringendorf, 1990.
10. London, 1802.

the importance of imagination and experience, and who believed that religious faith was kindled not by argument but by experience. Coleridge had Paley in mind when he wrote:

> Evidences of Christianity! I am weary of the word. Make a man feel the want of it; rouse him, if you can, to the self-knowledge of his need of it; and you may safely trust to its own Evidence.[11]

Newman held that people cannot be argued into faith. In a famous passage he writes:

> If I am asked to use Paley's argument for my own conversion, I say plainly I do not want to be converted by a smart syllogism; if I am asked to convert others by it, I say plainly I do not care to overcome their reason without touching their hearts. I wish to deal, not with controversialists, but with inquirers.[12]

For Coleridge and Newman, the imagination is what makes things come alive in the mind. It has been said of Coleridge that he continually seeks 'the radiance of the eternal in the particular'. Both he and Newman belong to the tradition of English empiricism, which favours the concrete over the abstract. For them, existents take precedence over essences. Coleridge professed: 'It is among the miseries of the present age that it recognises no medium between Literal and Metaphorical'.[13]

Newman made a celebrated distinction between the 'notional' and the 'real', which is roughly equivalent to the distinction between essence and existence and theology and religion. The real is personal, individual and particular. It is deep but it is also narrow. It is the conservative principle of knowledge. The notional is general, abstract and impersonal and is the principle of advancement, and therefore of cultural relevance. In Christianity we are saved by the real (faith); but faith is communicated by the notional (theology). The real on its own would be intellectually superficial (like fundamentalism). The notional on its own would amount to 'vague speculations'.[14]

11. S.T. Coleridge, *Aids to Reflection,* cited by Bernard M.G. Reardon, *From Coleridge to Gore: a Century of Religious Thought in Britain* (Longman, London, 1971) p. 65
12. John Henry Newman, *An Essay in Aid of A Grammar of Assent* (Longman, London, 1895), p. 425.
13. *The Collected Works of Samuel Taylor Coleridge*, vol. 6 *Lay Sermons* (Routledge and Kegan Paul, 1972(, p. 30.
14. Newman, *Grammar*, p. 34.

One of the many reforms instigated by Vatican II is reaction against the dualism of body and soul, which is paralleled by the dualism of nature and supernature, both of which have prompted church leaders to create for themselves an enclave designed to be separate from, and superior to, the world. It is important to appreciate that moderate reform of this dualism does not consist in replacing essence by existence. True reform strives to bring about a balance between the two, which will correct the imbalance that has long been promoted by an inflated emphasis on essentialist ideas and deductive methods in Catholic theology.

The radical essentialism of much papal thought has influenced every aspect of its teaching on sexual morality, including its views on homosexuality. Popes have felt constrained by the traditional papal understanding of the 'intrinsically' determined nature (essence) of the sexual act. A metaphysical approach to the matter, of the kind inherited from unquestioned, and possibly even from unconscious, Platonism tends to fend off any contribution that science might make to the subject. This is why lay participation in synods and other high-level assemblies is so important. Lay people will in most cases not have been schooled in essentialist thinking, though they may have been indirectly influenced by the essentialist mindset of their pastors. Their active participation in deliberative assemblies will help to bring a commonsense approach arising out of a lived experience that a celibate clergy does not have. Much the same needs to be said about homosexuality. The Lesbian, Gay, Bisexual and Transgender (LGBT) community needs to be listened to by the heterosexual community, if straight people are to understand how gay people actually feel in society and the church today. There is much to be learnt and acted upon, if we are to see how the Gospel expects us to think and behave. Short-sighted authority can stand in the path of reform in this respect.

Joseph Ratzinger's attitude to homosexuality, for instance, is strangely crude and astonishingly rigid for someone who initially played a significant role in bringing about the reforming ideals of Vatican II. His change of institutional attitude, which occurred towards the end of the 1960s, is difficult to understand. By the time John Paul II made him Prefect of the Congregation for the Doctrine of the Faith in 1981, he had become a fierce critic of homosexuality, and, by virtue of the power that his office gave him, he was able to impose his views on the entire Catholic Church, most notably in the US. In 1986 Ratzinger issued a letter, entitled *Homosexualitatis Problema*, which was directed to the whole church but was inspired mainly by American Catholic attempts to act pastorally towards gays and lesbians. Although he of course approved of pastoral care in the matter, he feared what he called 'an overly benign interpretation' of the homosexual condition, which, while it is not in itself a sin, 'the inclination itself must be seen as an objective disorder'.[15]

The language is forbiddingly essentialist, to say nothing of its insensitivity, and it puts Ratzinger in a curiously convoluted situation. On the one hand, he did not forbid pastorally minded Catholics to minister to homosexuals; on the other hand, he told them that, while doing so, they must always emphasise the morally 'disordered' nature of the homosexual condition – which is rather like a doctor telling patients always to remember that they are responsible for the congenital illness that has afflicted them. Guilty but not guilty. No wonder that many Catholic homosexuals were brought to the edge of despair, and tragically many of them have left the church. Ratzinger never seems to have appreciated that his attitude to homosexuality, not merely treats gay people with total lack of compassion and pastoral concern, but raises a crucial theological question about God the Creator.

It is an unreasonable reflection on the goodness of God's work to attribute the existence of homosexuality to sin, or to describe it as a 'disordered' condition. Ratzinger was, needless to say, accused of lack of compassion, but in John Allen's words, 'For Ratzinger ... compassion means telling homosexuals the full truth about church teaching, rather than encouraging what he sees as a flight from reality'. [16] He liked to speak of 'the right of the faithful to be given the truth', simply assuming that his own views are the truth. It cannot be said too often that he has a right to his own convictions; however, he had no right to use his powerful office to impose them on others in the name of orthodoxy. As a respected theologian aware of the traditions of academic freedom, he must have felt some tension between his life as an academic and the duty he seems to have felt as head of the CDF to impose what many would see as an unacceptable moral judgement on the entire church. His attitude to homosexuality has given scandal to many, inside and outside the church, and his advancement to the papacy has aggravated the harm done by him while he was Prefect of the CDF.

15. Cited in John L. Allen, Jr., *Cardinal Ratzinger: The Vatican's Enforcer of the Faith* (New York and London, 2000), pp. 201-2.
16. Ibid. p. 203.

On the one hand, Rome has adopted an exaggeratedly essentialist and deterministic view of the world, while atheistic existentialism, on the other hand, has regarded human beings as individuals who define themselves in total freedom from any predetermining essences, and who create their own values which give meaning to their world. Both views polarise opinions gratuitously and distort how Christians should see the world.

Nevertheless, the second horn of the dilemma is mainly philosophical in character: if we subscribe to *moderate and limited* essentialism in which there is an exclusive marital relationship between a man and a woman, that relationship belongs to nature and is, to that extent, permanent and unique. It cannot be changed by cultural and moral circumstances. It happens to be called 'marriage' in English; but the word is not significant. I agree with Archbishop Welby, however, that a gay relationship is entitled to all the legal recognition that is granted to married people; but that, as he points out, does not mean that there is no essential difference between the marital union of homosexuals and that of heterosexuals. I remain unimpressed by the claim that allowing gay men and lesbian women to marry members of their own sex necessarily has an effect on the Christian idea of marriage. Christians are perfectly free to carry on without any threat to their customary understanding of marriage.

I have described my situation as a dilemma. How is this dilemma to be met? In my view, from a Christian standpoint its solution needs to be pastoral rather than philosophical. It means balancing a gay claim to a right to marriage against a philosophical and moral conviction that the relationship we call 'marriage' is exclusively heterosexual in nature. To put the matter in practical terms, the referendum proposing a change to the constitutional idea of marriage was, in the last analysis, a case, not of religious or philosophical reference, but one of civil law. I believe that Catholics could legitimately vote in its favour for pastoral reasons.[17]

It is widely accepted by Catholic theologians today that since the Second Vatican Council's Declaration, *Dignitatis Humanae*, on religious liberty, one should not expect one's religious or philosophical convictions to be enshrined in a secular Constitution designed to be an instrument of government for all the people of a nation, irrespective of class, race or creed. In short, one can agree to respect a position which, for philosophical or

17. In this context, by 'pastoral' I mean care for the rights and dignity of all human beings, together with compassion for the victims of homophobia. We have allowed the word 'pastoral' to apply mainly to clerics. It is, of course, a feature of all Christian life, clerical *and lay*.

religious reasons one cannot share, and yet support the legal situation that gives gays and lesbians the dignity of seeing themselves, and allowing others to see them, as equal in every respect to the straight community in God's sight. The amendment to the Irish Constitution – 'Marriage may be contracted in accordance with law by two persons without distinction as to their sex' – does not mean that one has to change one's own idea of marriage; it simply means that others have a legal right to share our estate of marriage whether or not we agree.

I believe that questions to do with the adoption of children are distinct from those of gay marriage, and I do not consider them here. I respect, but do not share, the view of those who argue that marriage cannot be adequately discussed without considering the rights of children.

My belief that the condition we call 'marriage' is uniquely heterosexual is not a religiously inspired one, imposed by an intransigent magisterium, or by an uncritical and unhistorical reading of the Bible. It is philosophical to the extent that it is the product of critical analysis; and it is moral to the extent that it informs my conscience. One can be conscientiously opposed to gay marriage without being guilty of homophobia. The charge that all opposition to same-sex marriage is homophobic is simply unjust, in addition to being untrue. It is self-indulgent to the extent that it seeks to score an emotional victory over its opponents, instead of engaging in honest dialogue on a topic that calls for dispassionate argument and respect for opposing views. 'Homophobia' is a word that is lightly thrown around today, and it is on occasion applied recklessly to all opponents of gay marriage – which is both inaccurate and unjust.

Since Rome has chosen to take sexual and reproductive behaviour as a prominent element in its claim to supreme authority in the church, an examination of the ecclesiological implication of its approach to moral theology has become more necessary than ever. It is my contention that an analysis of the situation from a philosophical standpoint of the relationship between essence and existence can help in a constructive way to examine the matter afresh and perhaps lessen the tension between the magisterium and many of the rest of the church. My thesis is that radical essentialism has been the mark of Catholic moral teaching and ecclesiology, and that, as Cardinal Suenens remarked after Paul VI had issued his encyclical, *Humanae Vitae*, the Pope's decision to reaffirm the old heavily essentialist position on marriage and sexuality, which ignores both modern science and Vatican II's teaching on collegiality, laid, and continues to lay, an unnecessary burden on the shoulders of many in the church. In an age when religion has been so conventionally disregarded in the West, and recently in Ireland, why are some believers acting in a manner that only confirms the church's opponents in their conviction that they are right to dismiss its message?

Why is it that Catholics who put rules and regulations at the centre of church life do not seem to realise that they are setting up a repellent and joyless association, a faithless substitute for the sort of community that Jesus created when he sat at table with the rejects of society and made them feel accepted and cherished? Mercy and compassion achieve immeasurably more than laying down the law and punishing those who offend against it. If, as Pope Francis believes, the essence of church life is mercy and compassion, that essence will form a harmonious partnership with its concrete day-to-day existence, thus removing a damaging conflict between essence and existence, and giving the church a new lease of life.

15

Tacit Religion and Negative Capability

Pope Benedict XVI, now retired, has for long condemned 'relativism' not merely as a false philosophy but as a tyranny. He sees it in combative terms as a despotic move imposed on the world and church by modern secular culture. This construction placed on events deserves careful consideration. For him relativism amounts to the destruction of fixed, objective standards of truth and morality. In radical relativism, truth cannot be affirmed or attained as something given, absolute and eternally valid.

On the other hand, to deny the presence of a relativistic element in historical and social circumstances would be philosophically indefensible. As I have already suggested, a philosophy that appreciates the need for a balance between essences and concrete existences can help greatly in the struggle for meaning in today's world.

Pope Benedict rightly detected in the contemporary world a flight from any predetermined meanings that might be considered an encroachment on human freedom as an absolute. His critics, however, would claim that he went to the opposite extreme by rejecting the freedom to escape from the stranglehold of fixed meanings some of which can, and ought to, be changed or modified. A break with the then predominant essentialism was a major feature of the Enlightenment and the birth of modernity.

Philosophically speaking, the modern world begins in the revolution brought about by the philosopher Immanuel Kant in the eighteenth century. It is no accident that Kant was regarded as the main enemy by the defenders of neo-scholastic orthodoxy in the late nineteenth and early twentieth century. Kant challenged the idea that had been firmly established by the Greek philosophers, especially Plato and Aristotle, that knowledge registers the effect on the mind made by external reality. In this way of seeing things the mind is a *tabula rasa*, a blank receptor on which the external world imprints itself. Plato's view is that while contemplating that world, the mind discovers the unchanging essences of things that pre-exist in the world of forms and are reflected into nature in an orderly pattern before they are contemplated by human minds. For Aristotle, truthful knowledge consists in an accurate correspondence between the objective world and the human mind. In short, the mind must conform itself to what it finds in the given objective reality of the world.

Kant coolly reverses this centuries-old notion that the mind conforms itself to objective reality. Instead of the mind conforming to objects, he proposes that objects must conform to the mind. In his view we cannot know things as they are in themselves; we can know them only as given to the knowing subject by the mind. Kant does not reduce knowledge to a purely subjective creation, as later idealist thinkers were to do. For him, in all true knowledge the 'thing in itself' exists independently of the knowing subject. However, it cannot be known as it is in itself but must be clothed in the forms of the mind in order that it may be known. This emphasis on the subjective element of all human knowledge was a major contribution made by the Enlightenment to modern thought. It helps to explain why Kant was the leading 'adversary' in neo-scholastic orthodoxy.

Kant is not a relativist as Pope Benedict understood the term; but by his introduction of the subjective principle into modern thought, Kant makes extreme relativism possible. Benedict's dominant concern was that we should recognise the pre-existence of truth and the power of the mind to apprehend it. Otherwise we are tyrannized by the doctrine that each person makes his or her own truth, and consequently, that morality is purely relative to the circumstances in which people find themselves. Some of this kind of thinking actively attacks revealed religion for allegedly infringing on the freedom to believe and practise whatever one wants. However, in condemning radical relativism, thoughtful Christians should concede that there is a relativistic element in all doctrinal and moral judgement. A later age may reject as unacceptable the values of an earlier age. A pertinent moral example would be the abolition of slavery. In the cultural sphere change occurs as a natural sequence of reactive values, for example, from classicism to romanticism.

Situation[al] ethics, propounded by the American Christian ethicist, Joseph Fletcher, was influential in the 1960s. It reduced all morality to the single commandment of love and proclaimed that the end justifies the means. Thus the nuclear bombing of Hiroshima and Nagasaki could be justified on the grounds that it would shorten the Second World War. The scientists consulted by President Truman differed in their response to his question about the morality of what he planned to do by bombing the two Japanese cities. In the event, he listened to those who favoured his project, and both cities were consequently destroyed by atomic bombs.

In the late 1940s, when I was a student in Rome, in view of a house debate I was taking part in, I once asked Franziscus Hürth, S.J., the professor of moral theology in the Gregorian University in Rome, for his judgment on the morality of the atomic bombing of Hiroshima. He defended it and quite gratuitously added that he would also defend the carpet-bombing of Dresden only a short time earlier. Hürth was German and was reputed to be the most distinguished Catholic moral theologian of his time. Pius XII consulted him regularly. (I need hardly add that, in an age when authority was the principal source of moral certainty, quoting Hürth's opinion won the debate handsomely for our side!) Hürth, of course, was a preconciliar theologian and was in no way a situation ethicist, though in this instance he was prepared to argue that the end justified the means. The bombing of the two Japanese cities could be justified in his view on the grounds that it would shorten the war. Today there are Catholic moral theologians who would disagree with Hürth's opinion and would be prepared to argue that any use of nuclear weapons is wrong. It is a good example of legitimate differences of opinion and the development of moral consciousness.

However, attacks on relativism can go too far by promoting a concept of the absolute that leads to its own kind of tyranny. It has been said that absolutising the relative leads to fascism. Benedict XVI, in an interview, remarked that attempts to make the church change its position on homosexuality and the ordination of women are attacks 'on her freedom to live out her own identity'. This kind of thinking adopts a self-pitying and intemperate attitude that casts him and those who think like him in the role of victim. Once again, it identifies its own opinions with 'the teaching of the church' and ignores the legitimacy of pluralism and the right of Catholics to take issue with him. One does not have to be a radical relativist to dispute the papal position on such contentious issues as homosexuality and female ordination.

An unbalanced preoccupation with absolute values can be an obstacle to recognising the need for necessary change. Subscription to an inflated philosophy of essences can lead to an inflexible attitude to how things are in the church and world. Absolutism can militate against recognition of the changes brought about by the normal processes of history, and by doing so it can be said to demonstrate a lack of trust in the providence of God, who, in Jesus Christ, entered history to manifest himself to the world in a thoroughly human way.

This is why it is so important to recognise the implications of the fact that Christianity is an historical faith, and is therefore in some respects changeable, not in its essence but in the mode of its manifestation in every age. The essence of Christianity remains constant while its modes of existence and expression change in the course of history. The Good Samaritan can approach the wounded wayfarer in a space ship in the same way he does by the side of the road from Jerusalem to Jericho. Christianity is never a pure abstraction: it needs historical embodiment to fulfil its meaning and purpose. It began in history, and it achieves its meaning and purpose in history. Faithfulness to its essence depends upon willingness to engage in free dialogue with the changeable world in which it lives. There is always a risk of getting things wrong; but Christians have been given talents that need to be put at risk, if the grace of God in Christ is to influence the world. (Matthew 25:14-30)

Deduction, which used to be the normal form of theological and moral discourse, has, in some matters today, given way to scientifically based induction. There is much that religious believers can learn about human nature from scientific research, especially into the brain and how it functions. Setting up an opposition between science and religion, as some fundamentalists do, is indefensible and foolish. Of course there may come a point in some areas of scientific enquiry where religious authority finds itself forced to disagree with the moral implications of certain scientific conclusions and technological projects. However, if each remains in its own sphere, without seeking to pontificate where it has little or no competence, fruitless conflict can be avoided. The authorities of the Catholic Church would lose nothing by admitting that they do not have the answers to many problems thrown up by the modern world. Questioning, instead of outright condemning, would be a refreshing development in their thinking and behaviour; and it might, by its acceptance of nescience and even doubt, give an edifying lead in humility.

Catholics who hold views that are legitimately different from those of the current magisterium should not be treated as delinquents. Nobody who listens to his or her conscience is morally delinquent in a subjective sense. They may of course be persuaded by rational argument that they are wrong and ought to change their conscientious conviction(s). The practice by Rome of sending them to a monastery to repent of their convictions is lamentable, both arrogant and illogical. To suppose that prayer and silence can bring about a change in conscientiously and honestly held opinions, instead of strengthening them, might be regarded as laughable, were it not for the fact that it is a gross assault on human dignity and an offence against justice. The magisterium has no right to impose a biased, and possibly defective, position on dissidents. Intimidation is not a defensible way of trying to change the opinions of anyone, least of all, of one's fellow Christians. In this way of thinking, obedience to the magisterium is made to take moral precedence over conscience, intelligence and informed dissent. Obedience can never be a controlling virtue to be invoked as a justification for enforcing conformity to a questionable mindset. In secular society this would be called fascism.

The church has been entrusted with a glorious message that can contradict many assumptions and values of the world. This message can sometimes be counter-cultural and critical of some of the world's values in any age; but, if the church models itself on secular institutions for reasons of power or control, the message is easily lost to sight. The Christian challenge has always been to be in the world but not of it, in other words, to strike a balance between involvement and withdrawal.

The philosopher Michael Polanyi introduced the term 'tacit knowledge' into the philosophy of knowledge in 1958, in his book, *Personal Knowledge*, the title of which gives some indication of the meaning of his theory.[1] Tacit knowledge is the silent dimension of all that a person knows, and it is usually contrasted with explicit knowledge. An apprentice learns from his or her mentor by observation, close interaction, trust and a shared understanding as well as by verbal or written instruction. Albert Einstein

---

1. Michael Polanyi, *Personal Knowledge: Towards a Post-critical Philosophy* (Chicago, 1958).

used to claim that he did not teach his students: he provided the conditions in which they could learn for themselves.

Tacit knowledge cannot be verbally communicated to others. Its content has emotional resonance and may be intuitively based rather than purely rational and articulate. Once one has abandoned the nineteenth-century Catholic view of faith as assent to certain doctrines, tacit knowledge is the principal reason for the existence of church schools that have an ethos peculiar to this or that church.

Tacit knowledge should not be seen as an alternative to explicit knowledge: the two go together; and one without the other is incomplete. Doctrines are explicit and external communications: but they must be 'received' and lived if they are to become truly religious. One can be examined in doctrine but not in tacit religion. In a religious institution such as the Christian Church there has to be a respect for tacit values at every level of communication, including that of its formulation of doctrines and moral precepts. The church, if it is to speak credibly in the name of Christ, simply cannot act in the manner of totalitarian secular regimes. The imposition of cold rules is no substitute for a warm and empathetic sharing of values that are shaped by an honest response to the Gospel. The condemnation of waywardness, or perceived waywardness, needs to be carried out in a manner that is caring, tolerant and compassionate.

Tacit knowledge is an indispensible element in Christian life as well as in life in general. It bears on community, on relationships at every level and on an encouraging and hopeful outlook on life. It is more concerned with practice than with theory. Through it one learns to do the truth rather than simply acquiring truths through instruction. If tacit knowledge of Christianity is not acquired at local and familial level, it will hardly be achieved at any other level, however legitimately structured. Only someone obsessed with regimentation and control would choose to belong to the Catholic Church simply because it behaves so autocratically. People who tell critically minded members of the church that they should leave and join another church, in addition to encroaching scandalously on freedom of conscience, are demonstrating a mentality that is foreign to Christianity. If, in addition, they compare the church to a club, they simply reveal that their own membership of it has more to do with an unhealthy psychology and politics than with religion.

Tacit knowledge is present in the celebration of the sacraments and especially in any well-conducted Eucharist, where there is less focus on what happens to the bread and wine and more on what happens to those who are participating in the sacred meal. Sacraments are occasions for doing the truth, which is why Paul Tillich claimed that Catholic substance (always to be critically partnered by Protestant principle), is an indispensable element in any properly functioning Christian society. The most important feature of any, but especially any sacramental, celebration in Christian life is that its participants feel accepted and cherished, secure in the knowledge that they share in the consciousness of being sinners, accepted by God, when they admit their guilt and seek forgiveness. In the world of today, attribution of culpability has become a popular compulsion. We are all aware of evil and wrongdoing in the world, and there is a natural and instinctive urge to do something about it. Doing something about it may be totally located in policing, judging and imprisoning. Our prisons are full; and our principal concern often seems to be with retribution rather than with reform. There is a common impression that our judges are too lenient in their sentencing.

This response, however understandable it may be, cannot be allowed to constitute a final answer to the deeper question of the mystery of evil in the world. At a deeper level, one has to reckon with the Christian injunction not to judge. As Christians we cannot remain satisfied with denunciation and punishment as a remedy for all wrongdoing.

In Ireland we have become notably moralistic and judgemental; and those of us who are Christian may feel genuinely uncomfortable about the moralism which is endemic in our society, and which can so easily infect the church. Moralism, it must be emphasised, is very different from concern for morality. Moralism is a compulsion to assign blame wherever possible.

What, then, are we to make of the Christian injunction not to judge? The Gospel is disturbingly clear on the matter of judgement:

> Do not judge, and you will not be judged; do not condemn, and you will not be condemned. Forgive, and you will be forgiven. (Luke 6:37)

A. E. Harvey in his commentary on this saying of Jesus remarks that 'if [it is] taken as this-worldly advice, [it] would sound like either opportunism or wishful thinking'.[2] It is true that one could interpret the saying in a crudely opportunistic sense: 'I will not judge you, so that I can expect that you will not judge me'; but does it have to be taken in this self-serving sense? I believe that it goes much deeper than that, and reaches a level where the Gospel has its most profound meaning, which secularism cannot attain or even understand. Since I take it in this deeper sense, I should make it clear that I fully accept that there must be appropriate judgement and retribution for serious crime. This will normally happen in a court of law, though in less serious matters the urge to condemn can occur in everyday life. Sometimes one's reaction, for example, to an assault on a defenceless person will be an instinctive disgust coupled with a demand for punishment.

While I was pondering the deeper meaning of the Gospel's injunction not to judge, I heard on the news an account of how five young men had forced an entry to the house of a woman in her 80s who lived alone. Their initial motive appears to have been robbery, which is bad enough, but they also beat and kicked her for no reason. My immediate and instinctive reaction was, as it would be for most people, one of revulsion and anger at what they had done, and I instinctively hoped that they would be caught and severely punished. Was my judgement in conflict with the Gospel? I am forced to admit that to some extent it was; although the offence against elementary justice and love could be said to call for such a response.

The guiding spiritual principle obtaining in this and other similar situations would be the thought that, given the same social, moral and psychological circumstances, I could behave similarly. For this reason, and at this deepest level, however repelled I might be by the thought, I would have to identify myself with the criminals as potentially guilty of their crime. What any other human being has done, I could do, given similar circumstances. Such a judgement calls for clear-sightedness and especially for genuine humility. In worldly terms it can be dismissed as excessively idealistic; but is it not the true pith of the Gospel?

In the Sermon on the Mount Jesus draws attention to the fact that inner dispositions normally precede sinful acts: adultery begins with a lustful look, and murder begins with a feeling of anger (Matthew 5:27-28, 21-

2. A. E. Harvey, *The New English Bible: Companion to the New Testament* (OUP and CUP, 1970) p. 242.

22). In a word, by virtue of being human, we are all potential offenders; and the fact that we may not have committed murder or adultery may be due as much to lack of opportunity or lack of courage as to a genuinely moral response.

Another less dramatic but more relevant example would be that this book has been impenitently judgemental about the attitude and behaviour of popes and the Roman curia. My defence of what I am doing here would be that I am not acting at the deepest level of my being. If I were, I would have to imagine what it would be like if circumstances had led to my being a member of the Congregation for the Doctrine of the Faith. I have no reason to assume that, due to defective theological education and spiritual training, I would not have acted in an oppressive fashion similar to that of some of the members of the present Congregation.

The moralism that I have been reflecting on displays itself as an instinct to find people to blame for everything we perceive to be wrong; and this may draw our attention away from our own defects. In addition, there is the disturbing example of an offender, especially a sexual offender, who cannot understand why he or she did what they knew to be wrong, but felt helpless and distressed in face of the impulse to do it. Taking this example into consideration in no way detracts from the seriousness of the offence or the need to attend to the distress and the rights of the victim in cases of violence and assault. Evil as blame, however, can obscure the presence and truth of evil as lament. A judge who appreciates the importance of this distinction could feel sympathy for an offender while sending him or her to prison for transgressing the law. There is a great deal more to moral and religious life than merely observing and safeguarding the law.

The most harmful consequence of obsessive moralism is the destruction of our sense of the tragic. By 'tragic' I mean that part of life that is beyond the power of human control, moral or psychological, and thus induces in us a feeling of helplessness. By 'sense of the tragic' I mean the ability to contemplate, and live tranquilly with, the occurrence of wrongdoing, without succumbing to the compulsion to judge instantly and to assign blame, perhaps prematurely and possibly unjustly. The sense of the tragic, perhaps more than anything else, enables us to comply with the Gospel injunction not to judge. We possibly know little about the genetic, psychological or social conditions that have contributed to the commission of a particular crime.

This is not to be indifferent to the gravity of the crime; it merely acknowledges that human judgement can never reach a total understanding of human wrongdoing. Recognising this helps to keep us fully human and aware of the deeper dimensions of life.

The sense of the tragic is the moral counterpart of John Keats' penetrating idea of 'Negative Capability', which is

> when a man [or woman] is capable of being in uncertainties, mysteries, doubts, without any irritable reaching after fact and reason.[3]

Keats was expressing a poet's sentiments about his art; but his theory of Negative Capability has wider applicability than merely to aesthetics and the philosophy of poetry. To regard what Keats is saying as no more than a manifestation of the romanticism of his age is to miss the point he is making. According to Raymond Williams, Keats was aspiring to much more than dreamy passivity in his use of the phrase 'negative capability'.[4] Thoughtful Christians, when they contemplate their beliefs, which include the doctrine of creation, are dealing with mystery and transcendence, where scientific clarities are to be taken seriously, certainly, but then transcended to a level where a special frame of mind appropriate to the contemplation of mystery becomes indispensable.

Recognition of the limited capacity of the human mind to ponder the things of God is an honoured tradition in Christian thought. Apophaticism has traditionally gone under the phrase, *'docta ignorantia'*, learned awareness of what we do not know about God, which Thomas Aquinas held to be far greater than what we do know. Such awareness produces in the mystics a sense of wonder and peace, into which they can relax, secure in the knowledge that they are loved by God in whom they trust without reserve, in spite of the distressing problem of innocent suffering in the world and their own experience of the 'dark night of the soul'.

The doctrine of creation, when understood in its deepest sense, calls for a similar response. Creation must not be handed over to the exclusive

---

3. Letter to George and Tom Keats, 27 December 1817.
4. R. Williams, *Culture and Society 1780-1950* (London, Catoo and Windus, 1961), p. 62.

attention of scientists or neglected by Christians who concentrate exclusively on the doctrine of redemption. It refers theologically not merely to the beginning of the universe, but to the totality of relationships between nature and God.

The sense of the tragic is the moral counterpart of 'negative capability'. It does not remove the impulse, or the will, to condemn moral evil; it simply, at its deepest level, suspends moral judgement and the allocation of blame, thus generating a sphere of non-judgemental peace where the Gospel may be lived in all its fullness. The sense of the tragic acknowledges the mystery of evil in the world, and it recognises that the theory of 'original sin' has been, since the time of St Augustine, an imperfect attempt in the Western church to make evil in some way intelligible to Christian faith. The doctrine of original sin demands careful reconsideration by theologians today. There are people who reject the very notion of original sin, because it offends their sense of justice and their conviction of the innate goodness of human beings.

This view was particularly evident in the nineteenth and early twentieth centuries before the First World War put an end to romantic optimism about the human condition. In spite of its moral and intellectual defects, the doctrine of original sin attempts to say something of deep religious significance: no understanding of the human condition is valid that does not take into careful consideration its combination of goodness with its potential for evil. The debate over the question of whether human beings are basically good or bad is wrongly premised. The real challenge consists in accepting that every human being is a mysterious combination of both good and not merely actual evil but, perhaps more significantly, the potentiality for evil.

Unfortunately the doctrine of original sin, if not reformed, can allow the twofold meaning of evil, namely, 'evil as blame' and 'evil as lament', to become interchangeable, thereby blunting the distinction between culpability and tragedy. Notoriously, it became entangled with a false interpretation of the early chapters of the Book of Genesis, which need to be read with the mind and imagination of a poet sensitive to symbolism and metaphor. To identify Adam and Eve as historically the first biological humans is to play into the hands of hostile scientists who rightly dismiss this belief as blatant disregard for scientific truth. Taken, however, as a symbolic story of 'the Fall' of humankind, it is a brilliant representation of a mystery that is far too profound to lend itself to literal treatment.

Neither science nor law can account for the existence of evil in the world. Religion cannot do so either; but it can approach it with a mind appropriate to awareness of mystery, and it can employ stories called 'myths' that must be interpreted as symbolic and metaphorical, if they are to reveal their truth. A literal interpretation of them destroys their true meaning and scope and exposes those who interpret them literally to the ridicule of scientists, who, like fundamentalists, can themselves be disturbingly literal in their understanding of the world. Thoughtful Christians should always be aware of the true character of religious language, which is nearer to the condition of poetry than it is to that of science. It is not unscientific; it looks at nature from a different perspective.

Science has an indispensable part to play in our understanding of the universe, but it cannot be allowed to have the last word on the existence of the universe or to provide the only language through which the universe can be spoken about. Genuine scientists would never tell a poet, who often has recourse to metaphor and symbolism, that he or she should not write about nature in a way that is not literally (*i.e.*, scientifically) true. There is more than one way to speak about nature. One thinks, for example, of the poet who speaks of dew as 'the early sobbing of the morn', which is clearly not a scientific understanding of dew.

Recognition that not all 'evil' is attributable to wrongdoing may induce in the believer a feeling of helplessness; and it calls for a deep and difficult act of trust in the goodness and wisdom of God who permits evil and suffering to exist in the world. The existence of suffering in the world is often given as a cogent reason for atheism: a good God could never allow the innocent to suffer, we may feel. This assumes that the wisdom of God is similar to human wisdom, and it fails to practise the *docta ignorantia* taught by theologians like Augustine and Thomas Aquinas. This may be, to some extent, a reaction to the readiness of some misguided religious people to interpret natural disasters, such as earthquakes and diseases like AIDS, as a punishment from God – a monstrous notion which no morally responsible religious conviction could ever justify. An imagination that lacks a sense of the tragic, and attributes suffering and misfortune to the act of a punishing God, grossly distorts our image of God and of God's action in the world. God does not inflict suffering as a punishment for our wrongdoing. God asks us to live trustfully in a world where suffering occurs. If that suffering is remediable, God expects us to do what we can to remedy it. If it is not remediable, God asks us to trust in the wisdom of divine knowledge, power and love, and to get on with our lives in peace. Faith and trust are the deepest possible response to the mystery of God's relationship with creation.

The Gospel injunction not to judge others touches on one of the greatest mysteries of human existence. We can never fully know the inner disposition of another person. The existence of mental illness is a warning of how little we know about human subjectivity. Correct diagnosis of symptoms does not necessarily imply accurate knowledge of the condition that causes them. We know others largely by reference to ourselves and to our own experience; and often we do not know even ourselves at any depth. There have been notable advances in psychiatry and psychology in our time; but there is so much more than even experts can understand about human intelligence and freedom; and they never will.

Sometimes in crime dramas the prosecution wants to determine the guilt of an offender, so that a case can be made in a court of law. A psychologist is brought to the witness stand and asked whether the accused was able to know the difference between right and wrong, and whether in this instance he knew that what he did was wrong. If he did know, it may be sufficient in a court of law to lead to his conviction. But that is no solution to the mystery of human subjectivity. Not even the most learned psychologist or psychiatrist can go beyond academic or legal convention. Legal guilt is the best that judges and juries can determine, and even under law they may totally fail to arrive at a verdict that is accurate or just.

Sometimes, in a perceptive drama, an offender will cry out in misery that he or she felt powerless before an impulse to kill, commit an assault or act out a twisted or forbidden desire. That may carry little or no weight in a court of law; but it takes us into the mysterious depths of human subjectivity, where knowledge constitutes only part of the mystery, and where freedom is equally pertinent yet difficult to understand, still less to define.

The nature of freedom has been one of the classical philosophical discussions down the ages. Opinions range from an affirmation of unqualified freedom to an affirmation of unqualified determinism. The fact that so wide a range of opinions has been the case is an indication that we are in mysterious territory here. As we have seen in the matter of essence and existence, philosophical problems can have serious implications for theology. I have no intention of going into the problem of freedom and determinism here, except to remark that awareness of it may warn us that we are in an area in which there are no easy answers and no coherent or agreed theory. For instance, the treatments of paedophiles, ranging from castration to the wearing of devices or making their presence known to the community, with a consequent risk of mindless vigilantism, can all be seriously questioned. We are dealing here with a situation which cannot be understood simply as criminality, and which Christians may be obliged by their faith to take into greater depth than others would consider relevant or appropriate.

It is at these depths that the Gospel injunction not to judge comes into play. A verdict of guilty in a court of law does not begin to come to terms with the problem of evil, with its difficult though vital distinction between evil as attributable to wrongdoing and evil as a mystery of the human condition. God alone exercises ultimate justice because God alone can read the human heart. Law is a human creation, altogether necessary as an alternative to brute force. Nevertheless it can be imperfect enough to offend against justice. That is what makes capital punishment morally indefensible and psychologically distasteful. It is deeply disquieting to reflect that there have been men and women who were later shown to be innocent of the crime for which they were executed.

In a real sense the revealed fact of divine forgiveness cuts the knot of the philosophical problem of good and evil. That is why the Christian church must always remember the ambiguity of evil rather than indulging in condemnation. Morose condemnation of the modern world achieves little, and arguably acts as a counter-sign to the Gospel message that the church was given to announce to the world.

Regarding the church as a supernatural enclave segregated from the world at large, so that it may be the solitary source of spiritual health, is not merely arrogant; it may provide an occasion for the cynical merriment of outsiders – a fate that the church can ill afford in these days of its loss of credibility. The church cannot escape from the world; it will always bring the world with it into whatever seclusion it chooses. There are so many signs of wrongdoing in the church, that only faith can affirm its holiness. Those with faith cannot afford to ignore its failures; while those without faith cannot see its holiness; and this should shape the approach of the church to them. So often church authorities seem to assume that theirs is the only valid and truthful approach to the world and to the human condition. The church should be able to approach the world with an awareness of the world's values – not all of which, after all, are opposed to the Gospel.

A sound theology of salvation sees the whole world as the theatre of God's liberating activities and graces. The privileges that God has given to the church are given with the commission to use them with humility, liberality, trust and joy. They have been given with largesse and they should be used generously, with due regard for the freedom of people to refuse them, and always with a sensitive and sustained awareness of their divine origin. Without this awareness, the Christian church has no call to speak to the world with an authority greater than that of any other human society; and even when it does speak to the world with awareness of its divine mandate, it should do so with humility, an equal sensitivity to the insights of others and, above all, with an awareness that the Holy Spirit can inspire and act outside ecclesial settings.

The model for Christians is of course Jesus of Nazareth who made no distinction between the people who came to him and enjoyed his company at table. Creation is God's gift to every human being. It extends to a far wider community than to those who have listened to his word and organised a society in his name. He has other sheep that do not belong to the fold of the church: 'I must bring them also, and they will listen to my voice. So there will be one flock, one shepherd.' (John 10:17)

Creation is not simply the background to God's redemptive purposes; creation is itself part of the divine mystery, and is in need of redemption. 'We know that the whole creation has been groaning in travail together until now'. (Romans 8:22) Through human existence nature becomes conscious of itself, at least on our cosmologically undistinguished planet. The WCC document, to which I have already referred, puts the matter aptly and gives it an ecumenical context:

The Holy Spirit enlivens and equips the Church to play its role in proclaiming and bringing about that general transformation for which all creation groans (cf. Rom. 8:22-23).[5]

Some scientists, like Richard Dawkins, think that the question 'Why is there something rather than nothing?' is otiose, for the arrogant reason that science is not competent to answer it. Thoughtful people can find it to be possibly the most profound question that we can ask.

5. *The Church: Towards a Common Vision*, Faith and Order Paper No. 214, Art 21, p. 13.

16

Pilgrim's Progress and the Melancholy of Fulfilment

John Bunyan's famous hymn 'All Who Would Valiant Be' arises out of his great allegorical dream, *The Pilgrim's Progress*. It has strong Protestant echoes, and today it is often sung in Catholic churches. Bunyan was a seventeenth century Non-Conformist who was imprisoned for his failure to comply with Established Church regulations. *The Pilgrim's Progress* is both an English classic and a deeply Protestant work that has never been out of print since it was first published in 1678.

Since Catholics may be put off by its hostile attitude to the papacy, it is worth remembering that recent popes have formally asked members of other Christian churches to tell them how the papacy has been an obstacle to church unity. Martin Luther himself used the term 'the Antichrist', as a description of the papacy, and it has remained an instinctive feature of classical Protestant thought ever since. In Northern Ireland, and in other localities of populist Protestantism, it would in most cases be intended as a term of abuse with little or no serious theological content. Protestant ecumenists would probably be reluctant to use it in dialogue with Catholics today. However, Catholics should appreciate that Luther was not using it as a term of abuse; he was making a serious theological judgement that deserves equally serious consideration by Catholics. I mention it here because I believe that Catholics, in view of Bunyan's anti-Catholicism, might be dissuaded from pondering the message of *The Pilgrim's Progress*. That would be a pity, since the theme of pilgrimage is fundamental to Christian life, Protestant and Catholic.

Bunyan's allegory casts Christian, the hero, in the role of a pilgrim on a journey to the end of life. He encounters many hazards and temptations on the way, but he remains faithful to the purpose of his journey. At the end of his pilgrimage, mission accomplished, 'all the trumpets sound for him on the other side'. The theme of pilgrimage has been constant in

Christian thought and spirituality since its forceful expression in The Letter to the Hebrews: 'For here we have no lasting city, but we are looking for the city that is to come'. (Hebrews 13:14) The image of pilgrimage can be appropriately linked with the Eucharist, for example in Thomas Aquinas' hymn, *O Esca Viatorum*, translated in *Hymns Ancient and Modern* (1861) as 'O Food That Weary Pilgrims Love'.

Although the theme of pilgrimage can be found in both Catholic and Protestant spirituality, its natural home would seem to be Reformed Protestantism, where it expresses freedom from all earthly, including ecclesiastical, restraints (Non-Conformists, like Catholics, were punished by the seventeenth century English establishment). It somehow catches the Protestant spirit, which, in an age of unreconstructed religious bigotry and sectarianism, would have made it distasteful to Catholics. Today, thank God, in a more ecumenical age Catholics have much to learn from what it has meant to many Protestants down the ages. It has particular resonance for reflection on reform, and it prompts all Christians to consider how pilgrims should behave on their journey.

In this spirit, Catholics can profitably, and with good reason, listen to the words of Jonathan Edwards, a distinguished American intellectual, a Protestant theologian and spiritual writer who was an intriguing blend of Enlightenment scholar and revivalist churchman. He was particularly eloquent on the theme of pilgrimage:

> THIS world is not our abiding place. Our continuance here is but very short. Man's days on the earth, are as a shadow. It was never designed by God that this world should be our home.[1]

As well as being interested in science, Edwards was sensitive to the beauty of nature, and it has been said that he anticipated the theological aesthetics of the Swiss Catholic theologian, Hans Urs von Balthasar more than two centuries later. This was especially evident in his treatment of pilgrimage:

> Fathers and mothers, husbands, wives, children, or the company of earthly friends, are but shadows. But the enjoyment of God is the sub-

---

1. This and the following quotations are from Jonathan Edwards, *The Works*, Vol. 2., London: william Ball, 1839.

stance. These are but scattered beams, but God is the sun. These are but streams, but God is the fountain. These are but drops, but God is the ocean.

He is aware of the limitations and imperfections of all, including ecclesiastical, life:

> Civil, ecclesiastical, and family affairs, and all our personal concerns, are designed and ordered in subordination to a future world, by the maker and disposer of all things. To this therefore they ought to be subordinated by us.

Finally, he observes that the life of a pilgrim has a strong social and moral character:

> Let Christians help one another in going this journey. — There are many ways whereby Christians might greatly forward one another in their way to heaven, as by religious conference, etc. Therefore let them be exhorted to go this journey as it were in company: conversing together, and assisting one another. Company is very desirable in a journey, but in none so much as this. — Let them go united and not fall out by the way, which would be to hinder one another, but use all means they can to help each other up the hill. — This would ensure a more successful traveling and a more joyful meeting at their Father's house in glory.

The vocation of a pilgrim, then, is to see our earthly life as one of shadows, including ecclesiastical shadows. Shadows, however, imply light, the source of which in this case transcends this world. Church institutions are never permanent resting places. Phrases like 'Holy Mother Church', or 'love of the church' should never be taken to mean that in the church we have an existence that is there for its own sake. The church is there to serve as a temporary dwelling-place, a place of encouragement and a shadow of what is to come. It is there to remind us of our status and obligations as pilgrims. Edwards' exhortation to pilgrims to help one another is a reminder of the primary commandment of love and of how it should be manifested in our bearing and attitude to all men and women, and this will often mean conveying an attitude of acceptance and encouragement.

This applies not merely to persons but also to institutions.

In a world seriously damaged by injustice and lack of love, the Christian church has no need to resort primarily to judgement, condemnation and punishment in order to prove that it is firm in its moral and doctrinal teaching. It does not have to be a primary agent for condemnation, still less for punishment of wrongdoing. Instead, the special calling of Christians is to radiate warmth, inclusivity and compassion. We must try to take people as they are, regardless of their good or bad circumstances, giving them hope, understanding and empathy in a frequently unfriendly and censorious world. There are of course some serious matters on which the church has to take a stand, perhaps the most important of which, as Pope Francis forcibly reminds us, is the plight of the poor. This can be done firmly, but also in a manner that is consistent with the dictates of love and human dignity.

We can be too easily diverted from the search for universal justice by institutional preoccupations. Some of the matters that the Vatican bureaucracy has chosen to highlight as essential to church orthodoxy today, have little to do with the condition of poverty and social injustice which Pope Francis is putting before us as primary issues for our religious and moral concern. He is engaged in a struggle to change the focus of moral and doctrinal attention from such matters as female ordination, hostility to homosexuality and gay marriage to attending to the 'fundamental option for the poor'. This does not seem to be a present preoccupation of the curial magisterium, which has, for the moment, ceased to be actively engaged in the condemnation of Liberation Theology. In the interests of reform, however, I am forced to consider some of the issues that remain prominent features of curial preoccupation.

In chapter 14 I tried to suggest an answer to the sensitive problem of gay marriage. The equally sensitive matter of abortion can also cause bitter conflicts in society. Both are at the head of the contemporary church's magisterial concerns and have been made test cases of orthodoxy.

I have no intention here of going into the morality of abortion, or of arguing for any particular case. I am personally opposed to it, while being also opposed to the tactics resorted to by some extreme 'pro-life' campaigners whose methods are sometimes unacceptably aggressive. People on both sides of the dispute have strong convictions about the matter, and this tends to strengthen sectarian and intolerant attitudes.

The two terms 'pro life' and 'pro choice' are thoroughly unsatisfactory, because they are slipshod and lazy slogans for belligerent attempts to stake out a territory that their supporters see as having to be promoted or defended at all costs and by all means. Each combatant sees his or her opponents as enemies to be defeated, and acts as if the search for truth and concern with righteousness are irrelevant to the matter in hand. Those of us who seek to protect the life of the unborn need to respect the views of those who argue for freedom of choice in the matter. One can disagree radically and fervently with a position, while at the same time respecting the sincerity of those who hold it. Some Christians find it difficult to credit their opponents with the possession of consciences that are as entitled to respect as their own. The holding of conscientious views does not necessarily imply correctness of judgement; but it needs to be respected nonetheless.

The Catholic Church is known throughout the world for its emphatic opposition to abortion, which it properly sees as denying the right to life of the unborn in circumstances that do not involve the life of the mother. Others look at the matter differently. Convictions run very deep, and this can sometimes be taken as a license for intolerance, and in extreme cases even for violent action. Christians should be ready to say clearly and honestly where they stand on a matter like abortion; but they should do it with gentleness and respect (I Peter 3:15). If they fail in this respect, they betray the cause for which they are fighting. Conviction about the rightness of a cause never dispenses us from attending conscientiously to the manner in which we give expression to that conviction.

I would like to make it clear that I am not seeking a mediating position between two extremes. I am trying to suggest how the possessors of two mutually exclusive convictions can live together in tolerance and harmony. I am opposed to abortion; but I accept that there are unclear medical and legal aspects that call for careful legislation and guidelines, as we have recently seen in Ireland, where some politicians have suffered abuse for their legislative action. It is important to keep in mind that heavy and relentless emphasis on a moral cause can leave an impression of a negativity and authoritarianism that obscures the primary Christian vocation of understanding and compassion. Pope Francis is rather insistent about this:

[I]t is not necessary to talk about these issues [abortion, gay marriage and the use of contraceptives] all the time ... We have to find a new balance, otherwise even the moral edifice of the Church is likely to fall like a house of cards, losing the freshness and fragrance of the Gospel.[2]

In a world where so many men and women are locked into the pursuit of social status, material concerns and a philosophy of self-sufficiency, Christians have a vocation to make the basic message of their faith heard. That message is a simple though demanding one; but people can be alienated, less by the message itself than by the manner of its presentation. Christians are faced with the daunting challenge of proclaiming their message to a sceptical and sometimes hostile world, yet doing so in a manner that shows gentleness and respect.

Today in the world around us we are witnessing an apparent loss of conventional religious faith. Believing parents are faced with the quiet and disturbing spectacle of their children's failure to follow them in their religious faith and practice. Much as they would like to change the situation, parents are powerless to do so; and the wiser among them know that it would be self-defeating, to try to do so by duress of any kind.

In the Northern hemisphere the Catholic Church is in crisis, suffering from a scarcity of candidates for the priesthood. Religious orders seem to be dying out, with the middle-aged caring for the elderly as they watch the structural disintegration of their way of life. The temptation to despair is real; yet true Christians know that despair is never the answer, and, especially in this crisis, trust in God is fundamental to their faith. They know that at least they are facing the situation as it actually is, and that is where the Holy Spirit is to be found, not in a situation of their own devising. The Hebrew Scriptures (which Christians read as The Old Testament) show how the chosen people had to learn that God's grace remains constant even though venerable structures, like the Temple in Jerusalem, are destroyed and the people sent into exile. We need to consider the possibility that we are living in a transitional age in which it is easy to lose one's nerve because of the uncertainty of things. The prophetic word of God has proclaimed: 'Behold, I am doing a new thing; now it springs forth,

2. Pope Francis, Interview with Antonio Spadaro, S.J., editor in chief of *La Civiltà Cattolica*, published in *America*, September 30, 2013.

do you not perceive it? I will make a way in the wilderness and rivers in the desert.' (Isaiah 43:19)

An appropriate prayer might be to ponder how best to respond to the call of the Holy Spirit in these dispiriting surroundings. To take a concrete instance: perhaps the Northern hemisphere must yield institutional pride of place to the South, and to Africa, where the institution seems to be thriving and the clerical priesthood is flourishing. Their opportunities and problems are calling for an attention that has been denied them owing to a European and North American focus. If the word 'global' is to have religious as well as socio-political reference, we Northerners will have to yield place to newcomers and to neglected Southern societies that have their own problems and a way of life that is different from ours. There are solid spiritual and theological reasons for doing so.

A prominent theme of The Letter to the Hebrews is that, like many of the patriarchs of old, God is calling us on a journey to a goal that defines everything in this life as relatively unimportant. Christians are pilgrims; and like Abraham they are sent on a journey, not knowing where they are to go. To that extent, their journey is an adventure that calls for frequent reform of the structures they build for themselves on the way, none of which is destined to be a lasting resting place. Hope may be found in the embers of presumption, and God's grace provides an ever-new map for a journey that prompts us, as Jonathan Edwards says, above all to care for our fellow-pilgrims.

The divine initiative that we call grace is mysterious, unpredictable and given freely without being merited. We have absolutely no control over it. We can but implore and trust God to grant it to us. We may dwell too much on how we must behave in order to please God. In fact, it is God who takes all the initiatives in approaching us; and that is what we mean by 'grace'. Good missionaries know that God always precedes them and is already present in all the circumstances that invite them to intervene. A programme of evangelisation can never neglect the fact that the Holy Spirit is already present and active in advance of all missionary effort.

Jesus from Nazareth was possessed by the conviction that God's reign was taking place in him, and that if his listeners wished to find God, they must believe in him. Some people in his own town took the view that because Jesus, his parents and his family, were well known to them, it therefore followed that he could not be who he claimed to be. Jesus responded with the comment: 'Prophets are not without honour except in their own country, and in their own house.' (Matthew 13:57) Grace given in domestic familiarity, as it often is, may be spurned or ignored, because familiarity, when not seen as a grace, notoriously breeds contempt. It would appear that even in Jesus, God still does not wish to be found too easily; for Jesus lacked all pretence of human high office or powerful status. People were free to listen to him and throw their lot in with him, or, like the rich young man, depart from him with regret.

Jesus was with his disciples for a very short time. In that short time they were inspired by his leadership and responded to his teaching with awkward and sometimes naive generosity. He could say that whoever saw him saw the Father. There was an immediacy about his presence among them which would not be possible for his followers after he had gone. He himself commented on this when he invited Thomas to touch his hands and his side; and immediately Thomas believed. Jesus then said to him, 'Have you believed because you have seen me? Blessed are those who have not seen and yet have come to believe.' (John 20:29) Only relatively few people saw the risen Jesus; there would be myriads in the centuries to come whose faith in him would not be based on sight but on report and their inner disposition to respond to him, and on the example and support of a believing community. John's Gospel has Jesus say to his disciples that he must go so that the Holy Spirit may come and that he will ask the Father to send another Helper who is the Spirit of truth, 'whom the world cannot receive, because it neither sees him nor knows him'. (John 14:16-17)

Peter in Acts of the Apostles on the day of Pentecost proclaimed to a crowd that had gathered to see some excited men and women speaking in 'tongues', that the Holy Spirit had been sent from the Father by 'this Jesus whom you crucified'. (Acts 2:33-36) This was the sort of scandalous particularity that spoke existentially to people, some of whom may have called for the crucifixion of Jesus in Pilate's courtyard only a few weeks earlier. They were shaken by Peter's words and asked what they could now do to make up for what they had done then. Peter told them to repent and be baptised. According to Luke, a small group of disciples were that day transformed into a large gathering of believers, an occasion which some have regarded as the birth of the Christian church in which the

Spirit would be carrying on the work of Jesus and would in a mystical sense be taking his place. Discipleship would no longer entail the type of faith achieved by Thomas. Jesus would have to be approached through the other 'Paraclete' who would be sent to take his place and to carry on his work. He would remain the model and the redeeming memory, but his present mode of existence would not make him physically available. Our own survival beyond death would be closely linked with his resurrection. St Paul puts the matter unequivocally: 'And if Christ has not been raised, then our preaching is in vain and your faith is in vain.' (1 Corinthains 15:14)

Some Christians today can establish an unproblematic relationship with Jesus, and much enthusiastically devotional language promotes this way of speaking. Other believers and would-be believers have to face critical difficulties posed for them by the historical and philosophical problem of relating to someone who lived 2,000 years ago. Those of critically untroubled faith may deal with this difficulty by invoking the divinity of Christ as a means of evading the 'scandalous particularity' of Christian revelation. This stratagem is not possible for those who are constrained to take historicity and hermeneutics seriously. They need an asceticism of the mind whereby they can accept the challenge of believing in the true humanity of Christ – a central and defined article of faith, so easily obscured by the more heavily emphasised doctrine of his divinity.

From the Hebrew Scriptures Jesus selected what he called the first and greatest commandment: that they must love God with all their heart, with all their soul and with all their mind. This first commandment was to be accompanied inseparably by a second one that resembles it, which was that they should love their neighbours as themselves. On these two commandments hang all the law and the prophets (Matthew 22:34-40). It was a strikingly simple and unambiguous message, delivered without qualification and with all the strength that comes from unqualified simplicity and conviction.

God has entered history in the guise of a modest craftsman who instructed his followers to take this good news to the ends of the earth. This is the faith of all Christians. As St Paul told the Christians of Corinth, the violent death of this craftsman-turned-preacher was at the heart of God's message to humanity; and it would be a scandal to Jews and folly to Gentiles (1 Corinthians 1:18-25). But it was God's folly, carefully designed to confound worldly wisdom and to give those who are called to disciple-ship an assurance that their salvation is to be found in Jesus Christ who is the power and the wisdom of God. This is the message entrusted to the gathering of Christians that we call 'the church'; and it is a message that has often been obscured by a preoccupation with the messenger, who, in the sight of God, is not a powerful landlord but an indigent pilgrim.

In the Catholic Church there are structures that have a long institu-tional history behind them and have developed with the passage of time. In spite of its longevity the Roman Curia is not an indispensable part of church governance; when it functions properly, it is a convenient instru-ment that enables the pope to communicate with the church. It should reflect the aims and values of the pope, and more importantly it should reflect the mind of Christ. A reforming pope should necessarily imply a reforming curia, since the curia exists for no other purpose than to serve the pope and the bishops. Reforming the institutional church is an evangelical task, and not a mere tinkering with structures in order to improve the quality of church membership. The Christian church is not a club; still less is it a military institution. It is a gathering that is an essential social consequence of responding to the message of Jesus Christ. That is why its constant reform is so important. Church structures are there to promote the ideals of the Gospel, not to achieve a status that suggests permanence and brings adulation to its office holders. Those structures, too, need to be adapted to pilgrimage, and their indwellers must never think of themselves as inhabiting a lasting city.

They are pilgrims belonging to a community of equals seeking to respond communally to the ideals and vision of the Gospel and helping each other on the journey. They are subject to the same judgement as those they presume to judge. Gratuitous demonstration of power by a small group of Christians over their fellows creates an atmosphere that is contradictory to their shared status as pilgrims and to the message of the Gospel. Magisterial oppression of legitimate dissenters, quite apart from its lack of moral probity, is unnecessary as a means for propagating genuine orthodoxies, as distinct from the views of one mindset in the church. Religious ideas, of whatever stripe, should have the ability to com-mend themselves without relying upon coercion and intimidation. Truth is its own vindicator, when it is allowed to commend itself in freedom. It is discovered through the normal commerce of discussion, dispute and argument. That is how God made us human beings. Certain situations in life, like falling in love or having a religious faith, cannot be commanded; they simply happen, and it is up to us to make our choices in our response to them. The circumstances that brought them about are fortuitous, but they call for decision-making about their consequences.

An intolerant and belligerent church authority is a counter-sign to everything that Jesus stood for. I have dwelt on the example of Pope John XXIII at many points in this book because he showed that a pope could be conservative in many respects yet be inclusive and loving. It seems likely that Pope Francis will be remembered with similar affection and approval. In a caring atmosphere Catholics could work together in peace and joy to bring to the world the good news of salvation in Christ Jesus and commend it in freedom to be received in freedom. A repressive regime, by its very existence, obscures the original message of Christianity. Francis commends John XXIII for remarking that in the government of the church one should adopt the motto: 'See everything; turn a blind eye to much; correct a little.'

A glance at canon law, even though it has been subject to revision, may suggest that it has little to do with the Galilean message. Canon law, though it is rightfully there to legislate for the institutional church, can seem to promote a sense of theocratic permanence that is at odds with the spirit of pilgrimage. Recently in Ireland the committee of an ecumenical conference appealed to the archbishop of the diocese in which it was held for permission to celebrate the Eucharist with fellow Christians from sister churches. His response was to consult a canon lawyer. The advice that he received confirmed him in his conviction that he ought to forbid the celebration. It would have been more pilgrim-like to consult, not canon law, but the Gospel. It is often ecclesiastically hazardous to ask what Jesus would do in this or that situation!

There is an apparent compulsion on traditionalist leaders to project Vatican power-obsessed ideas about authority back onto the lives of unsophisticated fishermen who were captivated by a fellow Galilean who spoke to them about God in a way that inspired them and made them feel cherished. These fishermen have been turned into a 'college' presided over by a 'head'. This cold model may fit one legalistic conception of the church today; but when it is applied to the apostolic age, it flies in the face of a true historical perspective arising out of a study of the New Testament; and it suggests that anachronistic propaganda is being deliberately employed for political purposes. A canonically structured church can, but need not, lend itself to the sort of governance that is blind to the demands of pilgrim status. In the view of those who are obsessed with ecclesiastical authority Galilee must be interpreted as far as possible in a way that fits in with the power-driven institution that the Catholic Church has become; and woe betide those who make the obvious point that today's institutional church is strikingly different from that of Galilee or the early church. Reform consists in rediscovering the institutional implications of the ideals presented by the Gospel, in all their freshness, as if for the first time.

Sometimes reform and church unity appear to be an unattainable dream. However, one cannot be a true reformer or authentic ecumenist without being able to sustain a dream that is often dimmed by institutionally inspired opposition, or simply by inertia. It is necessary for us to have an idealised picture of a perfect church so that we may have a goal to strive for while knowing that we shall never achieve it. We must dream; and we need the wisdom to appreciate that the dream will never be fully realised in earthly existence; but that does not mean that we must stop dreaming. An approximation to the dream is well worth the effort.

As Protestants recognized not long after the Reformation, the task of reform is never done. The force of 'semper' in the phrase 'semper reformanda' is not condemnation to a hopeless Sisyphean exercise of rolling a heavy stone up a hill only to see it fall again to the bottom. According to the famous French Algerian philosopher and literary figure, Albert Camus, Sisyphus' task does not have to be seen as hopeless. Camus wrote an essay in 1942 on 'The Myth of Sisyphus', in which he admires Sisyphus as a hero for his courage in facing his endless task each day, knowing that he can never finally succeed. Camus' claim that 'one must imagine Sisyphus happy' is a counter-intuitive interpretation of an ancient myth. In short, he asks us to accept with joy the never-ending effort to endow the world with meaning. 'The struggle itself towards the heights is enough to fill a man's heart'.

Having rejected suicide as one possible answer to the problem presented by the absurdity of existence, Camus next considers the religious solution and judges it to be equally deficient. He found the world to be 'absurd', lacking meaning and purpose. As an atheist he repudiated what he saw as an irrational attempt to replace the absurd with a falsely transcendent world of meaning and comfort, thus evading the challenge presented by what seemed to him to be the obvious absurdity of life in the world.

His rejection of religion, however, was arbitrary and selective. Like many atheists, he chose a version of religion that is superficial and falsely comforting, and, as such, easy to repudiate. The view of religion that he rejects is not an accurate depiction of all religious belief, and indeed it can be seen as a serious distortion of the truth of authentic religion. What he was determined to do was to face the absurdity of human existence with truth, courage and determination, and in doing so, to revolt against it, knowing that he could never succeed: the struggle, he claims, is enough to satisfy the human heart. A well-informed Christian could agree wholeheartedly with this perspective on life in this world.

Camus was a distinguished and influential thinker, and one can only regret that he did not recognise that his view of life's absurdities could be reconciled with a truly religious view that tries to accept the meaninglessness of so much human and animal existence in the world, such as innocent suffering, while affirming, in an act of faith, that God knows how we feel but asks for our trust. The prospect of eternal reward for living faithfully and morally in this life can, but does not have to, be a cheap grace and an evasion of the true Christian vocation, which strives to understand and appreciate the Christian enterprise of daily life in the world. The Christian is called upon to find transcendent meaning in the spectacle of a crucified man who died seemingly abandoned by God, but in three days was raised to new life, to sit on the right hand of God.

A warped theology of merit – a sort of religious capitalism – together with too comfortable an idea of reward and punishment, can offer a superficial interpretation of Christian life in the world. Camus unfortunately saw all mysticism as a flight from reality; whereas, differently understood, it is a never-ending search for union with God in the face of the frequent absurdity, instability and shadows of everyday life.

Science has shown that we are living in an evolutionary world controlled by the mechanism of natural selection. In human beings, who have evolved from earlier and more primitive forms of life, nature becomes conscious of itself and achieves the possibility of taming the raw force of natural selection by intelligence, freedom and, above all, by the capacity to love. Christian faith contributes a distinctive feature to this awesome leap within the story of evolution: the weak need no longer perish, nor the fit be the only survivors. The practice of love, spectacularly demonstrated by Jesus in his own life and death, and given as his own special commandment to his followers, has the capacity to change the world and to redirect the thrust of a deterministic evolutionary force. God has created us at a distance from himself; and through grace has given us the means to travel as pilgrims on a journey through life to our final home; and through divine forgiveness we are rescued when we wander from the path set before us by One who cares for and cherishes us while respecting our freedom and autonomy and pardons the failures resulting from them. The gathering that we call the church consists of frail men and women who stumble on the path to their Creator whose Son once shared in their frailty and who understands from his own experience what it means to be human (Hebrews 4:15).

There is no prospect of a perfect church; there never was and there never will be; but there must be a dream of what a perfect church could be like with constant reform, contrition and forgiveness, if the pilgrimage is to be sustainable through hope and trust. On that pilgrimage there will be many falls and some drifting from the designated path (perhaps the best model for sin). Christians belong to a church that understands itself as sinful and, because its members are forgiven, in gratitude they need to be ready to forgive those who trespass against them, as the Lord taught us to pray. In certain circumstances even structural reform may be the proper response to knowing that we have been forgiven. Imperfection is a feature of all the societies we create or belong to; and it takes a graced wisdom to live placidly in them, and when necessary seek their reform.

Human beings are flawed and wounded; hence so are the societies they form within the cultural webs they have woven for themselves. When eternity enters time, the flaw is magnified in our perception, because it gives us a religious and moral horizon that we can never finally reach in this world; but it offers us the vision, the dream, of what is possible and an encouragement to strive for it. We need the dream, while recognizing that it can never be completely realized. The dream is indispensable to Christian life; and we must look for ways to give it vivid expression, so that we can experience it as a pledge of eternal meaning and glory given in this world as an earnest of what is to come.

An emphasis on pilgrim status could be taken to mean reduction in enjoyment of the good things that this world has to offer. This would be a tragic mistake. God has given us a world to be enjoyed to the full. All that God asks of us is to realise in faith that the greatest enjoyments given to us in this world lack finality and are but shadows of what is to come. Jonathan Edwards put this thought about those enjoyments in memorable words:

> We should be so far from resting in them, that we should desire to leave them all, in God's due time. We ought to possess, enjoy and use them, with no other view but readily to quit them, whenever we are called to it, and to change them willingly and cheerfully for heaven.

Christian faith inspires us always to remember that in the full enjoyment of earthly things God has destined us for greater than this. Heaven should be thought of not so much as a reward for virtuous living in this world, but rather as the final splendour of God's gift to those he has made in his own image and likeness. We are not to cling to what we have in this world, but be ready when we are called 'to change them willingly and cheerfully for heaven'. Seán Freyne quotes The Gospel of Thomas : '"Jesus said: Be a passerby" (*Gos. Thom.* 42) that is, do not become engaged with the world'.[3]

We know little about existence beyond death. Most religions profess a belief in an afterlife of contentment, delight and an end to pain and suffering, which they express in mythological language and images. If taken literally, these images would invite derision. Critically minded faith can accept the mystery of human existence as transcendent to, as well as immanent in, this world. In this life men and women can experience a desire for God not always recognised for what it is.

Desire is enormously important in St Augustine's theology and spirituality. He saw it as an indispensable element in human life. The memories of what he came to see as his sexually misspent youth illustrated how a desire could be diverted from its true end and twisted towards a false goal.

---

3. Seán Freyne, *The Jesus Movement and Its Expansion: Meaning and Mission*, (Grand Rapids, Eerdmans, 2014), p. 254.

His conversion was not pure gain: because of it, he threw sexuality and eternal love into mutual contradiction. Augustine on desire as the road to God is splendid; whereas Augustine on sexual desire is puritanical and unbalanced. He bequeathed to Western Christian experience a profound aversion to sex; but it would be a pity if we allowed this to blind us to the nobility of his teaching on desire. Despite his abhorrence of sex, he did not to try to banish desire from Christian life; he directed it towards the goal that would satisfy it at its deepest level. His most profound insight into the human condition is that our nature and our existence are defined by desire; to seek to banish desire would be to deny one's very humanity. For Augustine desire is the engine of human life and is intrinsic to any definition of what it means to be human. He had a profound dislike for any philosophy that sought as it final object, the stilling of desire. He would have had little time for Nirvana, presented as an ultimate aspiration by non-theistic Buddhism.

Many people have had a feeling of disappointment on having achieved a long-desired object or ambition, and when it arrives, have wondered, 'is that all?' The German Marxist philosopher Ernst Bloch used a memorable and typically Augustinian phrase to describe this feeling, which he calls 'the melancholy of fulfilment'. In this way of thinking, the pilgrim's journey consists of a succession of plateaux each of which, instead of being a final resting-place, reveals a further summit to be climbed. Reform, personal and structural, is a necessary feature of the journey, and without reform there is no pilgrimage, only a paralysed inertia - a seeking of final rest in something that falls short of God.

A sentence from Augustine's *Confessions* is celebrated and frequently quoted: 'For you have so made us that we long for you, and our heart is restless until it rests in you.'[4] A little later he asks an intriguing question: 'Must we know you before we can call upon you? ... How can people call upon someone in whom they do not yet believe?' In Augustine's way of thinking, desire precedes knowledge and faith. Influenced by the notion of Platonic contemplation, he has been called a theologian of the heart; Thomas Aquinas, influenced by Aristotle, is usually seen as a theologian of the mind. These are differences, not of substance but of emphasis, and

---

4. Augustine, *Confessions*, translated by Benignus O'Rourke (DLT, London, 2013), p. 3.

as such they enrich Christian thought.

The Apostles experienced the risen Jesus as the same Master they had come to love and follow during the short span of his missionary life. In his risen state he could appear and disappear and could pass through walls, thus defying the laws of physics and the commonsense experience of everyday life. Whereas Thomas was invited to feel his wounded hands and side, and so come to believe in him (John 20:24-29), Mary Magdalene initially mistook him for the gardener, but when he called her by her name, 'Mary', she recognised him, but he told her not to hold on to him (John 20:17).[5] It seemed as if the risen Lord had passed to a new existence; but being who he was, he could make a mysterious and perplexing contact with those he had known and lived with during his earthly life. It was clear that he was the same Jesus that they had known and loved, but he was now living in a very different mode of existence for which they knew no precedent. In Luke's gospel the risen Jesus appears to the disciples, saying, 'Look at my hands and my feet; see that it is I myself. Touch me and see; for a ghost does not have flesh and bones as you see that I have.' (Luke 24:39)

Traditionally understood, eschatology (literally the study of the last things) is the branch of theology that has originally dealt with death, what happens after death, and how the world will end. It arises out of what the Bible says about the last things, notably as contained in the Book of Revelation in the New Testament. Some Christians interpret this book, together with cognate texts in the Old Testament, literally. In much modern theology attention is diverted from concern with the last things and falls instead on the history of salvation. In this wider sense eschatology is concerned with God's overall plan for humankind's destiny, and it accepts a graceful nescience about the world that is to come.

Scientific cosmology gives an account of what will be the physical destiny of the solar system billions of years in the future; but this knowledge was not available to the biblical writers, whose perspective was different from that of scientific cosmologists and was expressed in symbols and

5. The Greek word can be translated as 'touch' or 'cling on to'. What John intends to convey is unclear and has given rise to different interpretations, including a Eucharistic one. At any rate, the story witnesses to the mysterious character of what is going on in the intermediate state between the earthly and the risen Jesus.

myths that are not always easy to interpret. Traditional eschatology and scientific cosmology have nothing in common, beyond a focus on the future. The world of traditional eschatology was fanciful, gnomic and greatly concerned with the justice that will be meted out to the faithful and the damned. Catholics have to reckon with traditional teaching on heaven, hell, purgatory and limbo. It is wise to take careful note of the context and symbolic character of traditional eschatology, which employs fanciful language that is open to literal interpretation and lends itself to melodramatic preaching.

In ordinary Christian parlance heaven and hell are represented as existences in the otherworld. 'Heaven' is an experience of total happiness; 'Hell' is an experience of intense pain and abandonment.[6] Christians may sometimes be asked menacingly, usually by literal-minded traditionalists, if they believe in hell – yes or no. The question will sometimes be asked in a belligerent and inquisitorial manner that is intended to put 'liberals' on the spot. There is no need to answer it, unless the questioner is prepared to discuss what he or she means by 'hell', and, perhaps more importantly, explain their interest in the question. Speculation about hell can bring out the worst in us; it can be characteristic of people who want to consign their opponents to it.

Hellfire sermons have often been self-indulgent and histrionic attempts to frighten people into a life of virtue. Correspondingly, heaven has been presented as a reward for virtue, thus reducing earthly morality to an exercise in prudential religious capitalism. Since the reforms of Vatican II, the hellfire sermon is heard less often in Catholic churches in the West; possibly leaving a vacuum that makes it harder to speak about the afterlife, which is difficult to visualise or imagine; failure to do so may seem like a loss of faith. Of course it is not a loss of faith. Faith is not a matter of being able to imagine what one believes. The wiser course may be to be guided by the simplicity of the Nicene Creed: 'I look forward to the resurrection of the dead, and the life of the world to come', and leave it at that, without trying to imagine what it might mean.

The Negro spirituals of nineteenth century America emphasise other-

6. Dante's *Divine Comedy* should be read as the literary masterpiece it is, or as a guide to fourteenth century religious and political history, and not as a guide to modern faith and morality.

worldly longings in a powerful way. African Americans had nowhere but the next life to turn to for relief from their sufferings. Heaven was the only home in which they could hope for justice and happiness. The spirituals, as the composer Michael Tippett (no admirer of conventional hymns) recognised, have something about them that transcends private devotion. Their universality embraces this world as well as the world that is to come. It should be impossible for a Christian to listen to these spirituals without accepting that the remedy for the sufferings they depict cannot be left to the next life alone. The Liberation and Black theologians have striven to emphasise our this-worldly obligations. Karl Marx's description of religion as the opium of the people is regrettably, but by no means necessarily, true. Authentic pilgrims recognise the moral and social implications of the journey that they undertake in faith.

Both Protestants and Catholics sing John Bunyan's hymn to a noble and rousing tune. Its first verse makes an appropriate conclusion to our reflections on pilgrimage:

> He who would valiant be,
> Let him come hither;
> One here will constant be,
> Come wind, come weather
> There's no discouragement
> Shall make him once relent
> His first avow'd intent
> To be a pilgrim.

17

A Reason for Hope

As I said at the beginning of this book, I wrote the greater part of it during the pontificate of Pope Benedict XVI, and I had almost completed it when the news broke of Pope Benedict's resignation and the election of Pope Francis. Not long afterwards Francis was interviewed by Antonio Spadaro, S.J., editor of the Italian Jesuit journal *La Civiltà Cattolica*. The interview changed the institutional scene by showing that the new Pope has a mentality critically at variance with that of many of his curia, most notably that of the Congregation for the Doctrine of the Faith. Some of his critics will probably claim that an interview with a journal does not constitute an officially valid and solemn papal pronouncement, thus demonstrating that they fail to understand Francis' mode of governance. Hitherto there had been few papal interviews, lest they portray some genuine papal thoughts as distinct from the polished language of formal utterances such as encyclicals and *motu proprio* documents.

It seems to me that Francis' use of the interview is no merely adventitious practice. There is reason to believe that he has deliberately chosen the interview as a tactic through the informality of which he can distance himself from the formal rigidities of traditional papal pronouncements, which have been closely bound up with absolute monarchical power; and that is simply not Francis' style. He is showing an acute distaste for grand and princely postures. Is this to read too much into what is no more than a matter of style? I think not. I do not think that his is a merely idiosyncratic style of behaviour. In his case I am convinced that the style is the substance, or in the jargon of the 1960s, 'the medium is the message', though it will take time to see whether it can defeat the opposition with which it will be greeted by hard-line traditionalists. We should not underrate the opposition it will meet: the Vatican Curia has centuries of authoritarian precedent behind it, and it will realise that genuine reform means a significant loss of power for it. Some American bishops are ill at ease with the alleged anti-capitalist tenor of his teaching.

Some may misguidedly believe that the arrival of Pope Francis has rendered some of the concerns of this book outdated. That would be to ignore the historic reality that curialism is now an endemic mentality in the Catholic Church, and one that has seen off earlier attempts to reform it. Francis will need all the support that we can give him. For many of us his arrival in the See of Peter is a cause for joy and rejuvenated hope, but we should not imagine that one man, however exalted, can single-handedly achieve success in the task of reform. That task calls for communal effort and determination. It has been said that Francis is more concerned with right practice (orthopraxis) than with right thinking (orthodoxy). This may put him at a disadvantage in his dealings with the Congregation for the Doctrine of the Faith (CDF) which is obsessed with orthodoxy and has shows little interest in orthopraxis, except to condemn Liberation Theology.

The problem, it seems to me, is whether he can introduce the changes he clearly favours without structural reform of the institution. Some commentators have observed that he is clearly conservative about 'church teaching' – an ambiguous phrase, at the best of times. It would seem that he considers himself bound by the teaching of his predecessors, some of whom were careful to preserve the church in its unreformed state; yet his pastoral instincts would seem to call for an institution marked by serious structural reform. Those instincts naturally seek consensus; but the question is whether there can be consensus between two parties with contradictory conceptions of church and its governance.[1]

Some traditionalists in high places talk menacingly about 'church teaching', using the phrase to include not only biblical and credal doctrine, but also, and perhaps especially, their own ultra-conservative opinions. Francis appears to be impressed by their emphasis on 'church teaching' to the extent of regarding encyclicals like *Humanae Vitae* and John Paul II's personal conviction that women can never be ordained, as doctrines binding the church permanently. Francis wishes to be seen as doctrinally conservative; but can he continue to do so in the light of his reforming zeal? He is trying to accord by their rules, keeping them onside, as he pursues a programme largely at variance with their instincts. His quest

1. See my article 'Let Battle Commence' in *The Tablet*, 10 January, 2015, pp. 12-13.

for consensus does credit to his heart; but surely his head must tell him that he is attempting a logically impossible task? True consensus is to be found, not in intellectual harmony, but in the willingness of both parties to live together in amity in spite of the mutual incompatibility of their convictions.

There is a Christian injunction to love one's enemies – which does not imply having to share their opinions. In the matter of church leadership, confrontation may be the Christian path, when it is necessary for much-needed reform. At Vatican II there was never a prospect of consensus between the conservative minority and the majority who were looking for change; the best that could be hoped for was the will to live peacefully together in the same church.

Pope Francis may have to face up to the structural implications of his preferential option for the poor; and this will entail extending his understanding of 'poor' to include faithful Catholics who are being harried for their legitimate beliefs and practices, and who do not have the power to defend themselves. To do so will involve confronting some of his own curia and vetoing their occasionally aggressive and intolerant behaviour. At the moment, Francis is trying to bring about justice and peace through structures that are sometimes ill suited to his attitude and plans. The truth is that if he wishes to implement his vision, he cannot avoid confrontation with the Vatican forces that are opposed to his vision and his aims. This will be extremely hard for him precisely because the Roman idea of 'the teaching of the church' stands four-square between him and the reforms that he knows to be necessary. He may not yet see that reform calls for structural change of a kind that would involve his breaking with the traditionalist dogma of the immutability of former papal statements that are not part of credal faith, and have often proved to be mutually incompatible.

Surely he must see that *Humanae Vitae's* condemnation of contraception has never been received by the church, that its purely essentialist basis has left it open to modern refutation? Paul VI's refusal to accept the advice offered to him by those whom he had invited to counsel him was remarkable. It has become an embarrassment in today's church and is being used by ultra-conservatives to oppose much that Francis is trying to achieve. His remark that the door is closed to women seeking ordination to the priesthood is untypically insensitive to so many Catholics who are looking to him for change.

If he is to bring about the sort of church that he so plainly favours, Francis will have to accept that the old monarchical structures, which he so obviously dislikes, are unsuited to bringing about the reforms which he clearly sees to be necessary, and that he will have to confront the opposition of those whose concept of church is dictatorial in its image of the papacy and its curia and authoritarian in its attitude towards the methods of governance and general control in the church. It is an attitude that is incompatible with genuine consultation of the entire people of God.

Impressed by the reforming will of the cardinals before his election, Francis has appointed a Commission of Cardinals to help him with reform of the curia – a task that has proved to be historically so difficult. There is perhaps some danger that the cardinals will limit the scope of reform to blatantly obvious examples of corruption and mismanagement, but they can hardly fail to have noticed that the quality of leadership that Francis is showing extends well beyond financial corruption and careerism. It signals a break not merely with the recent past, but with centuries of papal rule. Aware that he is breaking with the tradition of centuries, he evidently feels the need to place emphasis on the continuity of his pontificate with that of Benedict. The question is whether he can continue *not* to see that his attitude (a word to which Francis gives notable prominence and importance) is recognisably different from that of Benedict.

It seems plain that the mentality and behaviour of the CDF is out of kilter with the spirit of the new pope, to say nothing of the difficulty of squaring it with the Gospel. Wishing to establish a link between himself and his predecessor, Francis chose to issue in his own name an encyclical, *Lumen Fidei*, that he himself openly states to have been written mainly by Benedict, whose attitude to the world and to the church seems rather different from his own. It is interesting to note that the encyclical is not as rebarbative about the post-Enlightenment world as we had come to expect from Benedict. It would be equally interesting to know if Francis has quietly edited out Benedict's glum view of the modern world while retaining his predecessor's learned theological treatment of the light of faith. Nevertheless, his reforming zeal and his anxiety to emphasise the continuity between his pontificate and Benedict's seem to lack consistency.

The traditional Roman instinct has been to accentuate the continuity between pontificates, while ignoring or playing down the significance of evident discontinuities. For many, however, it is the discontinuities that inspire hope of change.

It remains to be seen whether Francis can reconcile his desire for continuity between himself and his predecessor, together with his commitment to previous papal teaching, on the one hand, with his instinctive inclusiveness and pastoral compassion, on the other. At the moment he appears to be attempting to pursue two contradictory courses of action. For example, he has re-appointed Gerhard Ludwig Müller, a close friend of Benedict, and an autocratic judge and administrator, to the post of Prefect of the Congregation for the Doctrine of the Faith, and has made him a cardinal. Müller, who has expressed anxiety about the division between traditionalists and progressives, is himself an uncompromising traditionalist. As Prefect of the CDF, he believes that the Congregation has 'a direct share in the Pope's teaching'. He shows no sign of recognising that punitive authoritarianism gives a powerful counter-sign to the Gospel. There can be no detached neutrality in this matter: either one is committed to reform; or one is not. Müller's conviction that the CDF takes priority over every other voice in the church puts the Congregation safely beyond criticism and therefore beyond reform. It needs to be competently and fearlessly challenged.[2]

There are Catholics who are in harmony with the pontificate of Benedict; and there are those who are not. Either view is legitimate, but honesty demands that we do not try to fudge the differences between Francis and Benedict. Misguided piety, confused ideology or misguided mysticism may prompt an affirmation of the continuity between them. Some traditionalists attack the claim that there are significant differences between the two popes; and the traditionalist attempt to praise Benedict is often intended as a backhanded rebuke to those who delight in the arrival of Francis. Realism and hope see undeniable differences. Benedict made a stark contrast between church and the world, especially the world of Europe and N. America since the Enlightenment. He saw the church's role as that of a crusader against a culture of unbelief. Francis is a far more

2. See *The Tablet*, 29 March 2014, p. 24.

inclusive thinker who reaches out to the poor and the suffering with no distinction of religion or nationality. Benedict came to the papacy directly from the CDF. Francis comes to it from a busy archbishopric. Benedict's background was that of academic theology, whereas Francis' theology is pastorally inspired. Francis may not fully appreciate that his pastoral instincts demand a supporting theology that is not afraid of necessary confrontation. This is what happened at Vatican II, and there is every reason to oppose, in the same spirit, those who dislike the new Pope's attitude.

No pope can legitimately impose his own theology on the whole church, though some have tried to do so. He can, however, commend it; and Francis has done so in his exhortation, *Evangelii Gaudium*, a document that is being read by people who would not normally read papal encyclicals. Christian faith must allow for different theologies in its support. Collegiality, properly conceived and exercised, would be a protection against despotic moves to bring about the enforced uniformity of thought that we have endured for so long. One must hope that the new pope will find the determination and patience actively to promote legitimate diversity of thought within the church.

Francis will continue to be faced with the problem of effecting reform within the present structures. He has committed himself to accepting what has been contentiously described as 'the teaching of the church' in an integralist sense which does not recognise a hierarchy of truths that distinguishes between the central and the peripheral in Christian beliefs. We must hope that he will challenge the view that such matters as former papal teaching on contraception, the ordination of women and the 'radical evil' of homosexuality are unchangeable. This will be difficult to do, because he will be charged with being unfaithful to 'church teaching' by those who identify that teaching with their own opinions. To someone of his impeccable loyalty to the church this charge will be painful, and he will need the support of theologians throughout the church who are willing to stand up to the autocracy of the CDF.

Papal nuncios who at present normally sponsor 'safe' candidates for the episcopate may find it difficult to adapt to the new scene; but Pope Francis speaks of the need for a greater recognition of regional input into church governance. It remains to be seen what steps he will take to promote the local election of bishops. I am only too aware that I am writing at an uncertain time in the history of the Catholic Church. In consequence, I write more of hopes than of sustainable achievements. It would be unwise to forget how a regressive curia undid some of the reforms of Vatican II. A pope may be head of the church, but there is only so much that a single man can achieve, when he is not a dictator. Radical reform of the curia has so far proved to be largely an unrealised dream. The curia has a Hydra-like way of reasserting itself when efforts to reform it seem promising but the will to bring about its reform is irresolute. The curia and some bishops will probably continue to employ the authoritarian tactics which prevailed in the past and which Francis shows every sign of wishing to avoid. The Pope will probably try to avoid confronting them directly, though some situations may leave him few alternatives to confrontation, if he is not to show weakness and thereby lose his authority. Francis may instinctively shy away from direct confrontation, but the CDF will have to be shown who is in charge, if reform is to come about. The Congregation assumes that everything it does is done with the authority of the pope. The new Pope will have to disabuse it of this presumption. There are some senior church officials who seem to feel the need to demonstrate their power by having recourse to ecclesiastical measures of repression, such as suspension and excommunication. Victims of this kind of behaviour will now be justified in resisting such measures and appealing directly to the pope himself, if the bullying still persists. One has to recognise, however, that Vatican bureaucrats will probably try to prevent such appeals from reaching him.

Pope Francis has several times repeated that the church's first responsibility to God and to the world is to show a compassionate, welcoming and non-judgemental face. This attitude would seem to be so plainly indicated by the Gospel, that it seems strange that, with a few exceptions, it has not hitherto been a prominent feature of papal and episcopal outlook. Church authorities, however, have made it their primary task to lay down the law, whether on belief or behaviour, and have condemned all whom they deem to have offended against either. In the process they seem to have neglected a crucial teaching of Jesus: 'Judge not, and you will not be judged; condemn not, and you will not be condemned; forgive, and you will be forgiven.' (Luke 6:37) 'Why do you see the speck that is in your brother's eye, but do not notice the log that is in your own eye?' (Matthew 7:3).

Francis has made plain his distaste for the habit of some church people, especially bishops and traditionalist ginger groups, to dwell obsessively on certain moral matters such as abortion and same-sex marriage. He clearly feels that unrelenting emphasis on these matters has obscured some primary features of Christianity, above all, mercy, compassion and forgiveness. Sexuality and reproduction have been a significant element in Vatican teaching, in spite of the fact that they play no great part in the New Testament. Some reflection on it may help to illustrate the need for reform, if not of the teaching itself then at least of the manner of its presentation and the doctrinal status to which it has been raised. To describe homosexuality as an 'intrinsic evil' is, to put it mildly, distinctly unhelpful, displaying, as it does, the unpleasant face of exaggerated essentialism. In the eyes of Pope Francis it is primarily the person, not the condition, that Christians need to care about.

In the matter of sexual orientation there has been a well-intentioned attempt to soften the impact of raw condemnation of homosexuality by differentiating between orientation and practice: the orientation being seen as morally neutral; the practice being reprehensible. This construction, however, forbids someone to give expression to a condition that occurs in nature – a prohibition that is unjust and unreasonable. Pope Benedict rightly saw the weakness in this distinction between the condition and its practice, but as a logical consequence he found himself forced to worry about the very existence of homosexual inclination, and not merely its practice. This has taken him into territory that is theologically hazardous, since, (as a seasoned theologian he must know) it poses the disturbing question of what the Creator is doing in permitting such an anomaly to occur in creation. Benedict chose, without a convincing explanation, to foreclose prematurely on the matter, in a bid to silence much-needed discussion.

Essentialist thinking coupled with deductive reasoning would seem to lie at the heart of the problem.[3] The magisterium needs to recognise the relevance of moderately existentialist thinking and inductive reasoning as a check on its own traditional dedication to unmitigated essentialism and deductive reason. This is a task not only for systematic theologians,

---

3. See *supra*, Chapter 14.

but also for moralists and canon lawyers with the courage to enter into institutionally sensitive territory in the interests of truth. Canon law will have to be radically reformed, if only because in its present form traditionalists can appeal to it as a justification for their intolerant behaviour. Canon law in its present form, even in its 1983 edition, closely reflects the theology prevailing in Vatican circles since Paul VI, whereas it should allow for the legitimate convictions of the entire contemporary church formed in the light of Vatican II.

Rome, by indulging in condemnation of those who have taken issue with some of its ill-chosen moral dogmas, has not evinced, as it seems to imagine, firmness in the face of misguided attitudes in the modern world. On the contrary, it has shown rigidity and intransigence in an area that calls for intelligence, humility and a willingness to learn. Identifying the magisterium with 'the church' is a discreditable way of elevating the opinions of one faction to the status of an authority binding the entire church. As long as this identification is allowed to prevail, there can be little prospect of reform.

Pope Francis has been criticised by conservatives for not coming out strongly enough on topics like abortion. He is correcting an imbalance that has occurred over the years in church attitudes to some moral questions. He is more concerned with the offended and the offender than with the offence. This is more Christlike than the fulminations we have grown used to from senior churchmen; and it is why many Catholics are rejoicing that Gospel values have at last returned to church governance, at least at the top.

In any kind of organized society, at any given time, there will normally be those who favour keeping things as they are, and those who are alive to the need for change. This is also true in the Christian church, which has been given the additional 'new commandment' of love (John 13:34) that should govern every other attitude in the church and be as attentive to means as to ends.

It is a fact of life that people differ over important concerns and when this happens within a church and bears upon church concerns, the Christian response is to strive to live peaceably, tolerantly and as caringly as possible in the same church. It is a hopeless task to try to find a consensus between two logically opposed parties. Each, however has a right to argue publicly for his or her case; and if authority is involved, it has the duty to act without prejudice and with compassion.

In the interests of justice and human dignity people need at least to feel that their views are being fairly considered by those who govern them. A stubborn and passively aggressive silence on the part of authority is no way to promote a healthy society that recognises the pastoral value of diverse opinions and convictions. A bishop should be able to say that he disagrees personally with a position that does not belong to the essence of the faith, while recognising the right of others to hold it with impunity. By doing so he would make himself more approachable and be more in touch with the spirit of the Gospel, rather than being preoccupied with ecclesiastical proprieties, canonical prescription and institutional conformity.

To hold that the church is always in need of reform is, by definition, to adopt a progressive attitude, taking the word 'progressive' to indicate movement and change, rather than simply as a term of approval. To hold that the church is fine as it is, and needs no change at all, can be fairly described as intransigently conservative. The two positions are mutually opposed but should be capable of co-existing in friendship and perhaps sometimes even with humour. The real challenge is to recognize the right to hold either position and to respect the other while arguing against it. Christians should, under grace, be able to disagree with each other on non-essential matters while maintaining the bond of love, tolerance and open-mindedness towards whatever truth may be found in each other's positions.

Communication is an indispensable function in Christian as well as in everyday human living; but communication between divergent wings in the Catholic Church seems to be difficult, both intellectually and psychologically. Conservatives and progressives need to listen to one another, with understanding, caring and mutual respect in spite of mutual disagreement. In this sense, at least, the church should be democratic.

Throughout this book I have used the word 'structure' to apply to the governmental offices of the church, as distinct from the people of God who make up the greater part of the church and are the reason for the existence of its structures. The structures are only instruments for the expression of attitudes. It is attitudes that have to change before structures can be utilised in a manner that is fair to all shades of opinion in the church.

One passage in Francis' interview with Antonio Spadaro calls for particular attention, where the Pope says:

> The first reform must be the attitude. The ministers of the Gospel must be people who can warm the hearts of the people, who walk through the dark night with them, who know how to dialogue and descend themselves into their people's night, into the darkness, but without getting lost. The people of God want pastors, not clergy acting like bureaucrats or government officials.

This is a stirring call to change. Humanity has not always been apparent in the attitudes of senior clergy. Reform is first and foremost a matter of attitude. It may therefore call for *metanoia*, conversion of mind and heart.[4] What was formerly taken for virtue may now have to be seen as a defect, as it was in the former life of Jorge Bergoglio. It can be painful to need conversion from what we once regarded as virtue.

The present pope is leading and teaching by example. He underwent a radical conversion from strict authoritarianism when as a Jesuit superior he came into contact with an oppressive government and later took himself to task for not doing enough for two of his fellow Jesuits who were resisting oppression and working among the poor. Without being an explicit supporter of Liberation Theology, he became ever more aware of the condition of the poor in his native Argentina. This brought him to see his authoritarian attitudes and actions as reprehensible: 'I am a sinner whom the Lord has looked upon.' When he constantly describes himself as a sinner, he is not speaking *pro forma*; he is thinking of real concrete wrongdoing of which he now fervently repents. He frequently asks others to pray for him, and he means it. The fact that he now regards authoritarian clericalism as sinful should give his fellow bishops, and especially his curia, pause for thought.[5]

Like John XXIII, Francis gives the impression of being within and not above the church. The period following John's pontificate, however, saw a revocation of his example. We can only hope that the same will not hap-

---

4. See *supra*, Chapter 3.
5. For an account of Francis' early life see Paul Vallely, *Pope Francis: Untying the Knots* (London, 2013). See also Austen Ivereigh, *The Great Reformer, Francis and the Making of a Radical Pope* (London, 2014). It is sometimes difficult to conflate these two books, perhaps because their authors consulted different sources .

pen after Francis. The examples of John and Francis can help those who might be tempted to despair of the very office of the papacy. These two popes show the human face of the papacy, and they do a real service to the church as a focus on unity, as distinct from uniformity, and as a convincing witness to the Gospel. They mitigate the historically disproportionate power of the papacy. The memory of John's life and charisma engages the imagination in a way that abstract descriptions of the nature and powers of his office could never do. The same is true of Francis.

However, the charismatic example of John's papacy was not reflected in the pontificates of three of his successors. John's first successor, Paul VI, was a peaceable though ambivalent man who was to some extent open to change, even attempting to reform the curia; but he was unhappily fixated upon the authority of his own office. The conservative minority at Vatican II knew this and tried to set him up as an alternative force to the council, by crowding him in his apartments and warning him against the dangers of collegiality.

The notorious '*Nota praevia*', intended as an interpretative papal commentary on chapter three of *Lumen Gentium*, set out to reaffirm the claim to the primatial superiority of the pope and implicitly to reduce the status and function of the College of Bishops. It flew in the face of the clear intention of *Lumen Gentium*. The *Nota praevia* is patently not part of the conciliar text and was relegated to the status of an appendix. As such it was an unhappy example of much that the conciliar majority was trying to change and of the determined attempts of the traditionalists to frustrate their efforts. Conservatives argue that the *Nota praevia* is part of *Lumen Gentium*, while liberals claim that it was a reactionary intervention of Paul VI, prompted by conservative pressure. (One report has it that the whole affair reduced Paul to tears.)

Paul's successor, John Paul I, looked like someone who was in the mould of John XXIII, but we can never know for sure, since he lived for only thirty-three days into his pontificate.

The next pope, John Paul II, was an imposing figure who, during a long pontificate, asserted his authority with vigour and remarkable self-confidence. Perhaps the most striking spiritual quality of John Paul was his Christian faith, which was not simply an important compartment of his life alongside his other qualities, but which shone through everything he did with a radiance that could dazzle his audiences. He played a major part in the fall of Communism, thus demonstrating his political weight and influence. He issued an encyclical, *Fides et Ratio*, on the relationship between faith and the pursuit of philosophy, which negated the position of his predecessors since Leo XIII and unknowingly shared the views of the Modernist, Lucien Laberthonnière. He carried out a large number of foreign visits which helped to centralise the church still further, leaving no one in any doubt about who was in charge. He reaffirmed the traditional Vatican stance on clerical celibacy, on the ordination of women and on what he saw as the radical evil of homosexuality. He reserved to himself the release of priests from the clerical to the lay state; and he made the process as difficult as possible. [6]

As a broad generalization, we can reasonably contend that Rome had moved away significantly from the spirit of John XXIII. Pope Benedict XVI continued in the same vein as his immediate predecessor. Because of the prominence given to Vatican authority in the Catholic Church, any programme for institutional reform must begin with the papacy, and especially with its court; but Benedict rejected the very notion of this kind of reform.

In addition to the conservative character of the papacy there is the worrying question of papal control over curial bodies. Theoretically the pope rules over the Vatican. There is, however, increasing evidence that Vatican personnel have for long enjoyed a life of their own, with nobody seemingly in control, and factions jealously jostling for power and influence. It may well be that it was this aspect of papal responsibility that caused Pope Benedict's resignation.

The task that Pope Francis has undertaken in reforming the curia is an onerous one, calling for exceptional political as well as spiritual skills. Already he is giving hope to a constituency in the church that has hitherto been neglected, defied and in some cases persecuted. For the sake of those, such as theologians, clergy and members of religious orders, who are particularly vulnerable to abusive authority in the church, reform will need to begin with dicasteries like the CDF which have achieved the

---

6. John Cornwell, *The Pope in Winter: The Dark Face of John Paul II's Papacy* (London, 2004) was written during the life of John Paul. Its title indicates clearly where Cornwell stood on his subject at a time when John Paul was lionized as one of the greatest of the popes.

grim power to threaten and assail those who do not share its questionable theological premises. If they persist in victimising faithful Catholics who happen not to share their narrow and rigid conception of orthodoxy, they will be flying in the face of the example of their papal master. They may resort to the cliché that the Vatican thinks in centuries and hope that they can wait out what is for them the difficult pontificate of Pope Francis, as they were able to do with Pope John XXIII.

According to the doctrine of collegiality, bishops are responsible for their local churches, but taken together they share with the Bishop of Rome responsibility for the governance and pastoral care of the whole church. They are theoretically described as teachers, but, as in the case of the pope, it is the manner of their teaching that matters. Some of them may not be notably competent in theology. It is therefore important that they have advisers who are representative of the different legitimate theological mentalities in the church. The danger is that they may consult only like-minded people – especially authoritarian canonists – whose advice may determine how they behave towards their flocks. They may simply refuse to listen to people who might challenge their assumptions, thus closing off a major source of reform. In today's church, many of them will hold predominantly conservative views, and they may find it hard to engage with pastors, theologians and laity who envisage a different, freer and more progressive, church.

Meetings between the bishops and the Association of Catholic Priests of Ireland seem to be marked by awkward, if polite, formality. There seems to be no meeting of minds. The reason for this probably has something to do with Rome's traditional dislike and distrust of all associations of priests throughout the church, who are occasionally critical of the establishment and who, for pastoral reasons, want to see change. Pope Francis remarks in his interview: 'I do not want token consultations, but real consultations.'

Each one of us must find his or her own artistic medium. For some it will be great painting or great literature. For many it is great music, which has the inestimable power to create, or sustain and enhance, a sense of the sacred. One evening recently I turned on my television, and quite by happy chance I happened on a concert that was about to start. It was Daniel

Barenboim and the West-Eastern Divan Orchestra, and they were about to play Beethoven's Ninth Symphony. Barenboim conducted without a score and clearly had a detailed and impressive grasp of the music. His effect on the orchestra was palpable. Apart from the fact that the performance was deeply satisfying, as one might have expected from a musician of Barenboim's distinction, the occasion was redolent of a powerful symbolism that melded perfectly with the majestic music. Something very like the dream of human perfection was being woven out of this occasion.

The orchestra comprised performers who came from both Israel and Palestine. Daniel Barenboim, an Israeli musician, and Edward Said, a Palestinian literary scholar, founded it in 1999. They named the orchestra after Goethe's collection of poems entitled *West-Eastern Divan*, a work intended to contribute to a concept of world culture. The concert was an occasion not only of great musical interest, but also of overpowering moral and spiritual inspiration. Here was an orchestra whose members were potential enemies, playing one of the greatest musical works by a composer who, by reason of his deafness, never physically heard a sound of it, when he wrote it near the end of his life. The occasion, involving a tragically deaf composer whose music was being played and sung by potentially hostile men and women, was a glorious manifestation of the human spirit when it triumphs over all its latent disabilities and rises to a vision of grandeur and promise.

Reflecting on the occasion afterwards, I realized that the aesthetic, the moral and the spiritual had merged into one overpowering experience of what human beings are capable of, when they are drawn, as in this instance, by great art into a world of transcendent beauty. Here was an evocation of the healing of the wounds of a world that so often and so easily falls to war, hatred, enmity and disillusionment. It raises human vision of the world to a level that seems out of reach in everyday life.

In theological terms, the occasion was sacramental; and although religion was never explicitly present, believers could take from the occasion a sense that 'All shall be well, and all shall be well and all manner of things shall be well.' 'The fullness of joy is to behold God in everything'. These celebrated words of the medieval English mystic, Julian of Norwich, offer a vision that can be missed when our concept of religion is ungenerous, inward looking, rule-driven and exclusive of a world that longs, at least tacitly, for an earnest of acceptance, fulfilment and salvation. Reform of the Catholic Church, however arduous and institutionally precarious it may be for those who pursue it actively, is the beginning of a glorious enterprise.

Index